Microsoft®Office

EXCEL 2003
Expert

Copyright - Editions ENI - December 2003
ISBN: 2-7460-2138-2

Editions ENI

BP 32125
44021 NANTES Cedex 1

Tél. 02.51.80.15.15
Fax 02.51.80.15.16

e-mail : editions@ediENI.com
http://www.editions-eni.com

English edition by Adrienne TOMMY

Collection directed by Corinne HERVO

Microsoft Office Specialist
Excel 2003 Expert

TEMPLATES, WORKBOOKS AND WORKGROUPS

CONFIGURATION

MACROS

This logo is your guarantee that you are using a Microsoft® approved preparation guide for the Microsoft® Office Specialist Excel 2003 Expert exam.

This complete preparation guide provides you with the theory that explains all the features tested in the exam and practical exercises that you can work through, to find out how much you really know. When you can work through all these exercises, successfully and easily, you are ready to take the Microsoft Office Specialist exam. At the end of the book, there is a list of all the Excel 2003 Expert exam objectives and the lesson number and exercise that relate to each objective.

For further information on the titles in the Microsoft Office Specialist collection, visit the ENI Publishing Web site, at **www.eni-publishing.com**; click the **Catalogue** link and then click the **Microsoft Office Specialist** link in the list of ENI collections.

What is the Microsoft Office Specialist certification?

The Microsoft Office Specialist exam gives you the opportunity to obtain a meaningful certification, recognised by Microsoft®, for the Office applications: Word, Excel, Access, PowerPoint, and Outlook. This certification guarantees your level of skill in working with these applications. It can provide a boost to your career ambitions, as it proves that you can use effectively all the features of the Microsoft Office applications and thus offer a high productivity level to your employer. In addition, it is a certain plus when job-seeking: more and more companies require employment candidates to be Microsoft Office Specialist certificate holders.

INTRODUCTION
What is Microsoft Office Specialist?

What are the applications concerned?

You can gain Microsoft Office Specialist certification in Word 97 and Excel 97 as well as the Office 2000, Office XP and Office 2003 applications: Word, Excel, Access, Powerpoint and Outlook. For Word 97 and Excel 97, only one level exists. However, there are two levels available for Word 2000/2002/2003 and Excel 2000/2002/2003, consisting of a Core level, for basic skills, and an advanced Expert level. If you obtain the Expert level for Word and Excel as well as Microsoft Office Specialist certification in PowerPoint, Access and Outlook (Office 2000, XP or 2003), you are certified as a Master.

How do you apply to sit the exams?

To enrol for the exams, you should contact one of the Microsoft Authorized Testing Centers (or ATC). A list of these centres is available online at this address: **http://www.mous.net**. Make sure you know the version of the Office application for which you wish to obtain the certificate.

There is an enrolment fee for each exam.

On the day of the exam, you should carry some form of identification and, if you have already sat a Microsoft Office Specialist exam, your ID number.

What happens during the Microsoft Office Specialist exam?

During the exam, you will have your own computer, on which you must perform a series of set tasks in the application concerned. Each action required to perform each task is tested, to ensure that you have done exactly what you were asked to do.

You are allowed no notes, books, pencils or calculators during the exam. You can consult the application help, but you should be careful not to exceed the exam's time limit.

Each exam is timed; it lasts in general between 45 minutes and one hour.

How do you pass the exam?

You must carry out a certain percentage of the required tasks correctly, within the allocated time. This percentage varies depending on the exam.

You will be told your result as soon as you have finished your exam. These results are confidential (the data are coded) and are only made known to the candidate and to Microsoft.

What happens then?

You will receive a Microsoft-approved exam certificate, proving that you hold the specified Microsoft Office Specialist level.

What happens if I fail?

You can take the exam as many times as you like, but will have to pay the enrolment fee again each time you apply.

How this book works

This book is the ideal companion to an effective preparation of the **MOS Excel 2003 Expert** exam. It is divided into several sections, each containing one or more **chapters**. Each section deals with a specific topic: managing data (such as named ranges, import/export, lists, publishing Web pages, using XML in Excel), tools for analysing data (audit, pivot tables and charts, simulation tools), workbooks, templates and workgroups, customising toolbars and menus and basic principles for working with macros. Each chapter is independent from the others. You can tailor the training to suit you: if you already know how to manage a list, for example, you can skip this lesson and go straight to the practice exercise for that chapter, then if you feel you need some extra theory, you can look back at the relevant points in the lesson. You can also study the lessons and/or work through the exercises in any order you wish.

At the end of the book, there is an **index** to help you find the explanations for any action, whenever you need them.

From theory...

Each chapter starts with a **lesson** on the theme in question, made up of a variable amount of numbered topics. The lesson should supply you with all the theoretical information necessary to acquire that particular skill. Example screens to illustrate the point discussed enhance the lesson and you will also find tips, tricks and remarks to complement the explanations provided.

...To practice

Test your knowledge by working through the **practice exercise** at the end of each chapter: each numbered heading corresponds to an exercise question. A solution to the exercise follows. These exercises are done using the documents on the CD-ROM accompanying the book, that you install on your own computer (to see how, refer to the INSTALLING THE CD-ROM instructions). In addition to the chapter exercises, five **summary exercises** dealing with each of the section themes are included at the end of the book. The solutions to these exercises appear as documents on the CD-ROM.

All you need to succeed!

When you can complete all the practice exercises without any hesitation or problems, you are ready to sit the Microsoft Office Specialist exam. In the table of contents for each chapter, the topics corresponding to a specific exam objective are marked with this symbol: ▦. At the back of the book, you can also see **the official list of the Excel 2003 Expert exam objectives** and for each of these objectives the corresponding lesson and exercise number.

Free online training

Editions ENI have developed a series of practice tests for certain Microsoft Office Specialist exams (Word 2000/2002, Excel 2000/2002, Power-Point 2000/2002). These tests are free and can be found on the **www.moustest.com** site. These tests take place online, within the application in question, just like in the official exam. To use this, you need an Internet connection on your computer, the application (e.g. Word 2000) and Internet Explorer 5.0 or later. At the end of the test, you can see your results in detail.

INTRODUCTION
How this book works

The layout of this book

This book is laid out in a specific way with special typefaces and symbols so you can find all the information you need quickly and easily:

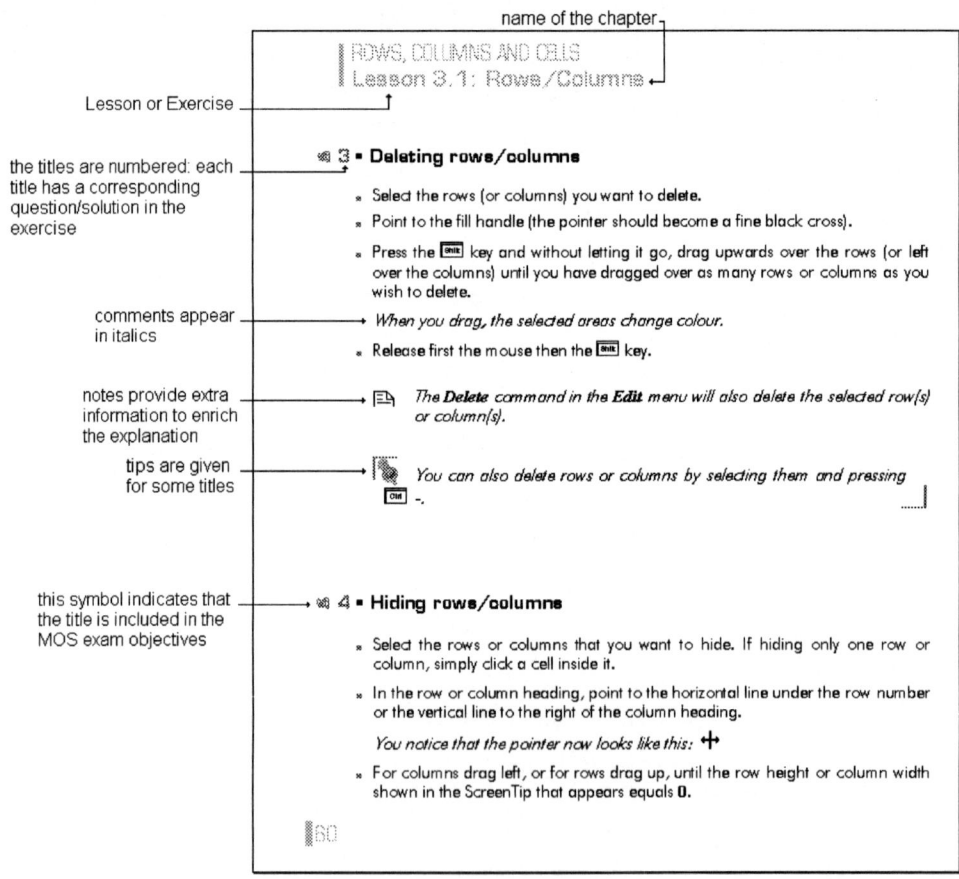

name of the chapter

ROWS, COLUMNS AND CELLS
Lesson 3.1: Rows/Columns

Lesson or Exercise

the titles are numbered: each title has a corresponding question/solution in the exercise

3 ▪ Deleting rows/columns

▪ Select the rows (or columns) you want to delete.
▪ Point to the fill handle (the pointer should become a fine black cross).
▪ Press the [Shift] key and without letting it go, drag upwards over the rows (or left over the columns) until you have dragged over as many rows or columns as you wish to delete.

comments appear in italics

When you drag, the selected areas change colour.
▪ Release first the mouse then the [Shift] key.

notes provide extra information to enrich the explanation

*The **Delete** command in the **Edit** menu will also delete the selected row(s) or column(s).*

tips are given for some titles

You can also delete rows or columns by selecting them and pressing [Ctrl] -.

this symbol indicates that the title is included in the MOS exam objectives

4 ▪ Hiding rows/columns

» Select the rows or columns that you want to hide. If hiding only one row or column, simply click a cell inside it.
» In the row or column heading, point to the horizontal line under the row number or the vertical line to the right of the column heading.
You notice that the pointer now looks like this: ✛
» For columns drag left, or for rows drag up, until the row height or column width shown in the ScreenTip that appears equals 0.

60

You can tell whether an action should be performed with the mouse, the keyboard or with the menu options by referring to the symbol that introduces each action: 🖱, 🎲 and 📄.

Installing the CD-ROM

The CD-ROM provided contains the documents used to work through the practice and summary exercises and the summary exercise solutions. You will need to copy its contents onto your hard disk before you can start working.

- Put the CD-ROM into the CD-ROM drive of your computer.

- Windows XP may ask you what to do with the CD; if this happens, choose the **Open folder to view files** option and enter. Otherwise, start the Windows Explorer, by right-clicking the **start** button on the task bar and choosing the **Explore** option.

- In the left pane of the Explorer window, scroll through the list until the CD-ROM drive icon appears. Click this icon.

The CD-ROM's contents will appear in the right pane of the window. Now copy the contents into your My Documents folder as described below.

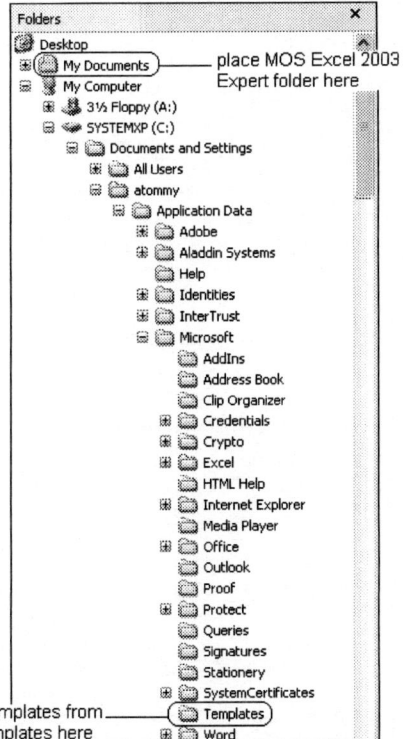

*The My Documents folder appears clearly in the file hierarchy, under the **Desktop** icon, in the folders pane on the left side of the Explorer.*

* In the CD-ROM's contents, select the folder called **MOS Excel 2003 Expert**. For the moment, do not include the folder called **ENI Templates** in your selection.

* Drag this folder into the left pane, into the **My Documents** folder.

  You now need to copy the templates from the folder called ENI Templates on the CD-ROM into your default templates folder.

* Find your default **Templates** folder in the left pane of the Explorer. On Windows XP, this is located at C:\Documents and Settings\your user name\Application Data\Microsoft\Templates.

  It may occur that you cannot find the folder called **Application Data**. Do not panic! In Windows XP, this folder is considered to be a system folder and so may be hidden automatically. To unhide this folder and copy the templates, follow this procedure:

  - In the **Windows Explorer**, use **Tools - Folder Options**.

  - Click the **View** tab.

  - In the **Advanced settings** list, activate the **Show hidden files and folders** option then click **OK**.

  You should now be able to see the Application Data folder in the hierarchy.

* Click the CD drive icon if necessary to see its contents in the right pane of the Explorer, then double-click the **ENI Templates** folder and select the two files that it contains.

* Copy them into the default **Templates** folder, by dragging them from one to the other as described above.

  You have now copied all the files necessary to work through the book's exercises.

- If you asked Windows to show its hidden files and folders, you may like to hide these items again. To do this, use **Tools - Folder Options - View** tab in the Windows Explorer and activate the **Do not show hidden files and folders** option then click **OK**.

You can now put away the CD-ROM and start working on your Microsoft Office Specialist exam preparation.

MANAGING DATA
Lesson 1.1: Named ranges

MANAGING DATA
Lesson 1.1: Named ranges

⊞1 ▪ **Naming ranges of cells**

A range of cells can be referred to by a name, which makes it easier to select or insert in a formula.

First method

- Select all the cells to which you want to give the same name.
- **Insert - Name - Define** or `Ctrl` `F3`

Excel proposes to take the contents of the cell above or to the left of the selection as the name of the range.

- If you prefer, enter another name for the selected cells.

There must be no spaces or hyphens in these names! You can use the ▩ button to collapse the dialog box and select cells on the sheet.

- Click the **Add** button.
- Name any other ranges in the same way.
- Click **Close** on the **Define Name** dialog box.

Second method

This method uses the existing column or row labels as the names of the selected ranges (but does not include those labels in the named range).

▪ Select the cells containing the names to be used <u>and</u> the cells you want to name.

▪ **Insert - Name - Create** or `Ctrl` `Shift` `F3`

▪ Indicate the position of the cells containing the names by ticking the appropriate check box.

▪ Click **OK**.

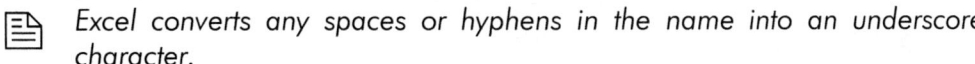

Excel converts any spaces or hyphens in the name into an underscore character.

▥2 ▪ Deleting a name

▪ Go into the **Define Name** dialog box.

▪ Select the name that you wish to delete in the list.

▪ Click the **Delete** button.

The deletion is instantaneous: Excel does not ask for confirmation.

▪ Click **OK** to close the **Define Name** dialog box.

▦3 ▪ Using named ranges in calculations

It can be simpler to use a named range in an argument instead of ordinary cell range references.

Using a name in a formula

▪ Start entering the formula and stop when you need to insert the required name.

▪ **Insert - Name - Paste** or F3

A dialog box appears listing all the pre-existing named ranges:

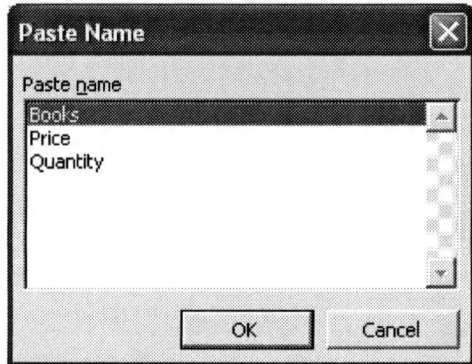

▪ Double-click the name you wish to use.

▪ Complete the formula.

 You can also type the name into the formula, substituting the name for the cell references.

Replacing cell references by their name

You can modify a formula to replace cell references by the corresponding name.

▪ Select the cell containing the reference you want to modify.

▪ **Insert - Name - Apply**

■ Click the name(s) you wish to use.

■ Click **OK**.

Excel replaces the range of cells in formula with the chosen name, providing that they match correctly.
If they do not, Excel displays an error message :

4 ▪ Using LOOKUP functions

VLOOKUP function

This function looks for a value in the first column of a table (the V in VLOOKUP refers to this vertical search) and produces the value found in the cell located on the same row, in the column you have specified.

■ Create a table grouping together the data that you will subsequently retrieve during your search, then sort the table in ascending order by the first column in it.
Name this cell range if you do not wish to select it when creating your calculation formula.

■ Click the cell where the information retrieved from the table should be displayed.

■ Create your calculation formula, respecting the following syntax:
=VLOOKUP(lookup_value,table_array,col_index_num,range_lookup)

lookup_value   is the compare value the function looks for in the first column of the table.

table_array	is the table from which the data is to be retrieved. This argument can consist of the reference of a range of cells or the name of a named range.
col_index_num	is the number of the column in the table (table_array) containing the value that is to be displayed as a result. For example, the first column in the table is column 1.
range_lookup	is a logical value that looks for an exact or similar match. If the range_lookup is TRUE or is left blank, an equal value or a value immediately inferior to the value you are seeking is returned. If the range_lookup is FALSE, only the exact match will be returned.

	D18	▼	*fx* =VLOOKUP(A18,Books,4)			
	A	B	C	D	E	F
11						
12						
13	Book code	Title	Quantity	Sale price	Total	
14	BI02	Light a Penny Candle	1	5.99	5.99	
15	CO03	Cruel and Unusual	2	5.99	11.98	
16	DE06	Way through the Woods	1	5.99	5.99	
17	GR01	Client	1	4.99	4.99	
18	KI03	Green Mile Compilation	1	7.99	7.99	
19						
20						
21			TOTAL AMOUNT DUE		36.94	
22						

In this example, the VLOOKUP function looks for the reference of the book (whose code is contained in A18) in a table (or in this case, a named range) called Books and then returns the price of the item located in the fourth column of that range.

* Confirm the formula by pressing ⏎.

HLOOKUP function

This function is used to locate a value in the first row of a table (the H in HLOOKUP refers to this horizontal search), and looks up the value contained in the same column and in the row you specify.

- Create a table grouping together all the data you will need to retrieve in your search then sort the table in ascending order by the data in the first row. To do this, select the table, activate the **Data - Sort** command, then click the **Options** button. Activate the **Sort left to right** option then confirm. Check that Excel is going to sort by the first **row** in the table in **Ascending** order then click **OK**.
Give this range of cells a name if you do not wish to select it when creating your calculation formula.

- Click the cell where you want the information found in the table to be displayed.

- Create your calculation formula, respecting the following syntax:
=HLOOKUP(lookup_value,table_array,row_index_num,range_lookup)

lookup_value	is the value the function looks for in the first row of the table.
table_array	is the table from which the data is to be retrieved. This argument can be the references of a cell range or a named range.
row_index_num	is the row number in the table containing the value that should be the search result. For example, the first row in a table is row 1.
range_lookup	is a logical value that looks for an exact or similar match. If the range_lookup is TRUE or is left blank, an equal value or a value immediately inferior to the value you are seeking is returned. If the range_lookup is FALSE, only the exact match will be returned.

- Confirm the formula by pressing ⏎.

MANAGING DATA
Exercise 1.1: Named ranges

Below, you can see **Practice Exercise 1.1**. This exercise is made up of 4 steps. If you do not know how to do one of the steps, go back to the title that corresponds to that particular lesson. When you have finished, you can check your work by reading the **Solution** that follows.

All the steps in this exercise are likely to be tested in the Microsoft Office Specialist exam.

☞ **Practice Exercise 1.1**

*To work on practice exercise 1.1, open the **1-1 Invoice.xls** workbook, which is in the **MOS Excel 2003 Expert** folder, then activate the **Invoice** sheet.*

1. Give the name **Quantity** to cell range **C14** to **C18** and the name **Price** to cell range **D14** to **D18**.

2. Delete the **UnitPrice** name.

3. Use the **Quantity** and **Price** names in a formula to calculate the total for the **BI02** book in cell **E14**.
   Copy this formula into cells **E15** to **E18**.

4. In cell **B14** create a formula that will look for the title of the book that corresponds to the code in cell **A14**. The cell range (**A1** to **D106**) that contains the data from the table is called **Books** and is located in the worksheet also called **Books.**
   Next, copy this formula into cells **B15** to **B18**.

If you would like to practise these features more, on another document, you should work through Summary Exercise 1, on MANAGING DATA. You will find the summary exercises at the end of the book.

It is often possible to perform a task in several different ways, but here, only the easiest solution is presented. You can go back to the corresponding lesson if you want to see other techniques you could use.

Solution to Exercise 1.1

1. To assign the name QUANTITY to cells C14 to C18, select cells **C14** to **C18**.
   Use **Insert - Name - Define**, leave **Quantity** in the text box, then confirm by pressing ↵.

   To assign the name Price to cells D14 to D18, select cells **D14** to **D18**.
   Use **Insert - Name - Define**, type **Price** in the text box, then confirm by pressing ↵.

2. To delete the UnitPrice name, use the **Insert - Name - Define** command and click **UnitPrice** in the **Names in workbook** list, then click the **Delete** button.
   Click **OK** to close the **Define Name** dialog box.

3. To use the Quantity and Price names to calculate the total for the BI02 book in cell E14, click cell **E14**.
   Type = then use **Insert - Name - Paste**.

   Click the **Quantity** name and click **OK**.

   Type * then use **Insert - Name - Paste**.

   Click **Price** then **OK**.

   Press ↵ to confirm the formula.

   To copy this formula into cells E15 to E18, select cell **E14**, then drag its fill handle down to cell **E18**.

MANAGING DATA
Exercise 1.1: Named ranges

4. To create a calculation formula in cell B14 to look up the title of the book that corresponds to the code in cell A14, click cell **B14**.
Type **=VLOOKUP(A14,Books,2)** then confirm by pressing ⏎.

To copy this formula into cells B15 to B18, select cell **B14**, then drag its fill handle down to cell **B18**.

MANAGING DATA
Lesson 1.2: Importing/Exporting

MANAGING DATA
Lesson 1.2: Importing/Exporting

🪟1 ▪ Importing data from other applications

Importing data from a text file

▪ Activate a cell outside a range of imported data.

▪ **Data - Import External Data - Import Data**

▪ In the **Files of type** list box, choose **Text Files**.

▪ Select the drive then the folder in which the text file is stored.

▪ Select the text file you wish to import and click the **Open** button.

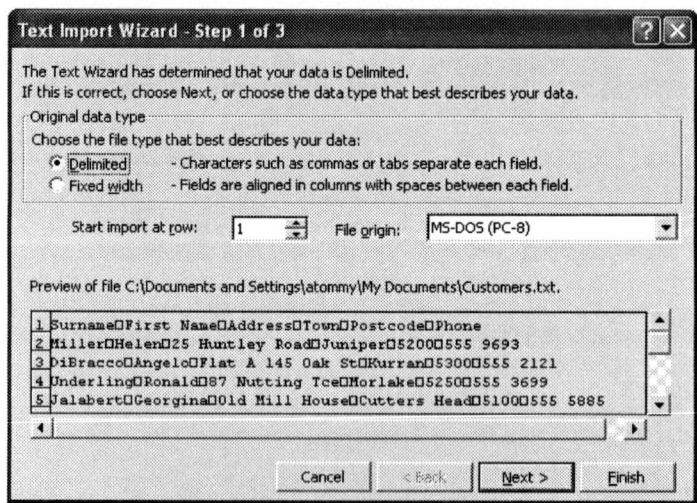

*The wizard will interpret the data as having either a **Delimited** style (the data is separated by commas or tabs) or a **Fixed width** (separated by spaces).*

▪ If necessary, modify the **Original data type** in the corresponding frame.

▪ If you do not want to import the data from the first row in the file, select or enter the required row number in the **Start import at row** text box.

▪ Click the **Next** button to go on the next step.

24

■ Select the delimiters contained in data that are **Delimited** or choose the field widths following the instructions in the first frame of the window, if they are of **Fixed width**.

■ Click **Next** to go on to the next step.

■ For each column, select the data format. Do this by clicking the column then choosing one of the options in the **Column data format** frame.

*The **Advanced** button enables you to check, and possibly modify numerical data settings on the imported data such as the decimal and thousands separators.*

■ Click **Finish**.

■ To insert the table in an **Existing worksheet**, activate this option then click the ▣ button. Access the worksheet then click the first destination cell for the external data. Click the ▣ button again to restore the dialog box.
To insert the table into a **New worksheet**, activate the corresponding option.

*The **Properties** button displays options for refreshing data and layout options.*

■ Click **OK**.

 *You can change the source file by activating an item of imported data and using the **Data - Import External Data - Edit Text Import** command or clicking the **Edit Text Import** 🔲 tool button on the **External Data** toolbar.*

*The **File - Open** command can be used to import a text file. Excel then guides you in importing the data with the **Text Import Wizard**. However, if you use this method you cannot update the data.*

Importing data by copying, without establishing a link

■ Open the application then the file in which the data you want to copy are stored.

■ Select the data you want to copy.

If you are copying text that is not separated by a delimiter (for example, a tab), it will be pasted into a single cell in the Excel sheet.

- Copy the data using the appropriate command. In Office applications, use **Edit - Copy** or ⬚ or [Ctrl] C

- Open the Excel application, if necessary, then open the workbook in which you want to paste the copied data.

- Activate the first destination cell for the copy.

- **Edit - Paste** or ⬚ or [Ctrl] V

Importing data by copying and establishing a link

When a link is established, any modifications to the data in the source file are carried over into the Microsoft Excel sheet.

- Open the application then the file in which the data you want to copy are stored.

- Select the data you want to copy.

- Copy the data using the appropriate command. In Office applications, use **Edit - Copy** or ⬚ or [Ctrl] C

- Open the Excel application, if necessary then open the workbook where you wish to paste the data.

- Activate the first destination cell for the copied data.

- **Edit - Paste Special**

- Activate the **Paste link** option.

- Using the **As** list, select the format in which the data should be pasted.

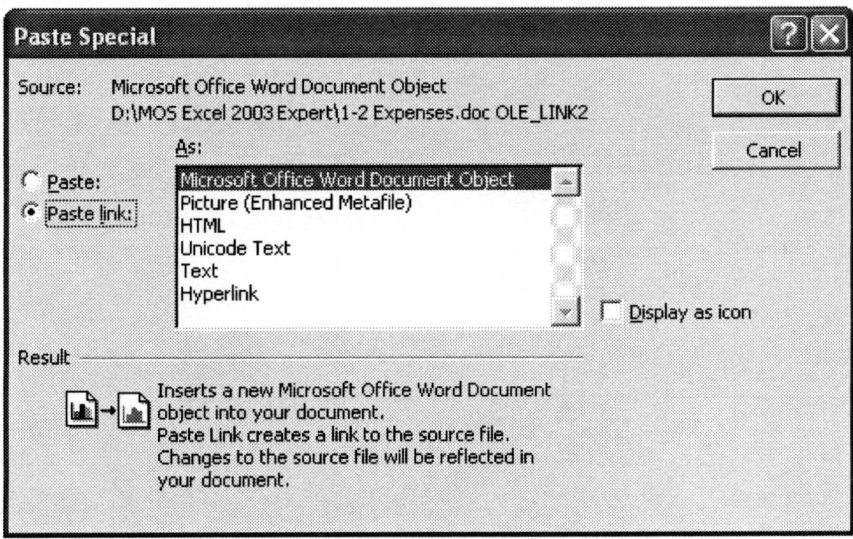

The data imported into the Excel worksheet will be linked to its source file.

■ Click **OK**.

Importing an object

An object is part or the whole of a document originating from another application.

■ Open the workbook then activate the sheet in which you want to embed the object.

■ **Insert - Object**

■ If you are embedding an existing file into the sheet, click the **Create from File** tab then enter the path and file name in the **File name** box or click the **Browse** button to select the file.

■ If you want to insert a new object, click the **Create New** tab.

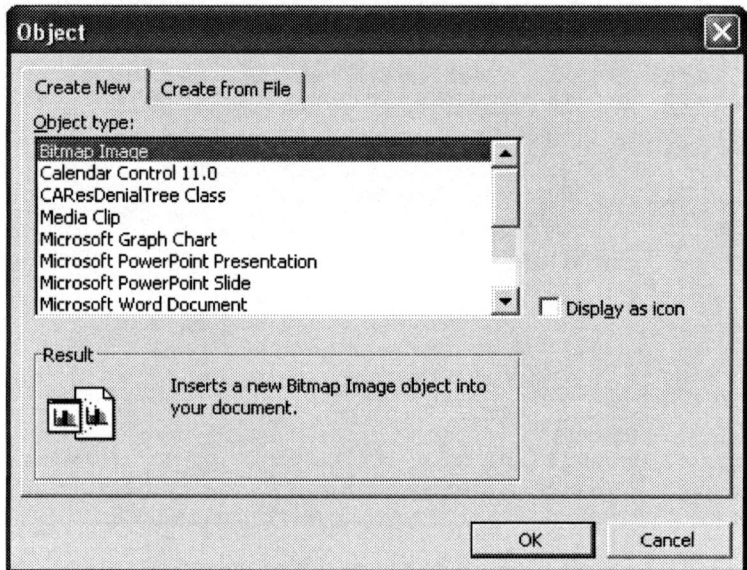

- In the **Object type** list, select the type of object you wish to embed into the worksheet.
- Click **OK**.

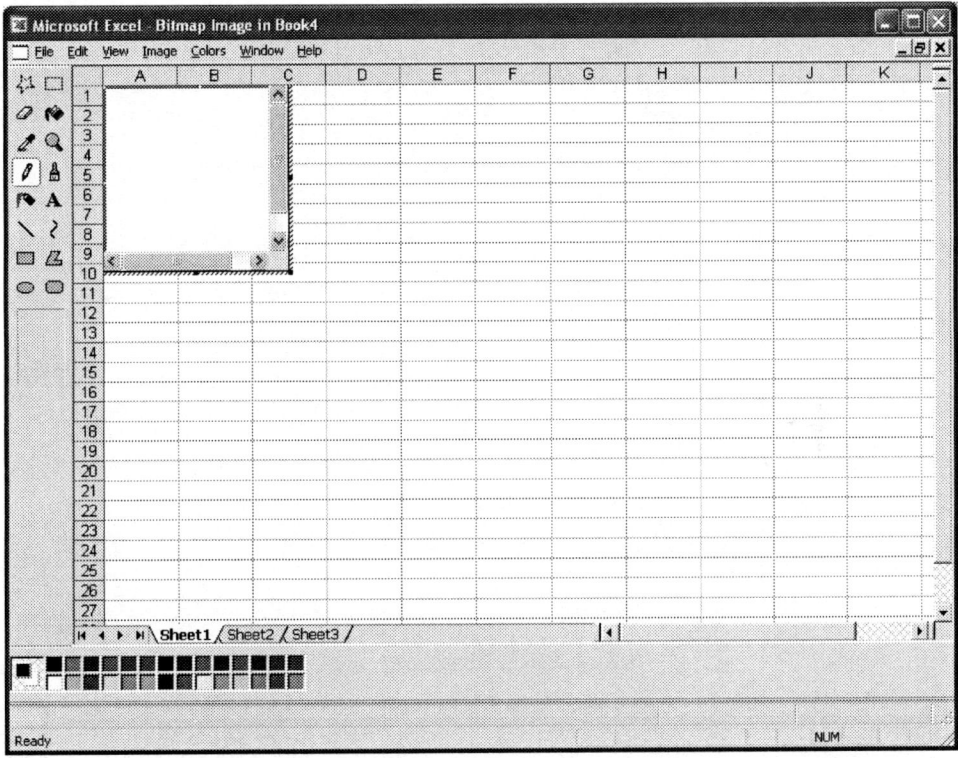

A frame with a hatched border appears. The menus and toolbars of the application that will be used to create the object replace the Excel menus and toolbars.

- Create the object using the tools and functions of the source (server) application.

- When you have finished creating the object, click outside the object frame on the Excel worksheet to view the object in the sheet.

- To edit the object, double-click the embedded object.

- Save then close the workbook.

Importing an entire file

It is possible to import a file saved in an application other than Microsoft Excel (Lotus1-2-3, Quattro Pro, Microsoft Works, text file...).

▪ **File - Open** or [image] or [Ctrl] **O**

▪ Open the **Files of type** list then select the format of the file you want to import.

▪ Select the file you want to import then click the **Open** button or double-click the file name.

▪ If the file you are importing is a text file, follow the instructions in the **File Import Wizard** to define how the text should be distributed in the columns.

The imported file can now be seen on the screen in its original format. You must now save the file in Microsoft Excel format.

▪ **File - Save** or [image] or [Ctrl] **S**

▪ Depending on the type of file being used, Excel may suggest that you keep the file's format. If this happens, click **No**.

▪ In the **Save as type** list, select the **Microsoft Excel Workbook (*.xls)** option.

▪ If necessary, change the drive and/or folder where the workbook should be saved then change the **File name**.

▪ Click the **Save** button.

2 ▪ Importing Web data without a query

This method can be used to copy data using the Internet Explorer Web browser (version 4.1 or later).

▪ In the browser, select the data you wish to copy.

▪ **Edit - Copy** or [image] or [Ctrl] **C**

▪ Go into Excel and activate the first destination cell for the copied data.

- **Edit - Paste** or 🖻 or [Ctrl] **V**

- To change the way Excel pastes the data, click the 🖻▾ icon at the bottom right of the range of pasted cells and choose to **Keep Source Formatting** or to **Match Destination Formatting**. The **Create Refreshable Web Query** option will create a query based on the Web page from which you copied the data.

3 • Importing Web data with a Web query

Creating a Web query

By using a Web query, you can import data into Excel from one or more tables on a Web page, with the option of updating the data in the future.

- Activate a cell outside a range already containing imported data.

- **Data - Import External Data - New Web Query**

- In the **Address** box, enter the URL of the Web page from which you wish to import data, or expand the list to choose a recently visited **Address**.

- Click **Go** to go to the required page.

- To import the data contained in one or more frames of the Web page, click the ➡ icon for each frame concerned. To import the data from the whole page, click the ➡ icon in the upper left corner of the page.

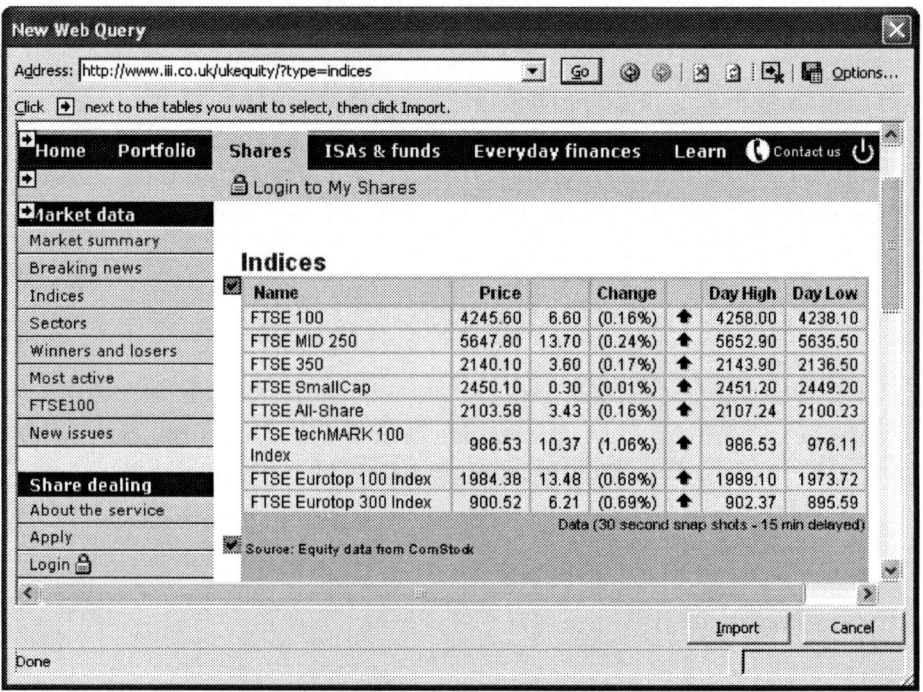

The icon changes to become ☑. If you cannot see any of these icons on the Web page, click the ⬛ button on the *New Web Query* window.

The **Options** button displays the default options for formatting and importing Web data, which you can modify.

■ If you wish to be able to extract the query data to use it in other workbooks or share the query with other users, you should save that query separately. To do this, click the ⬛ button on the dialog box, select the file in which you want to save the query and enter the **File name**, then click **Save**.

A Web query is saved as a file with an *.iqy* extension. If you do not save the Web query in a separate file, it will be saved as part of your current workbook and can only be run from that workbook.

■ Click the **Import** button.

- In the **Import Data** dialog box, specify where to place the imported data. To insert the table in an **Existing worksheet**, activate the appropriate option, click the ⬛ button, go to the worksheet concerned and click the first destination cell. Click the ⬛ button to restore the dialog box. To insert the table into a **New worksheet**, activate the corresponding option.

  *The **Properties** button leads to the data update settings, which you can modify. (cf. Changing data update settings).*

- Click **OK**.

Modifying a Web query

- To modify the source of a Web query, activate one of the items of imported data on the worksheet.

- **Data - Import External Data - Edit Query** or click the ⬛ tool button on the **External Data** toolbar.

- Use the ⬛ icons to redefine what should be imported then click the **Import** button.

Running a saved Web query

- In the worksheet, activate a cell outside any ranges of previously imported data.

- **Data - Import External Data - Import Data**

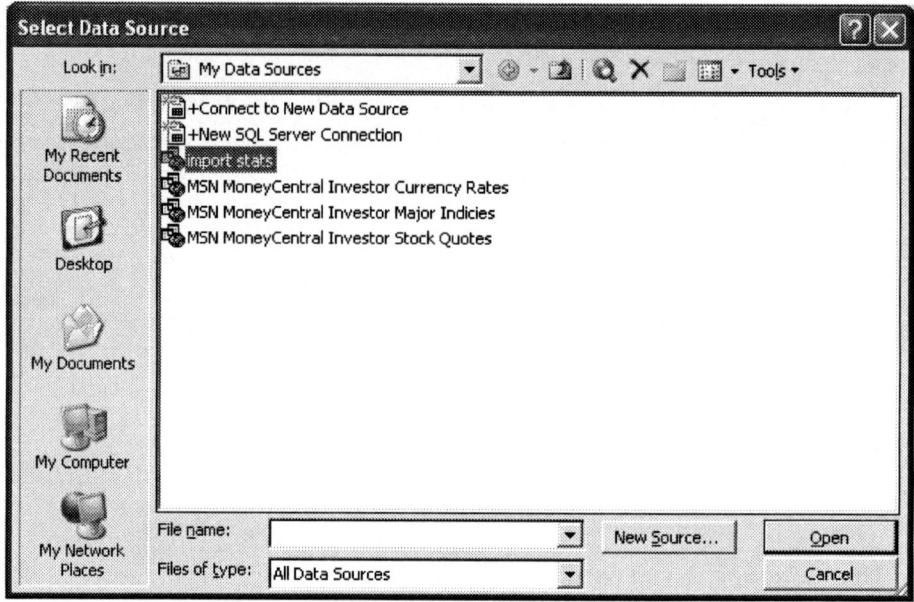

By default, Excel opens the **My Data Sources** folder, which contains **.iqy** type queries, among other things.

* Select the query you wish to run and click the **Open** button.

* Activate the appropriate option, according to where the data should be inserted in the workbook.

* Run the query by clicking **OK**.

Updating imported data automatically on opening the workbook

* Click one of the cells in the range of imported data then click the **Data Range Properties** ▣ button on the **External Data** toolbar.

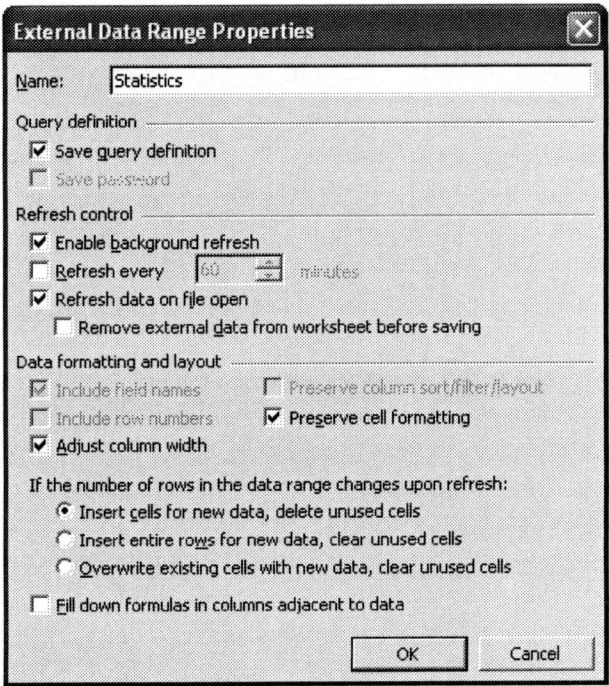

- Tick the **Refresh data on file open** option.

- To save the workbook and the query definition but not the external data, tick the **Remove external data from worksheet before saving** option.

  This action helps reduce the file size.

- Click **OK** to confirm.

Updating several ranges of imported data located on the same worksheet

- If necessary, display the **External Data** toolbar using the **View - Toolbars** menu.

- Click the **Refresh All** button.

■ To refresh data in several open workbooks, click the ![button] button in each workbook.

Updating data from an imported text file

■ Select the worksheet containing the imported text file.

■ Click the **Refresh Data** ![button] button on the **External Data** toolbar.

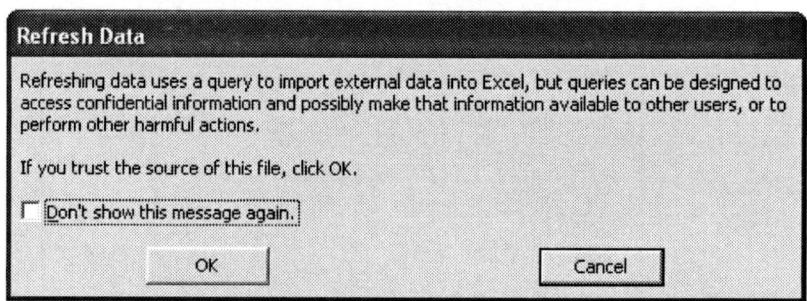

■ If necessary, click **OK** on the message asking you to confirm whether or not the file is trustworthy.

The **Import Text File** dialog box opens.

■ Select the text file you wish to update then click the **Import** button.

Changing data update settings

■ Activate one of the cells containing imported data.

■ **Data - Import External Data - Data Range Properties** or click ![button] on the **External Data** toolbar.

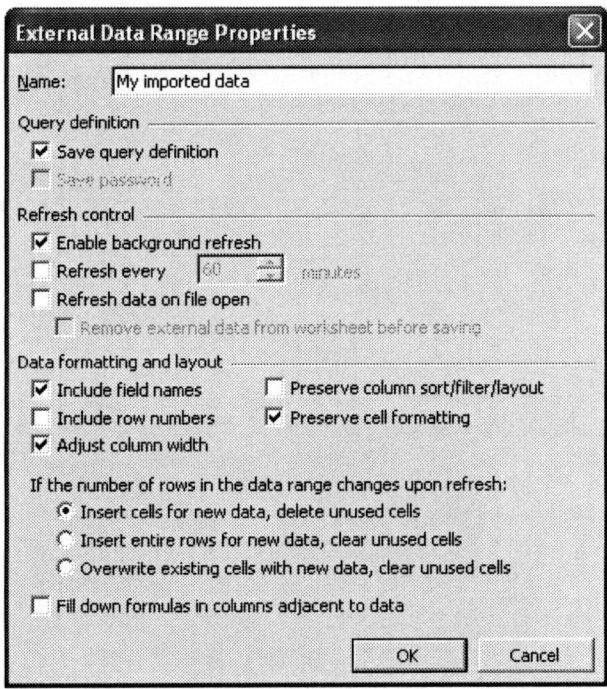

- Keep the **Save query definition** option active if you want to be able to update the imported data.

- If you need a password to connect to the data source, Excel can create a compulsory prompt the first time the data is updated per work session; to do this, deactivate the **Save password** option.

  This feature does not apply to data from a text (*.txt) file or a Web query (*.iqy). Take note that saved passwords are not encrypted.

- In the **Refresh control** frame, determine how and when Excel should refresh the data.

- Use the **Date formatting and layout** options to select how imported data should be formatted.

- Indicate what Excel should do **If the number of rows in the data range changes upon refresh** in the frame of the same name.

- If the **Fill down formulas in columns adjacent to data** option is active, Excel will allow automatic copying of formulas added after the data was imported.

- Click **OK**.

> *Depending on the type of data imported, some of the options in the **External Data Range Properties** dialog box may be unavailable.*

4 ▪ Exporting data to other applications

Exporting data by copying without establishing a link

- If necessary, open the Excel application then the workbook containing the data you wish to export.

- Select the cells containing the data to be exported.

- **Edit - Copy** or [icon] or `Ctrl` C

- Open the application, then the file in which you wish to paste the data.

- Click the place where you want to paste the data.

- **Edit - Paste** or [icon] or `Ctrl` V

Exporting data by copying and establishing a link

When a link is in place, any changes made to the data in the original Microsoft Excel workbook are carried over into the file containing the exported data.

- Open the Excel application if necessary, then open the workbook containing the data you want to copy.

- **Edit - Copy** or [icon] or `Ctrl` C

- Open the application and the file into which you want to paste the Excel data.

- Click the position where the data should be pasted.

- **Edit - Paste Special**

- Activate the **Paste link** option.

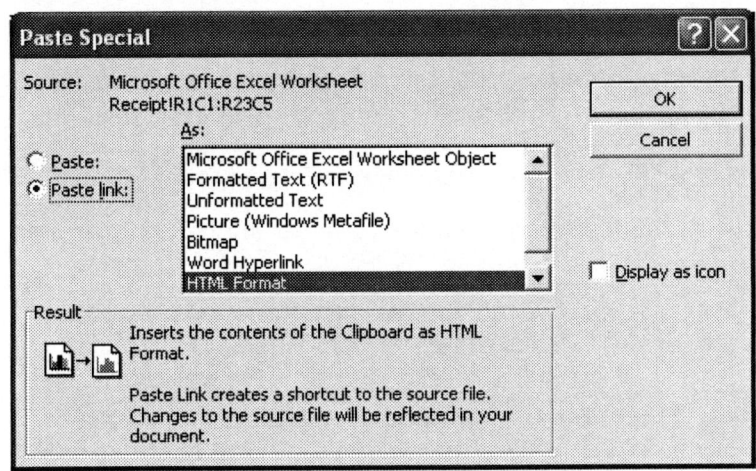

- From the **As** list, select the format in which you want to paste the data.

- Activate the **Display as icon** option if you want the linked data to be displayed in the form of an icon.

- Click **OK**.

Exporting an entire file

The aim of this technique is to open a Microsoft Excel file in another application. To do this, the other application must be able to manage Excel files.

- Open the application in which you want to open the Microsoft Excel workbook.

- **File - Open** or 🗁 or Ctrl O

- Open the **Files of type** list then select the **Microsoft Excel** format.

- Select the drive and folder in which the Excel workbook is stored.

- Select the file then click the **Open** button or double-click the file name.

- If necessary, fill in any dialog boxes that appear subsequently; the contents of these dialog boxes change depending on the application you are using to open the Microsoft Excel workbook.

The Excel file can now be seen on the screen in its original format (.xls). You should save the file in the format of the application to which you are exporting it.

- **File - Save As**

- In the **Save as type** list, select the format of the active application.

- If necessary, modify the drive or folder where the file will be saved, then change the **File name**.

- Click the **Save** button.

Inserting a workbook into another application as an object

- Open the application then the file in which you want to insert a Microsoft Excel object.

- **Insert - Object**

- Activate the **Create from File** tab.

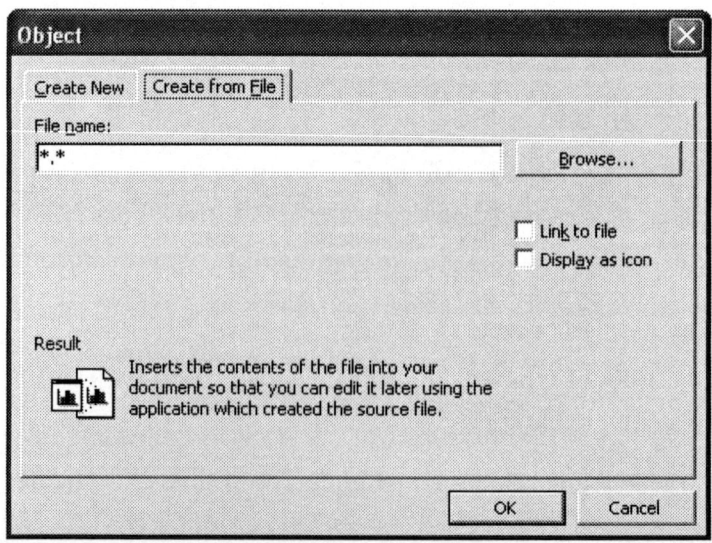

- Enter the path and name of the file you want to insert or click the **Browse** button to select it.

- Click **OK**.

- To edit the object, double-click the embedded object.

  A frame with hatched borders appears. The Microsoft Excel menus and toolbars replace those of the active application.

- To view the object within the other application again, click outside the object's frame.

5 • Creating a Web page from a workbook/worksheet

Creating/publishing a non-interactive Web page

*A **non-interactive Web page** contains information that can be consulted by users visiting your Internet/intranet site but cannot be modified. You can publish a selection of cells, a worksheet or a workbook, without interactivity.*

- Create or open the workbook (in xls or htm format) that you want to publish.

- If necessary, select the data you wish to publish, or if you want to publish a whole sheet or workbook, do not make any selection.

- **File - Save as Web Page**

- Select the location in which you want to publish your Web page, using the **Save in** list or the **Places Bar**. Depending on your version of Windows, the **Places Bar** can take you rapidly to one of the previously created **Web Folders** (in Windows NT 4.0) or to the existing **My Network Places** (in Windows 2000/ Me/XP).

  It is a good idea to test your Web page before publishing it on a Web server. To do this, first save the Web page on your hard disk, test it, make any necessary changes then when you are satisfied with the results, go ahead and publish it on the Web server, where any authorised user can access it. The publication procedure is identical, whether you are publishing on your own workstation or on a Web server; the only thing that differs is the place chosen to publish the page.

MANAGING DATA
Lesson 1.2: Importing/Exporting

- Use the **Web Options** in the **Tools** menu to modify the settings for the Web page you are publishing: the browser used for viewing, how published files are managed, encoding, fonts and so on.

- Specify whether you are saving the **Entire Workbook** or just a **Selection** by activating the appropriate option.

- Make sure the **Add interactivity** option is not active.

- If you wish, click the **Change Title** button and enter the text that will appear on the browser's title bar when the Web page is opened, then click **OK.**

- If necessary, change the proposed **File name**.

  You should avoid putting spaces and accents in file names as they are not always managed correctly by Web servers.

- To save the Web page, without accessing the publication options, click the **Save** button.

  *The Web page appears in htm format and the original file closes automatically. Along with the Web page, Excel generates a folder that contains all the components of the Web page, which are called "supporting files". This folder is called **Web page name_files**; the supporting files folder and the Web page are indissociable.*

- To publish your Web page onto a Web server, choosing more advanced options if you wish, click the **Publish** button.

A new dialog box appears:

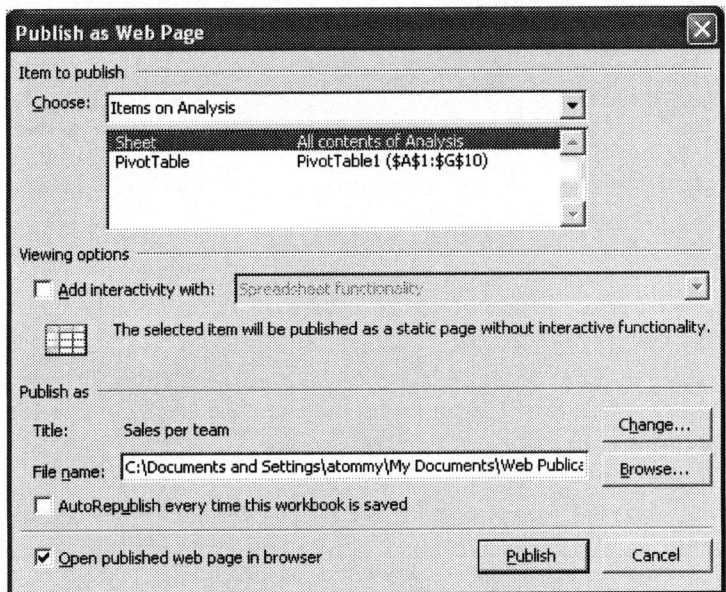

- In the **Choose** list, select the element you want to publish.

  What appears in this list depends on the contents of the Web page.

- Make sure the **Add interactivity with** option is not active.

- Click the **Change** button if you want to modify the name entered for the page during the previous step.

  *By default the place of publication followed by the file name defined in the previous step appear in the **File name** text box.*

- If you are publishing the Web page on a web server, modify this address (if necessary), making sure you use this syntax: http://server_address/file.htm.

- Tick the **AutoRepublish every time this workbook is saved** check box if you want Excel to update the Web page each time you save changes to the source file.

■ To preview the Web page in the default browser once you have published it, tick the **Open published web page in browser** check box.

■ Click the **Publish** button.

If you chose to see a preview, the default browser opens and displays the Web page.

■ Once you have finished checking your page, close the browser window.

 If you saved your Web page on your own workstation, you can check the result by viewing the file in your Web browser. If necessary, modify the original workbook you used to create the Web page then when you are satisfied with the result, publish the Web page on the server using the same procedure but replace the address of your own computer by the address of the Web server concerned.

*If you saved (not published) a whole workbook as a non-interactive Web page, you can still preview the page without publishing it. To do this, open the htm file in question then use the **Web Page Preview** command in the **File** menu.*

Creating/publishing an interactive Web page

A visitor to an interactive Web page can modify the page, but he/she must have Internet Explorer (4.01 or later) installed on his/her computer and also have the appropriate Microsoft Office licence to use worksheets, charts and pivot table lists published exclusively from Microsoft Excel.

■ Create or open the workbook (in xls or htm format) from which you wish to publish one (or all) of the sheets.

While you can publish a whole workbook or individual sheets, only published sheets can contain interactive elements.

■ If you want to publish only one of the sheets in the workbook, activate it by clicking its tab.

■ **File - Save as Web Page**

- Select the location in which you want to publish your Web page, using the **Save in** list or the **Places Bar**. Depending on your version of Windows, the **Places Bar** can take you rapidly to one of the previously created **Web Folders** (in Windows NT 4.0) or to the existing **My Network Places** (in Windows 2000/Me/XP).

- Use the **Web Options** in the **Tools** menu to modify the settings for the Web page you are publishing: the browser used for viewing, how published files are managed, encoding, fonts and so on.

- Activate the **Selection: sheet** option then tick the **Add interactivity** check box.

  You can only publish individual worksheets interactively.

- If necessary, click the **Change Title** button to enter the text that will appear in the browser's title bar when you open the Web page then click **OK**.

- If you wish, modify the suggested **File name**.

  You should avoid putting spaces and accents in file names as they are not always managed correctly by Web servers.

- To save the Web page, without accessing the publication options, click the **Save** button.

  The Web page appears in htm format and the original file closes automatically. For an interactive Web page, Excel does not generate a supporting files folder.

- To publish your Web page on a server, choosing more advanced options if you wish, click the **Publish** button.

A new dialog box appears:

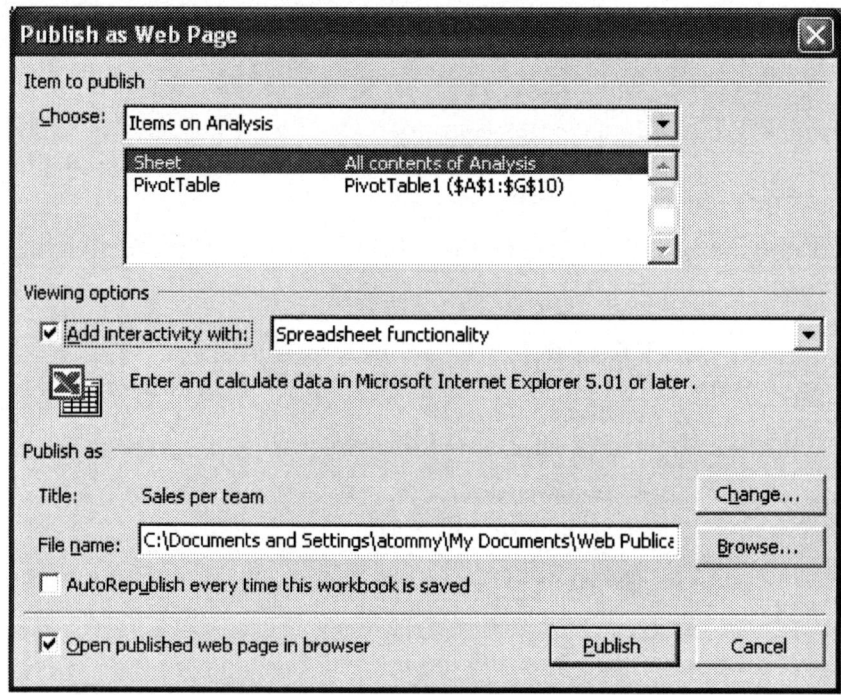

■ In the **Choose** list, select the element you want to publish (except the **Entire workbook** option).

What appears in this list depends on the contents of the workbook.

■ Make sure the **Add interactivity with** check box is still ticked and if necessary, open the attached drop-down list to choose which Excel functionality you want to make available to users of the page. This depends on what type of interactive element you are publishing (you can offer spreadsheet, chart or pivot table functionality).

■ Click the **Change** button if you want to modify the name entered for the page during the previous step.

- By default the place of publication and the file name defined in the previous step appear in the **File name** text box; if you are publishing the Web page on a web server, modify this address (if necessary), making sure you use this syntax: *http://server_address/file.htm*.

- Tick the **AutoRepublish every time this workbook is saved** check box if you want Excel to update the Web page each time you save changes to the source file.

- To preview the Web page in the default browser once you have published it, make sure there is a tick in the **Open published web page in browser** check box.

- Click the **Publish** button.

If you are publishing a pivot table, your browser may inform you that the source data for your table is located in another domain.

- In this case, click **Yes** to continue.

Excel publishes the Web page in htm format in the chosen place (on your workstation or on a Web server) but the source file, in xls format, remains in its original location.

Here is an example of a published interactive worksheet:

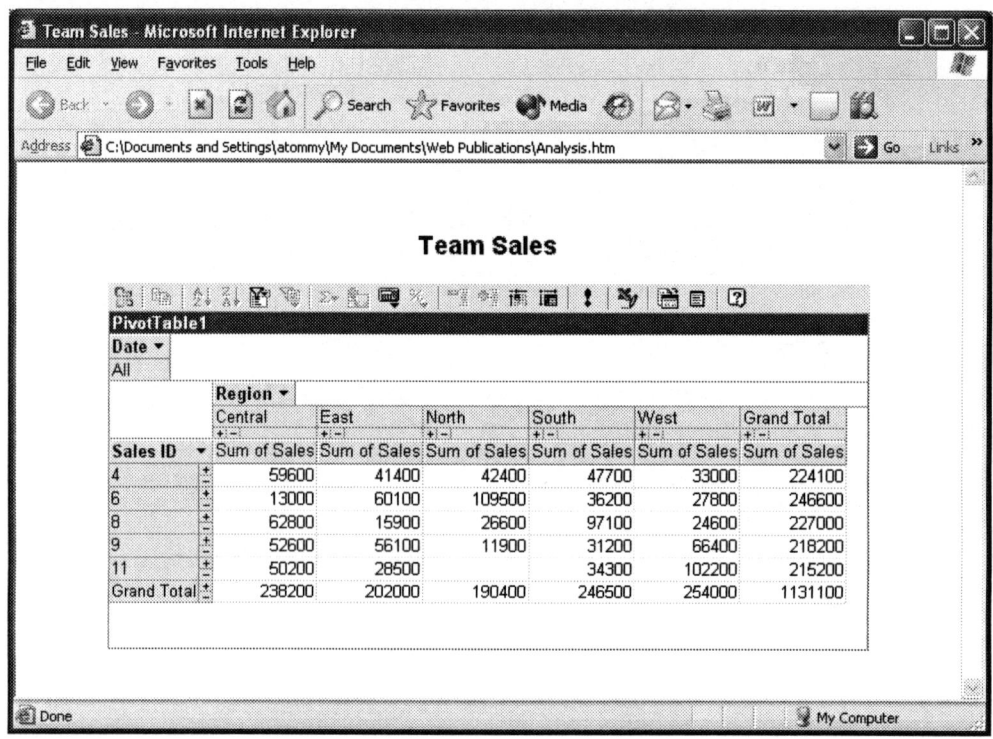

You can see that in the example above, which is a pivot table, each field has its own drop-down list, containing the details of that field. You can modify the table by activating or deactivating one or more of these detail items. A user visiting this page can change the table as he/she likes, without needing the Microsoft Excel application, as the changes are made directly in the Web browser (the user does however need the appropriate Microsoft Office licence to use the Excel functionalities).

Here is an example of a published workbook:

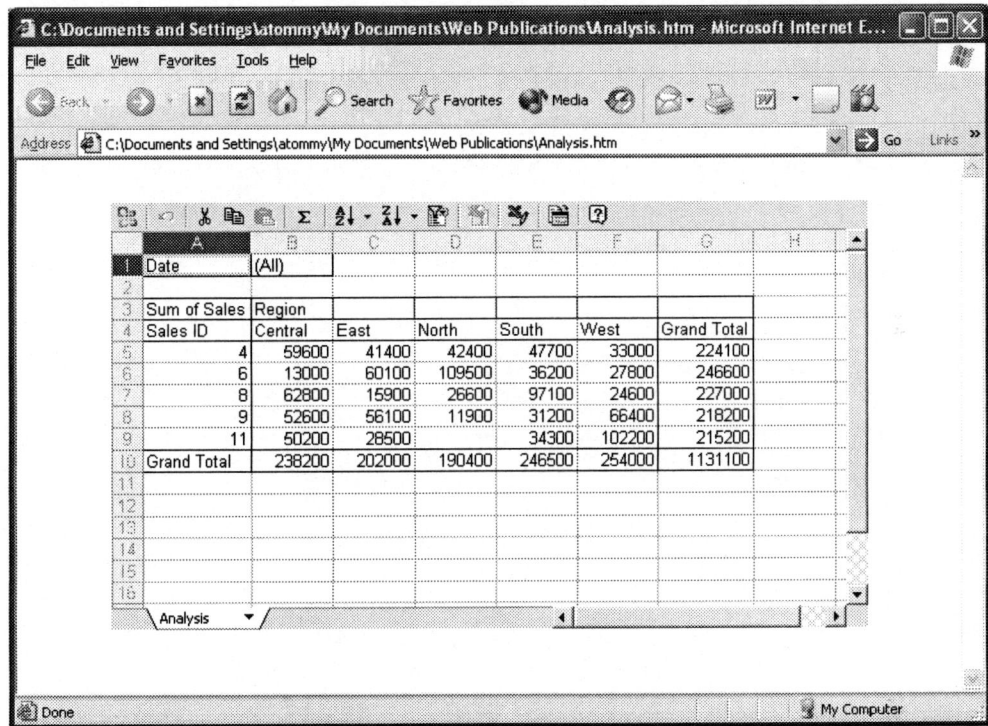

You can see that the network user cannot work with the pivot table in the same way as with the previous example. Here, some of the fields are inactive, there are less tools available and so on. A user visiting this page can, however, look at all the sheets in the workbook, by clicking the down arrow that appears on the sheet tab at the bottom left of the screen and choosing the name of the required worksheet.

- When you have finished your work, close the browser window.

- If you wish, close the Excel file.

To delete a Web page, use the Windows Explorer to go to the server and/or folder where the Web page is located. Select the Web page (file_name.htm) and its supporting files folder (filename_files), if there is one. Press the Del *key and click* **Yes** *to confirm the file deletion.*

Below, you can see **Practice Exercise 1.2**. This exercise is made up of 5 steps. If you do not know how to do one of the steps, go back to the title that corresponds to that particular lesson. When you have finished, you can check your work by reading the **Solution** that follows.

All the steps in this exercise are likely to be tested in the Microsoft Office Specialist exam.

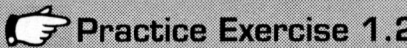 **Practice Exercise 1.2**

1. Import the table from the **1-2 Expenses.doc** document into **Sheet1** of the **1-2 Expenses sheet.xls** workbook. Copy the data without a link; the first destination cell for the copied data is cell **A14**. You can find the **1-2 Expenses.doc** Word document and the **1-2 Expenses sheet.xls** workbook in the **MOS Excel 2003 Expert** folder. Save your changes.

2. From the Web page located at this address: http://www.eni-publishing.com/Examples/Excel2003Expert/Members.htm, import the list of members that make up the **SEN** category into the **SEN** sheet in the **1-2 Members.xls** workbook. Save your changes.

3. Using a Web query, import all the data from the **Statistics.xml** file into a new workbook. This file's URL address is: http://www.eni-publishing.com/examples/Excel2003Expert/Statistics.xml. Save this query as **Import stats**.

4. Export the contents of cells **A1** to **E23** from the **Receipt** sheet in the **1-2 Receipt.xls** workbook, located in the **MOS Excel 2003 Expert** folder, into the second page of the **1-2 Letter.doc** document (also in the **MOS Excel 2003 Expert** folder). Establish a link when you make the copy. Save your changes.

5. Create a new folder within your My Documents folder and call it **Web Publications**. Publish the pivot table in the **1-2 Analysis.xls** workbook (in the **MOS Excel 2003 Expert** folder) as an interactive Web page into this Web Publications folder. Call the new Web page **Analysis** and the title of the page should be **Sales per team**.

If you would like to practise these features more, on another document, you should work through Summary Exercise 1, on MANAGING DATA. You will find the summary exercises at the end of the book.

It is often possible to perform a task in several different ways, but here, only the easiest solution is presented. You can go back to the corresponding lesson if you want to see other techniques you could use.

 **Solution to Exercise 1.2**

1. To import the table from the 1-2 Expenses.doc document into Sheet1 of the 1-2 Expenses Sheet.xls worksheet, start the Microsoft Word application then open the **1-2 Expenses.doc** document (in the **MOS Excel 2003 Expert** folder).
   Click inside the table, use the **Table - Select - Table** command then click the ⬚ tool button.

   If it is not open, start the Excel application then open the **1-2 Expenses Sheet.xls** workbook.

   Click cell **A14** on **Sheet1** then click the ⬚ tool button.

   Click the ⬚ tool button to save your changes.

2. To import the list of members belonging to the SEN category from the Web page   http://www.eni-publishing.com/examples/Excel2003Expert/ Members.htm into the SEN sheet of the 1-2 Members.xls workbook, open the **1-2 Members.xls** workbook in the **MOS Excel 2003 Expert** folder then click the **SEN** sheet tab.

   Open your Web browser (Internet Explorer for example), type **http://www.eni-publishing.com/examples/Excel2003Expert/Members .htm** in the **Address** box then press the ⏎ key.

   Scroll through the list until you can see the members in the **SEN** category.

   Position the pointer just before the **A** in Anderson (Terry), then drag down to the **N** in the **Paid** column of the row for O'Brian (Sean).

Use ⌈Ctrl⌉ **C** then return to cell **A2** on the **SEN** sheet in the Microsoft Excel application window and use ⌈Ctrl⌉ **V**.

Click the 🖫 tool button to save the changes made in the **1-2 Members.xls** workbook, then close your browser if you need to.

3. To import the data from the Statistics.xml file into a new workbook using a Web query, click the 🗋 tool button to create a new workbook.

Activate cell **A1**.

Use the **Data - Import External Data - New Web Query** command.

In the **Address** text box, type: **http://www.eni-publishing.com/examples/ Excel2003Expert/Statistics.xml** then click **Go**.

Click the ➡ icon in the top left corner of the page to select the whole of the Web page.

To save the query, click the 🗔 tool button, enter **Import stats** into the **File name** text box and click the **Save** button.
Click the **Import** button on the **New Web Query** dialog box to start importing the data.

Make sure the **Existing worksheet** option is active and check that the active cell reference shown is =**$A$1**.

Click **OK** to confirm.

Close the new workbook but do not save it.

4. To copy cells A1 to E23 of the Receipt sheet in the 1-2 Receipt.xls workbook into the second page of the 1-2 Letter.doc Word document, open the **1-2 Receipt.xls** workbook in the **MOS Excel 2003 Expert** folder and activate the **Receipt** sheet tab.

Select cells **A1** to **E23** then click the 🗎 tool button.
Open the Word application then the **1-2 Letter.doc** file (this is in the **MOS Excel 2003 Expert** folder) and scroll down the document so you can click at the top of the second page.

Use the **Edit - Paste Special** command and activate the **Paste link** option. In the **As** list, click the **Microsoft Office Excel Worksheet Object** option and click **OK**.

Click the ⊞ tool button to save the changes made to the document.

5. Start by creating a new folder for your Web page. Go to your **My Documents** folder (for example, on Windows XP, click the **start** button and choose **My Documents** from the **start** menu). Once you are exploring the My Documents folder, use the **File - New - Folder** command and type in the new name for the folder, which is **Web Publications**. You can now close the Explorer window.

To publish the pivot table in 1-2 Analysis.xls (in the MOS Excel 2003 Expert folder) as an interactive Web page in the Web Publications folder, open the **1-2 Analysis.xls** workbook with the **File - Open** command.

Next, use the **File - Save as Web Page** command.

In the Places Bar, click the **My Documents** shortcut and double-click the icon of the **Web Publications** folder to open it.

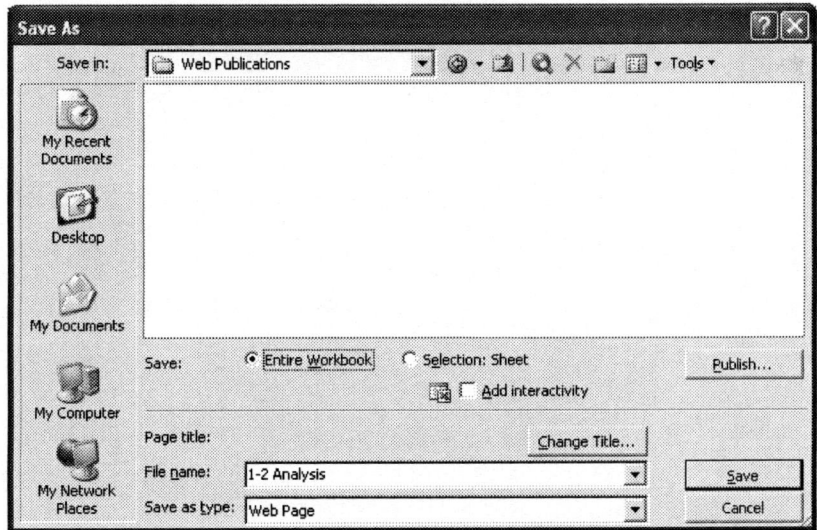

For this example, do not modify the current Web page settings with the **Tools - Web Options** command.

Activate the **Selection: Sheet** option and tick the **Add interactivity** check box.

Click the **Change Title** button, type **Sales per team** and click **OK**.

Drag to select the contents of the **File name** box and enter **Analysis**.

Click the **Publish** button.

In the **Choose** list, select the **Pivot Table** option.

Make sure the **Add interactivity with** option is active then, if it is not already selected, choose the **Pivot Table functionality** option in the drop-down list.

Tick the **Open published web page in browser** check box.

Click the **Publish** button.

The default browser opens and displays the interactive pivot table.

Sales per team

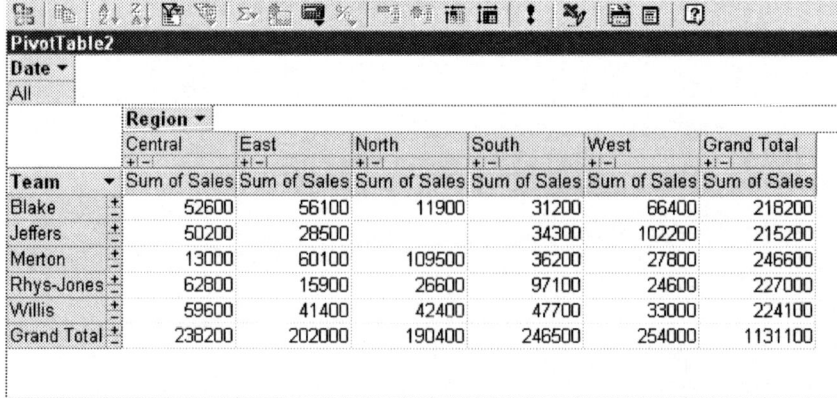

	Region ▾					
	Central	East	North	South	West	Grand Total
Team ▾	Sum of Sales	Sum of Sales	Sum of Sales	Sum of Sales	Sum of Sales	Sum of Sales
Blake	52600	56100	11900	31200	66400	218200
Jeffers	50200	28500		34300	102200	215200
Merton	13000	60100	109500	36200	27800	246600
Rhys-Jones	62800	15900	26600	97100	24600	227000
Willis	59600	41400	42400	47700	33000	224100
Grand Total	238200	202000	190400	246500	254000	1131100

MANAGING DATA
Lesson 1.3: Formatting

MANAGING DATA
Lesson 1.3: Formatting

1 ▪ Formatting numerical values

▪ Select the values concerned by the formatting.

▪ Choose one of the formats below:

Currency	(£10,000.00)		Dollar	($10,000.00)
Percentage	(1000000%)		Euro	(€10,000.00)
Comma	(10,000.00)			

▪ Select the values concerned.

▪ **Format - Cells** or Ctrl **1**

If you use the keyboard shortcut, press the 1 on the alphanumerical keyboard.

▪ Click the **Number** tab.

▪ In the **Category** list, select the category of the format you want to use.

▪ If necessary, modify the format settings; for example, you can specify the number of **Decimal places** or use a thousands separator.

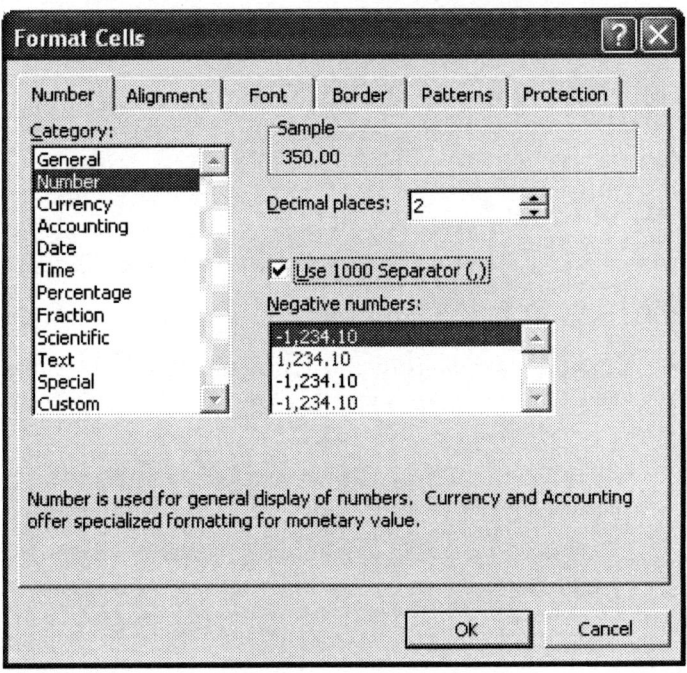

- Click **OK**.

 Hash symbols (#) may appear in some cells if the column is not wide enough to display the selected format; if required, widen the column concerned.

*To display one more or one less decimal place, click the **Increase Decimal** tool button on the **Formatting** toolbar or display one less decimal place with the **Decrease Decimal** tool button.*

⊞2 ▪ Creating a custom number format

▪ Select the cells concerned by the formatting.

▪ **Format - Cells** or ⌷Ctrl⌷ **1**

   If you choose to use the shortcut key, use the 1 on the alphanumeric keyboard.

▪ If necessary, activate the **Number** tab.

▪ Select the **Custom** format from the **Category** list, then enter or complete the required custom format in the **Type** text box.

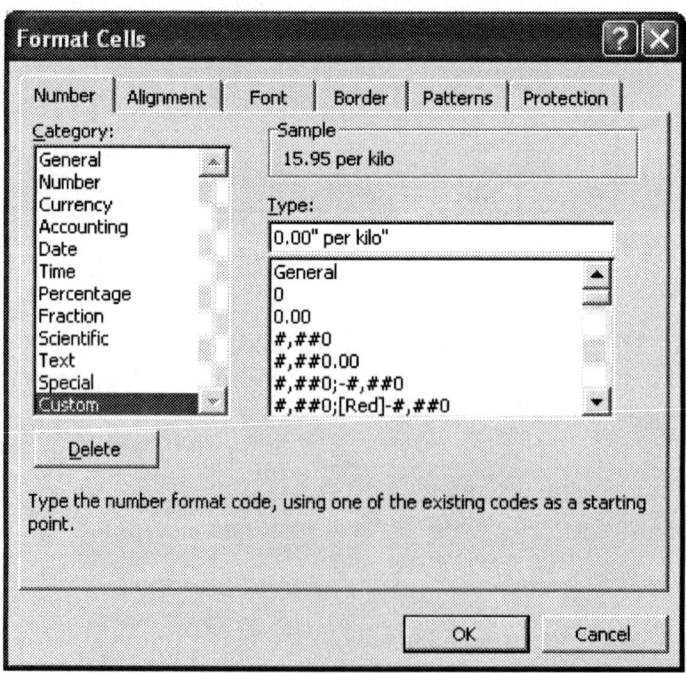

▪ A custom format can contain up to four sections, separated by semi-colons which define, respectively, the format of positive numbers, negative numbers, null values and the format of text.

For example: 0.00" kg";[red]-0.00" kg";0;[blue] This example shows positive values with two decimal places followed by the text "kg", negative values in red, preceded by a minus sign and followed by the text "kg", null values as zero and any text in the colour blue. Leaving a section empty applies no special format to that type of value.

- If you define only one section, it is used for all number types.

  For example: #,##0" net" With this format, whatever the value (positive, negative or null), the hundreds and thousands are separated by a comma and the value is followed by the text "net".

- Remember that you can use the following syntaxes when creating a custom format:

  <u>To add text to a custom format</u>: Text added to a format must be surrounded by quotation marks.

  <u>To customise a number format</u>: # ##0 puts a space between the thousands and hundreds; #,##0 adds a thousands separator (a comma).
  0 shows values without decimals,
  0.00 shows two decimal places.
  For example # ##0.00" net" displays **2415** as **2 415.00 net**.

  <u>To customise a date format</u>: For days use the codes d (1), dd (01), ddd (Sun) or dddd (Sunday),
  For months use m (1), mm (01), mmm (Jan) or mmmm(January),
  For years use yy (04) or yyyy(2004).

  Use the character of your choice as the separator.

  For example, the format **ddd dd mmm yyyy** displays **25/4/04** as **Sun 25 Apr 2004** (the position of days and months will depend on your regional options).

  <u>To include a text entry section</u>: to display whatever is entered in the cell, use the @ character. For example, **"State: "@** displays **State: Queensland** when you type **Queensland** into the cell.

- Click **OK** to confirm.

You can also display data as text using the TEXT function.

3 ▪ Creating conditional formats

▪ Select the cells concerned by the format.

▪ **Format - Conditional Formatting**

▪ In the **Condition 1** frame, open the first drop-down list and select:

Cell Value Is   if the condition refers to the value contained in the cells (a constant or the result of a formula).

Formula Is   if the condition refers to a logical formula.

▪ In the first case, the next thing to do is select a comparison operator then a comparison value. In the second case, define the logical formula (the result of this type of formula is TRUE or FALSE).
If the condition concerns a formula, start it with an equals sign (=).

▪ Click the **Format** button.

▪ Use the options in the **Font**, **Border** and **Patterns** tabs to define the format that is to be applied to the cells when the condition is fulfilled.

▪ Click **OK**.

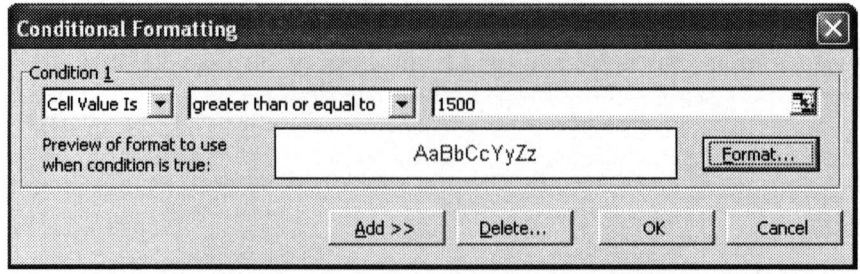

Here, if the cell value is 1500 or over, the cell contents will change colour to red.

- To define other formats to be applied under different conditions (particularly to define a format to be used when the preceding condition is not fulfilled), click the **Add** button then define another conditional format in the same way.

- Click **OK**.

The cell format changes automatically according to the contents of the cell.

4 • Formatting drawing objects

Selecting objects

- Click the ![tool button] tool button on the **Drawing** toolbar.

- Click an object to select it.

- To select several objects, hold down the [Shift] key and click each object to select it.

📄 *When several objects are selected, no name appears on the formula bar.*

🐾 *You can also select several objects by dragging an invisible rectangle around them.*

Resizing/moving an object

- Select the drawing object concerned.

*The small circles surrounding the selected object are called **handles**. When you place the mouse pointer over each type of handle, the pointer changes shape.*

- To resize an object, drag one of the selection handles. If you drag a corner handle, the object's proportions are unaffected.

- To move an object, point to one of its edges (not a handle) and when the pointer becomes a four-headed arrow, drag it into its new position.

📄 *Use the* Alt *key as you drag to align the object with the cell grid.*

Scaling objects to an exact size

- Select the object concerned.
- **Format - Name_of_object** or Ctrl **1** or double-click the object
- Click the **Size** tab.
- To give the size of the object as a precise height and width, enter the values required in the **Size and rotate** frame, in the **Height** and **Width** text boxes.
- To resize the object using a percentage of its current size, enter the required percentages in the **Scale** frame, in the **Height** and **Width** text boxes.
- If you wish to keep the object's original proportions, make sure the **Lock aspect ratio** option is ticked.

  If it is not, you may find that the object appears distorted after resizing.
- Click **OK** to confirm.

Cropping a picture

- Select the picture concerned.
- If necessary, display the **Picture** toolbar (**View - Toolbars - Picture**).
- Click the **Crop** tool button.

Cropping handles appear around the image.

- ■ To crop one side, point to the middle cropping handle on that side then when the pointer takes the shape of a "T", drag into the picture.

- ■ To crop two perpendicular sides, drag a corner handle.

- ■ To crop two opposing sides in an identical way, hold down Ctrl, then drag one of the corresponding middle cropping handles, towards the centre of the picture.

- ■ To crop the four sides simultaneously, hold down the Ctrl key and drag one of the corner cropping handles, towards the centre of the picture (the pointer will take the shape of a right-angle).

- ■ To end the cropping process, click the **Crop** tool button again.

📄 *To cancel a crop, drag the corresponding cropping handle outwards on the picture, holding down the Ctrl key if appropriate.*

Rotating an object/a picture

■ Select the object or picture concerned.

■ Point to the small green circle at the top of the object or picture and drag to rotate the object.

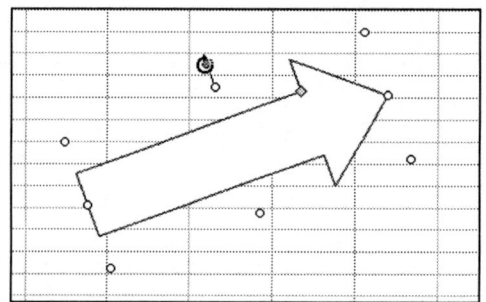

📄 *You can also rotate an object by clicking the* ***Rotate Left 90°*** 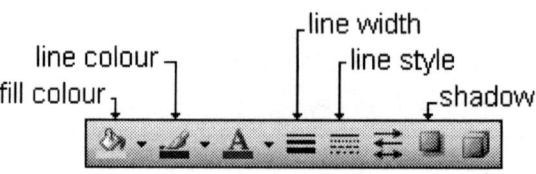 *tool button on the* ***Picture*** *toolbar (****View - Toolbars - Picture****).*

Changing the appearance of a 2D/3D object

■ <u>For a 2D object</u>: select the object and use the tool buttons on the **Drawing** toolbar:

The [⇄] *tool button is used to define arrowheads for line objects.*

*To remove an object's borders, select it then choose **Format - Text Box** or **Picture - Colors and Lines** tab. Go into the **Color** list and choose the **No Line** option.*

- For a 3D object: select the object then click the [▦] tool button on the **Drawing** toolbar to select a pre-set 3D style. If none of these styles is suitable, click the **3D Settings** button to create a specific 3D effect:

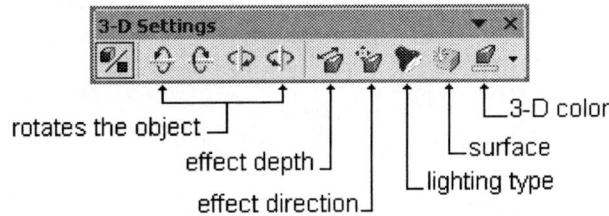

Some of these effects can be found in the **Format** dialog box: double-click the object to display this dialog box.

Adjusting brightness and contrast on a picture

- Select the picture concerned.

- If necessary, display the **Picture** toolbar (**View - Toolbars - Picture**).

- To change the picture's contrast, use the **More Contrast** [◐] or **Less Contrast** [◐] tool buttons.

- To change the picture's brightness, use the **More Brightness** [☀] or **Less Brightness** [☀] tool buttons.

📘5 ▪ **Formatting charts**

Selecting the different objects in a chart

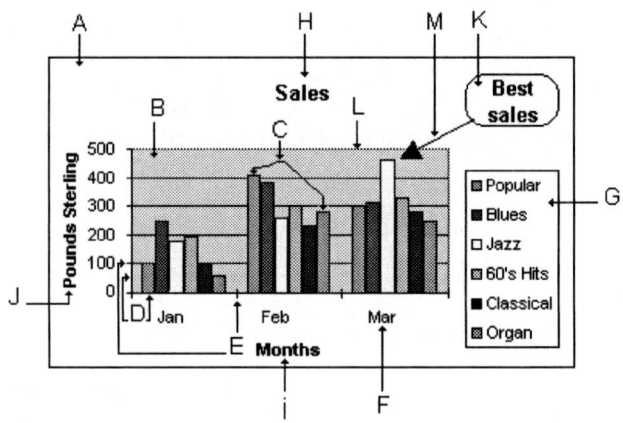

	Object	How to select it	What it contains
A	Chart area	Click in the chart but not in any object	All the chart objects
B	Plot area	Click in the plot area but not in any object	The axes and data markers
C	Point	Click the series then click the point	Each value in a series
	Series	Click one of the data markers in the series	All the points that constitute a data series
D	Value axis Category axis	Click one of the tick mark labels	

	Object	How to select it	What it contains
E	Tick marks	No selection	Lines which divide up the axes
F	Tick mark labels	No selection	Texts attached to tick marks
G	Legend	Click the object	Shows the names of the series represented in the chart and identifies the symbol or colour used for the data markers
H	Chart title	Click the object	Attached text
I	Value axis title	Click the object	Attached text
J	Category axis title	Click the object	Attached text
K	Text box	Click the object	Unttached text
L	Gridlines	Click one of the lines	Lines crossing the plot area to make it easier to read the chart
M	Arrow	Click the object	

 *When you point to an object in a chart, its name and value appears in a ScreenTip, providing that the **Show names** and **Show values** options are active in the **Options** dialog box, **Chart** tab (**Tools - Options**). You can also select a chart object by opening the list box on the **Chart** toolbar (**View - Toolbars - Chart**) and clicking the object's name.*

*To access a dialog box in which you can format a chart object, select the object then use the first command in the **Format** menu. This command name changes depending on the object. You can also double-click the item you wish to modify.*

Changing chart type

■ If you want to change the chart type for all the data series in the chart, select the entire chart (the square black handles that appear around the edge of the chart show that it has been selected).
If you want to change the chart type for just one of the series, select the series in question.

■ **Chart - Chart Type**

■ Choose the **Chart type**.

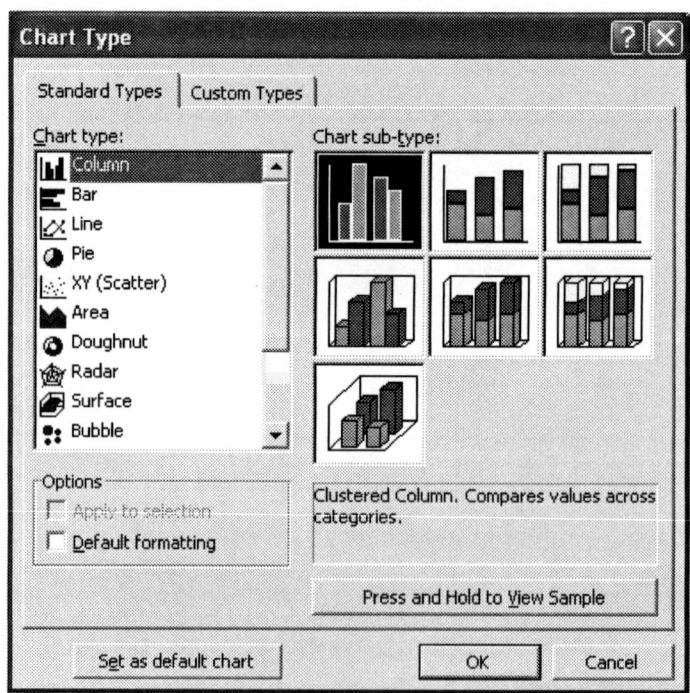

The **Apply to selection** option is not available when you are changing the chart type of the whole chart.

■ Double-click the **Chart sub-type** of your choice.

The *button on the* ***Chart*** *toolbar can be used to change chart type but does not allow you to choose between the various sub-types.*

The ***Source Data*** *option in the* ***Chart*** *menu allows you to redefine the different series in the chart.*

All the options for managing the chart can be found in ***Chart - Chart Options****.*

Inserting gridlines in a chart

- Select the chart.

- **Chart - Chart Options - Gridlines** tab

- Activate the options in the **Category (X) axis** frame to add vertical gridlines to the chart.

- Activate the options in the **Value (Y) axis** frame to add horizontal gridlines to the chart.

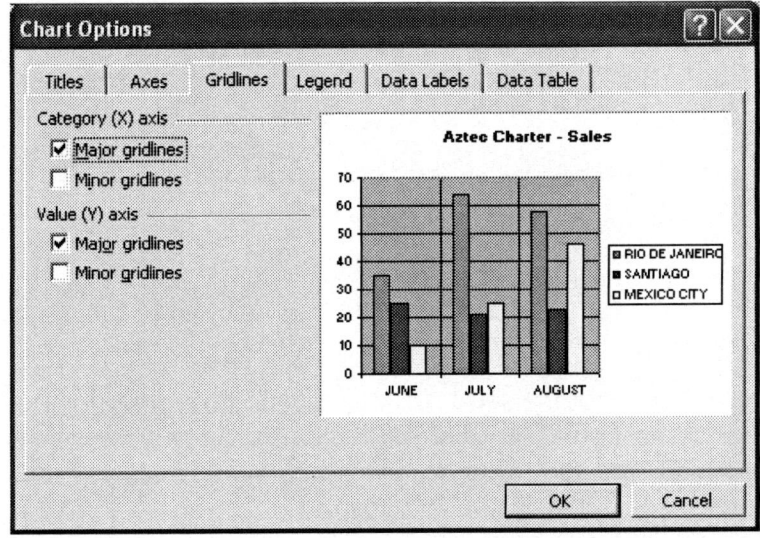

■ Click **OK**.

Managing a chart legend

■ If necessary, activate the chart.

■ **Chart - Chart Options - Legend** tab

■ Choose whether or not to **Show legend** by ticking or deactivating the check box.

■ In the **Placement** frame, choose the required position for the legend.

The legend is displayed horizontally when moved to the top or the bottom of the chart.

■ Click **OK**.

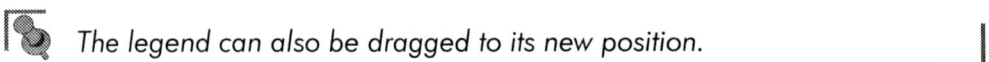 *Click the* ▣ *tool button on the* ***Chart*** *toolbar to display or hide the legend.*

🖰 *The legend can also be dragged to its new position.*

Adding a data series

First method

This can be used only when the series to be added is next to a series already included in the chart.

■ Select the chart area.

On the worksheet, the cells containing the data series are enclosed in a green rectangle.

■ Drag the handle of the green rectangle until it has encompassed the values of the new series (make sure the pointer looks like a double-headed, and not a four-headed, arrow).

Second method

- Select the cells containing the values corresponding to the series.
- Drag the selection onto the chart.

 This method is very quick but can be used only for embedded charts when the source data is close by. If the chart is in a chart sheet, you can copy the source data using the clipboard.

Third method

- **Chart - Source Data - Series** tab
- Click the **Add** button.

  Excel creates a new series called Series1.

- Click the **Name** box and give the new series a name.
- Click the **Values** box and click the ▣ button to work in the sheet. Select the cells containing the values for the new series and click ▣ to restore the dialog box.
- Click **OK**.

 This command can also be used to change the cells associated with a series.

*You can also use the **Chart - Add Data** command.*

If you wish to add a series or category to a chart sheet, you must select and copy (▣) the cells corresponding to the series or category then paste (▣) them into the chart sheet.

Deleting a data series

- Select the chart.
- **Chart - Source Data - Series** tab
- In the **Series** list, select the series you want to delete.
- Click the **Remove** button.
- Click **OK**.

> You can also delete a data series by clicking it in the chart then pressing the [Del] key.

Modifying the chart type for a data series

- Select the series concerned.
- **Chart - Chart Type**
- Select the required **Chart type** and **Chart sub-type**.
- Make sure the **Apply to selection** option is active.
- Click **OK**.
- If you wish, modify the presentation of this series by making sure the series is still selected and using **Format - Selected Data Series**.

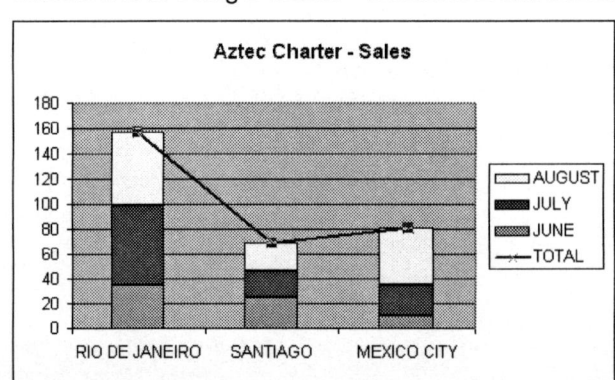

In this example, a Line chart type has been applied to the Total series.

Changing the order of the series

- Select one of the series on the chart.

- **Format - Selected Data Series - Series Order** tab

- Click the series you wish to move in the **Series order frame** and click the **Move Up** or **Move Down** button as appropriate.

- Click **OK**.

 When a series is selected, the SERIES() function appears in the formula bar. The last argument in this function refers to the place of that series in the order.

Adding/deleting a data category

Either the mouse or the menus can be used to add or delete a category in an embedded chart.

- Select the chart area.

- To add a new category, and its corresponding data points, drag the handle of the purple rectangle until it encompasses the cells containing the new category. To delete a category, reduce the rectangle so the data in question is excluded from it.

 This method can be used only in the case of an embedded chart, with the source data close by.

If the category you wish to add is not adjacent to the existing categories, you can select the corresponding cells and drag them into the chart.

- Select the chart area.

- **Chart - Add Data**

* In the **Range** text box, give the references of the data you want to add then click **OK**.

    The *Paste Special* dialog box may appear.

* If this occurs, activate the **New point(s)** option. In the **Values (Y) in** frame, indicate whether the series are in rows or columns. Activate the **Categories (X Labels) in First Column** (or **Row**) option if the selected range contains category labels.

* Click **OK**.

6 ▪ Formatting diagrams

You can change the look of an organization chart or other type of diagram by changing its size, layout or colours:

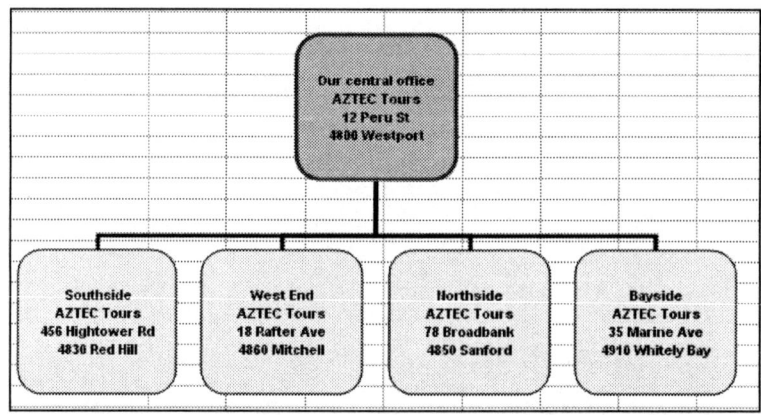

Resizing/colouring a diagram

* To select a diagram, click within its plot area, without clicking directly on one of its objects.

    *When a diagram is selected, the **Organization Chart** or **Diagram** toolbar appears, depending on the type of object.*

- To resize a diagram, select it and point to one of its corners. When the pointer becomes a double-arrow, drag in or out to decrease or increase the size.

  This resizes all the objects in the diagram proportionally.

- To colour the objects within a diagram, do one of the following:

  - To change a shape's fill, click the edge of the shape to select it then use the ⬜ tool button on the **Drawing** toolbar.

  - To change the border of a shape, use the ⬜ tool button to change the border colour, the ⬜ tool button to change the line width and the ⬜ tool button to change the line style. These tools are all on the **Drawing** toolbar.

- To change a shape's text, drag over the text to select it then change its style, size, colour, etc. as you would with normal text.

  📄 *Advanced formatting options can also be found in the **Format AutoShape** dialog shape: click a shape to select it then use **Format - AutoShape**.*

Changing a diagram's layout

- To add another shape to a diagram, choose the shape to which you wish to add a new one then open the **Insert Shape** list on the **Organization Chart** or **Diagram** toolbar and select the type of shape you wish to add.

- To delete a shape from a diagram, click the edge of the shape to select it then press ⬚Del⬚.

- To change a diagram's layout, open the list on the **Layout** button on the **Organization Chart** or **Diagram** toolbar and select the type of layout you require.

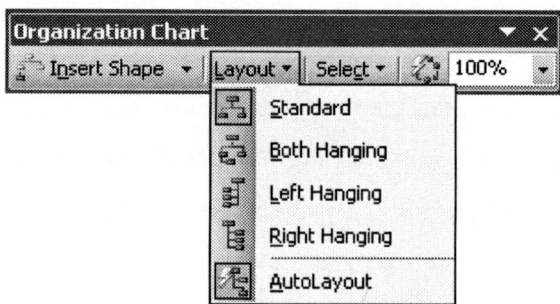

 The ☐ *tool button on the* **Organization Chart** *or* **Diagram** *toolbar can be used to apply an automatic format to the diagram.*

To delete a diagram, select it then press the ⌨Del⌨ *key.*

Below, you can see **Practice Exercise 1.3**. This exercise is made up of 6 steps. If you do not know how to do one of the steps, go back to the title that corresponds to that particular lesson. When you have finished, you can check your work by reading the **Solution** that follows.

Steps in the exercise that are likely to be tested on the exam are preceded by this symbol: ⊞. However, it is a good idea to complete all the steps in the exercise, to ensure that you have understood all the points discussed in the lesson.

☞ Practice Exercise 1.3

*To work on practice exercise 1.3, open the **1-3 Beef.xls** workbook in the MOS Excel 2003 Expert folder and activate Sheet1.*

1. Apply a **Comma** format to cells **B5** to **B13** then remove the decimal places.

⊞ 2. Create a custom number format for cells **C5** to **E12** that will display the values with two decimal places, followed by a space then the words **per kilo** (for example: 15.95 per kilo).

⊞ 3. Create conditional formats that will show total profits (F5 to F12) greater than or equal to 1500 in red and the others in blue.

*To continue this exercise, close and save the **1-3 Beef.xls** workbook and open the **1-3 Aztec Charter.xls** workbook.*

⊞ 4. Make the following changes to the objects on the **Aztec Charter** worksheet:

- Select the WordArt object that displays the title **Aztec Charter** and make it slightly smaller.

- Select the picture of a stone temple that is above the chart and rotate it until is correctly horizontal again, give it more contrast then move it closer to the WordArt object (try to centre it along column G).

5. Make the following changes to the chart on the **Aztec Charter** worksheet:

- Change the chart type to a clustered column type.

- Add major gridlines to the value and category axes.

- Display the legend below the chart.

- Remove the **Caracas** series from the chart. Move the **Mexico City** series to it appears furthest to the left on the chart.

- Add the **Caracas** series again and give it a line chart type.

- Delete the **August** data category from the chart.

6. In cell A34 there is a diagram. Make the following changes to it:

- Insert a **Coworker** shape to the Southside shape and enter this text:

West End AZTEC Tours
18 Rafter Ave
4860 Mitchell

- Change the text in the new shape by putting it in bold type.

- Change the colour of the topmost shape, giving it a **Gold** fill colour, then apply a 2 ¼ pt line width and a **Brown** line colour.

Save the changes made to the **1-3 Aztec Charter.xls** workbook and close it.

If you would like to practise these features more, on another document, you should work through Summary Exercise 1, on MANAGING DATA. You will find the summary exercises at the end of the book.

It is often possible to perform a task in several different ways, but here, only the easiest solution is presented. You can go back to the corresponding lesson if you want to see other techniques you could use.

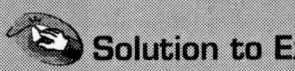 **Solution to Exercise 1.3**

1. To apply the comma format to cells B5 to B13, select cells **B5** to **B13** then click the ⬛ tool button.
   To remove the decimal places, keep cells B5 to B13 selected and click the ⬛ tool button twice.

2. To create a custom number format for cells C5 to E12 that displays the values with two decimal places, leaves a space, then displays the words "per kilo", select cells **C5** to **E12**, use the **Format - Cells** command then click the **Number** tab.
   Select the **Custom** format in the **Category** list, then click the **0.00** option in the **Type** list.
   Click after **0.00** in the **Type** text box and type "⬛Space⬛ **per kilo**".
   Click **OK** to confirm.

3. To create conditional formats that will show profits made that are greater than or equal to 1500 in red and the others in blue, select cells **F5** to **F12** then use **Format - Conditional Formatting**.
   Leave the **Cell Value Is** option selected, select the **greater than or equal to** operator in the second list and enter **1500** in the following text box.
   Click the **Format** button then the **Font** tab. Select the colour red in the **Color** list and click **OK**.
   Click the **Add** button to define the second format that is to be applied (condition 2). Leave the **Cell Value Is** option selected and select the **less than** comparison operator in the second list. Enter **1500** in the following text box. Click the **Format** button then the **Font** tab and select the colour blue in the **Color** list then click **OK**. Click **OK** to finish.

MANAGING DATA
Exercise 1.3: Formatting

Click the ⊟ tool button to save the **1-3 Beef.xls** workbook then close it with **File - Close**.

*Start by using **File - Open** to open the **1-3 Aztec Charter.xls** workbook in the **MOS Excel 2003 Expert** folder.*

▦ 4. To select the WordArt object (the **Aztec Charter** title) on the Aztec Charter worksheet, click it. To make it smaller, point to the handle in its bottom right corner and when you see a two-headed arrow, drag inwards.

Click to select the picture of a stone temple. To rotate it, point to the green rotation handle at the top of the picture. When the pointer takes the shape of a rotation circle, drag counter-clockwise until the temple is straight again.

To increase the picture's contrast, display the **Picture** toolbar if it is not on the screen: right-click a toolbar and choose **Picture**. Next, click the ▣ tool button on the **Picture** toolbar until you see a more marked contrast (about 5 clicks).

To move the picture, point inside it and when the pointer takes the shape of a four-headed arrow, drag the picture closer to the **Aztec Charter** WordArt title. Release the mouse when the centre of the picture is approximately on column G.

▦ 5. To edit the chart on the Aztec Charter worksheet, start by clicking it to select it.

To change the chart type, use the **Chart - Chart Type** command and click the **Standard Types** tab if necessary. In the **Chart sub-type** list, click the type at the top left corner, called **Clustered Column**. Click **OK** to confirm. To add major gridlines to the value and category axes, make sure the chart is still selected then use the **Chart - Chart Options** command and click the **Gridlines** tab. Tick the **Major gridlines** option under both **Category (X) axis** and **Value (Y) axis** then click **OK** to confirm.

To display the legend below the chart, make sure the chart is still selected then use **Chart - Chart Options** and click the **Legend** tab. Under **Placement**, activate the **Bottom** option and click **OK** to confirm.

To remove the Caracas series from the chart, make sure the chart is still selected then use **Chart - Source Data** and click the **Series** tab. Select **Caracas** in the **Series** list, click the **Remove** button then **OK**.

To move the Mexico City series so it appears furthest to the left on the chart, select the Mexico series on the chart then use **Format - Selected Data Series**. Click the **Series Order** tab. In the **Series order** box, click the **Mexico City** series if necessary then click the **Move Up** button twice. Click **OK** to confirm.

To add the Caracas series to the chart, select cells **A23** to **D23** on the worksheet and drag these cells into the chart area. To change the chart type for this series, select it if necessary then use **Chart - Chart Type**. On the **Standard Types** page, choose **Line** in the **Chart type** list then leave the default sub-type suggested by Excel. Click **OK** to confirm.

To delete the August category from the chart, select the chart area if necessary. Drag the blue selection handle that appears at the bottom right of cell **D12** on the worksheet across to the right until you reach cell **C12**.

6. To make the described changes to the diagram in cell **A34**, start by clicking the diagram area to select it.
To add a Coworker shape to the Southside shape, click the edge of the **Southside** shape to select it, then open the **Insert Shape** list on the **Organization Chart** toolbar and choose **Coworker**. The insertion point is in the shape, so type this text: **West End ⏎ AZTEC Tours ⏎ 18 Rafter Ave ⏎ 4860 Mitchell**

To put the new shape's text in bold type, drag over the new text and click the **B** tool button.

To change the look of the topmost shape (Our central office...), click the shape's edge to select it. To give it a Gold fill colour, open the list on the tool button and choose the colour called **Gold** in the palette. Next, open the list on the toolbar and choose a 2 ¼ pt line width. Open the list and choose the colour **Brown** to change the border colour.

Save and close the 1-3 Aztec Charter workbook by clicking its button then clicking **Yes** when Excel prompts you to save the file.

MANAGING DATA
Lesson 1.4: Outlines

MANAGING DATA
Lesson 1.4: Outline

⊞1 ▪ Creating an outline

An outline allows you to see or print only the main results of a table without the detail of the data.

Creating an outline automatically

If your table was created with formulas, such as sums or averages, you can create an automatic outline.

▪ Select the table concerned.

▪ **Data - Group and Outline - Auto Outline**

		Golden Delicious	Williams Pears	Bananas	Nectarines	TOTAL
1		FRUIT PRODUCTION (in kilos)				
2		Golden Delicious	Williams Pears	Bananas	Nectarines	TOTAL
3	January	14000	14800	12000	1000	41800
4	February	17500	21300	11270	850	50920
5	March	13450	14050	13600	800	41900
6	**1st Quarter**	44950	50150	36870	2650	134620
7	April	18000	21500	13600	760	53860
8	May	18250	22800	13000	700	54750
9	June	15000	18900	12800	4500	51200
10	**2nd Quarter**	51250	63200	39400	5960	159810
11	**1st Semester**	96200	113350	76270	8610	294430
12	July	13000	18000	10000	8600	49600
13	August	14900	18200	11500	16000	60600
14	September	15000	18300	10000	22000	65300
15	**3rd Quarter**	42900	54500	31500	46600	175500
16	October	27000	26700	8000	15000	76700
17	November	23640	23500	7500	6050	60690
18	December	17600	17430	8640	4030	47700
19	**4th Quarter**	68240	67630	24140	25080	185090
20	**2nd Semester**	111140	122130	55640	71680	360590
21	**ANNUAL TOTAL**	207340	235480	131910	80290	655020
22						

Buttons that allow you to manage the different levels of the outline appear to the left and at the top of the worksheet. This outline is made up of four levels: level 4 contains the detail rows (for each month), level 3 corresponds to the quarter rows, level 2 corresponds to the semester totals and level 1 is the annual total. In the illustration above, all the levels have been expanded.

- If you cannot see the ⊟ and/or ⊞ buttons, use **Tools - Options - View** tab and tick the **Outline symbols** option.

Creating an outline manually

- Select the rows (or columns) that should belong to the same outline level.

  Do not select any summary rows that may be connected with the rows you want to group.

- **Data - Group and Outline - Group**

- To insert a column (or a row) in the preceding level group, select the column (or row) then use **Data - Group and Outline - Group**.

- To remove a column (or a row) from a group, select the column (or row) and use **Data - Group and Outline - Ungroup**.

- Use the ⊟ and ⊞ buttons to collapse or expand the outline.

▣2 ▪ Using outlines

- To hide lower-level columns or rows, click the corresponding ⊟ button.

- Click a numbered button to hide all the levels below that level (for example, to hide level 3 and below, click the button numbered 2).

	A	B	C	D	E	F
1		FRUIT PRODUCTION (in kilos)				
2		Golden Delicious	Williams Pears	Bananas	Nectarines	TOTAL
6	1st Quarter	44950	50150	36870	2650	134620
10	2nd Quarter	51250	63200	39400	5960	159810
11	1st Semester	96200	113350	76270	8610	294430
15	3rd Quarter	42900	54500	31500	46600	175500
19	4th Quarter	68240	67630	24140	25080	185090
20	2nd Semester	111140	122130	55640	71680	360590
21	ANNUAL TOTAL	207340	235480	131910	80290	655020

On this illustration, button 3 was clicked, which collapsed the level 4 rows and left the rows of level 3 and higher. The ⊟ buttons become ⊞.

■ To restore hidden rows or columns, click each ⊞ button or click the numbered button that corresponds to the row you wish to reveal.

3 ▪ Clearing an outline

■ Activate the worksheet that contains the outline.

■ **Data - Group and Outline - Clear Outline**

> *If you clear an outline while the detail data is hidden, the detail rows or columns might remain hidden. If this occurs, show the data again by dragging the pointer over the row numbers/column letters that can still be seen then open the **Format** menu. Point to the **Rows** or **Column** option as appropriate then click the **Unhide** option.*

4 ▪ Inserting rows of statistics

By inserting automatic subtotals, you can obtain rows of statistics in a list.

■ Sort the table by the column that contains the entries you want to group together, as a first step to producing a subtotal for each group.

■ Select the table concerned by the statistics rows.

■ **Data - Subtotals**

■ In the **At each change in** list, select the column that contains the groups that are to be used for the statistical calculation.

■ Choose the calculation to be made in the **Use function** list.

■ Tick the columns that contain the values that you want to use in the calculation.

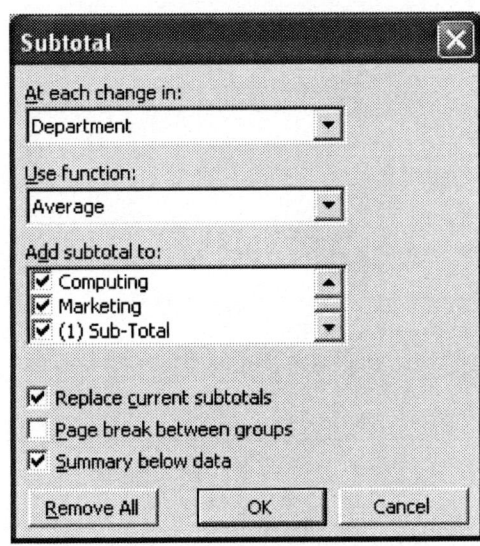

*Here, an average will be calculated for each different **Department** (**Computing**, **Marketing** and so on).*

- Leave the **Replace current subtotals** option active if you want to replace any existing subtotals with those that you are creating.

- Tick the **Page break between groups** check box to automatically insert a page break after each group of subtotals.

- Leave the **Summary below data** option active if you want to create subtotals and totals beneath detailed data. If this option is deactivated, only the subtotals will appear below the detailed data.

- Click **OK**.

1 2 3		A	B	C	D	E	F	G	H	I
	1	Exam Results								
	2									
	3	Department	Candidate	Computing	Marketing	*Sub-Total*	Project	Interview	*Sub-Total*	*Overall Total*
	4	Accounting	Blake, Sophie	14	15	29	24	56	80	109
	5	Accounting	Szuke, Jan	11	9	20	32	51	83	103
	6	Accounting	Cohen, Joshua	11	13	24	34	46	80	104
	7	Accounting	McPherson, Paul	14	12	26	39	44	83	109
	8	Accounting	Ferguson, Sandra	3	6	9	36	40	76	85
	9	**Accounting Average**		11	11	22	33	47	80	102
	10	Marketing	Pearson, Guy	12	16	28	26	54	80	108
	11	Marketing	Lee, Vanessa	11	15	26	20	30	50	76
	12	Marketing	Bancroft, Helen	14	12	26	32	48	80	106
	13	Marketing	Pringle, Owen	16	14	30	38	42	80	110
	14	**Marketing Average**		13	14	28	29	44	73	100
	15	**Grand Average**		12	12	24	31	46	77	101
	16									
	17		Average	12	12	24				
	18		Maximum	16	16	30				
	19		Minimum	3	6	9				
	20									

Excel calculates the subtotals that provide statistics you have requested and creates an outline that allows you to show or hide the detail rows that correspond to each subtotal.

 The **Remove All** button in the **Subtotal** dialog box removes all the subtotals, plus the outline, from the selected table.

Below, you can see **Practice Exercise 1.4**. This exercise is made up of 4 steps. If you do not know how to do one of the steps, go back to the title that corresponds to that particular lesson. When you have finished, you can check your work by reading the **Solution** that follows.

All the steps of this exercise are likely to be tested in the Microsoft Office Specialist exam.

☞ **Practice Exercise 1.4**

*To work on exercise 1.4, open the **1-4 Exams.xls** workbook in the **MOS Excel 2003 Expert** folder.*

1. Create an Auto Outline of the cell range **A3 (Department)** to **I12 (85)**; now remove columns **F (Project)** and **G (Interview)** from the outline.

2. Collapse the outline using the ⊟ button so that the **Computing** and **Marketing** columns are hidden, then use a numbered button to display only the first level.

3. Clear the whole outline.

4. Insert rows of statistics for all of the columns in the table of exam results, using the **Average** function. You will need to sort the table by the **Department** column first.

If you would like to practise these features more, on another document, you should work through Summary Exercise 1, on MANAGING DATA. You will find the summary exercises at the end of the book.

MANAGING DATA
Exercise 1.4: Outline

It is often possible to perform a task in several different ways, but here, only the easiest solution is presented. You can go back to the corresponding lesson if you want to see other techniques you could use.

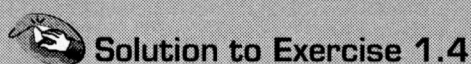 **Solution to Exercise 1.4**

1. To create an auto outline for cells A3 to I12, select this cell range then use **Data - Group and Outline - Auto Outline**.

   To remove columns **F** and **G** from the outline, select them by dragging over their column-headers, then use **Data - Group and Outline - Ungroup**.

2. To hide the **Computing** and **Marketing** columns, click the ⊟ button above column **E**.

   To show only the first level of the outline, click the ① numbered button in the top left corner of the worksheet.

3. To clear the whole outline, click one of the cells in the table, then use **Data - Group and Outline - Clear Outline**.

4. Before inserting **Average** statistic rows, click a cell in the **Department** column (**A3** to **A12**) then sort the data in the table using the [A↓Z] tool button.

   Once the data have been sorted, stay in the table and use the **Data - Subtotals** command.
   In the **Use function** drop-down list, choose the **Average** function
   In the **Add subtotal to** list, tick the options for which a calculation is to be made, in this case: **Computing**, **Marketing**, **(1) Sub-total**, **Project**, **Interview**, **(2) Sub-total**, leave the **OverallTotal** option active, then click **OK**.

MANAGING DATA
Lesson 1.5: Lists of data

📖1 ▪ Creating a list

A list is a set of interconnected data on an Excel sheet. Excel provides you with convenient features to help you manage and analyse lists of related data.
You can define several ranges as lists on the same worksheet, which can be useful if you want to separate your data into distinct groups for a better analysis.

▪ Open the workbook containing the data that you wish to define as a list.

This must not be a shared workbook.

▪ Select the range of cells that you want to convert into a list.

▪ **Data – List – Create List** or Ctrl **L**

	A	B	C	D	E	F	G	H	I
1	Surname	First Name	Address	PC/City	Sex	Age	Subs	Paid	
2	Alderman	Christine	56 Harvey St	4100 Tewesbury	F	13	2.50	Y	
3	Andrews	Melissa	27 Ridley St	5600 St Lucia	F	15	3.00	Y	
4	Barnett	Frances	38 Harrison Cres	4500 Greerton	F	15	3.00	N	
5	Charles	Yolanda	29 Bartlett Cres	6000 Lorton	F	14	3.00	Y	
6	Cray	Hannah	77 Kennedy Drive	5800 Rafter	F	17	4.50	Y	
7	Dell	Tammy	13 Read Road	4300 Dryden	F	16	4.50	Y	
8	Dorcas	Michelle	10 Kings Ct	5400 Fern Grove	F	16	4.50	Y	
9	Grant	Jessica	14/196 Red Sand Road	6100 Herston	F	17	4.50	N	
10	Grey	Josephine	89 Green St	5500 Killybill	F	22	8.00	N	
11	Greene	Louise	45 West Road	5600 St Lucia	F	25	8.00	Y	
12	Hunt	Rosemary	32 Fern Drive	5000 Gunston	F	18	4.50	Y	
13	Loxton	Marie	12/149 G			22	8.00	Y	
14	Marsh	Sarah	19 River			19	8.00	Y	
15	Martingale	Joanne	9/27 Thu			19	8.00	Y	
16	Norton	Vera	18 Quinn			24	8.00	Y	
17	Peak	Alison	26A Pine			21	8.00	Y	
18	Peyton	Theresa	141 Mt G			25	8.00	N	
19	Rowe	Patricia	265 Ash			15	3.00	N	
20	Sanders	Heather	16 Marigo			12	2.50	N	
21	Smith	Liza	15 Tall Tr			12	2.50	N	
22	Stanes	Ashley	3/28 Bartlett Cres	5200 Abbeyville	F	15	3.00	Y	
23	Stowerton	Laura	12 Oak St	4200 New Grove	F	12	3.00	Y	
24	Stoner	Carla	56 Lawrence St	4000 Westport	F	15	3.00	N	
25	Youmad	Alanna	58 Eagle St	5400 Fern Grove	F	13	2.50	Y	
26	Anderson	Terry	67 Milton Road	5200 Abbeyville	M	17	4.50	N	
27	Barton	John	37 Chambers St	4000 Westport	M	16	4.50	Y	
28	Blake	Peter	35 Nichol St	5600 Killybill	M	18	4.50	Y	
29	Clifton	Bill	29 William St	5800 Rafter	M	31	8.00	Y	
30	Drew	Gordon	78 Abbey Road	5200 Abbeyville	M	20	8.00	N	
31	Evans	Michael	35 Prior St	6300 Stoughton	M	33	8.00	Y	
32	Federicks	Neil	159 George St	4200 New Grove	M	24	8.00	Y	

Create List

Where is the data for your list?

=$A$1:$H$47

☑ My list has headers

OK   Cancel

- If you need to modify the reference of the selected cell range, click the 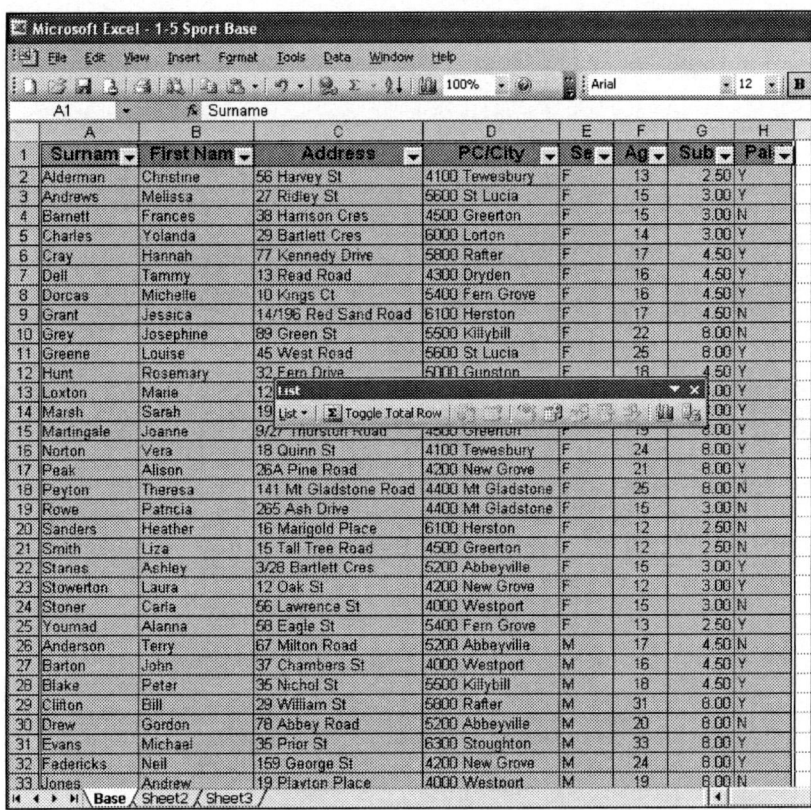 button, make a new selection, then click the button to expand the **Create List** dialog box.

- Tick the **My list has headers** option if the selected data includes headings.

- Click **OK**.

	A	B	C	D	E	F	G	H
1	Surnam ▾	First Nam ▾	Address ▾	PC/City ▾	Se ▾	Ag ▾	Sub ▾	Pai ▾
2	Alderman	Christine	56 Harvey St	4100 Tewesbury	F	13	2.50	Y
3	Andrews	Melissa	27 Ridley St	5600 St Lucia	F	15	3.00	Y
4	Barnett	Frances	38 Harrison Cres	4500 Greerton	F	15	3.00	N
5	Charles	Yolanda	29 Bartlett Cres	6000 Lorton	F	14	3.00	Y
6	Cray	Hannah	77 Kennedy Drive	5800 Rafter	F	17	4.50	Y
7	Dell	Tammy	13 Read Road	4300 Dryden	F	16	4.50	Y
8	Dorcas	Michelle	10 Kings Ct	5400 Fern Grove	F	16	4.50	Y
9	Grant	Jessica	14/196 Red Sand Road	6100 Herston	F	17	4.50	N
10	Grey	Josephine	89 Green St	5500 Killybill	F	22	8.00	N
11	Greene	Louise	45 West Road	5600 St Lucia	F	25	8.00	Y
12	Hunt	Rosemary	32 Fern Drive	5000 Gunston	F	18	4.50	Y
13	Loxton	Marie	12				.00	Y
14	Marsh	Sarah	19				.00	Y
15	Martingale	Joanne	9/27 Thurston Road	4500 Greerton	F	19	8.00	Y
16	Norton	Vera	18 Quinn St	4100 Tewesbury	F	24	8.00	Y
17	Peak	Alison	26A Pine Road	4200 New Grove	F	21	8.00	Y
18	Peyton	Theresa	141 Mt Gladstone Road	4400 Mt Gladstone	F	25	8.00	N
19	Rowe	Patricia	265 Ash Drive	4400 Mt Gladstone	F	15	3.00	Y
20	Sanders	Heather	16 Marigold Place	6100 Herston	F	12	2.50	N
21	Smith	Liza	15 Tall Tree Road	4500 Greerton	F	12	2.50	N
22	Stanes	Ashley	3/28 Bartlett Cres	5200 Abbeyville	F	15	3.00	Y
23	Stowerton	Laura	12 Oak St	4200 New Grove	F	12	3.00	Y
24	Stoner	Carla	56 Lawrence St	4000 Westport	F	15	3.00	N
25	Youmad	Alanna	58 Eagle St	5400 Fern Grove	F	13	2.50	Y
26	Anderson	Terry	67 Milton Road	5200 Abbeyville	M	17	4.50	Y
27	Barton	John	37 Chambers St	4000 Westport	M	16	4.50	Y
28	Blake	Peter	35 Nichol St	5500 Killybill	M	18	4.50	Y
29	Clifton	Bill	29 William St	5800 Rafter	M	31	8.00	Y
30	Drew	Gordon	78 Abbey Road	5200 Abbeyville	M	20	8.00	N
31	Evans	Michael	35 Prior St	6300 Stoughton	M	33	8.00	Y
32	Fadericks	Neil	159 George St	4200 New Grove	M	24	8.00	Y
33	Jones	Andrew	19 Playton Place	4000 Westport	M	19	8.00	N

Notice that the selected cell range, which is now a list, contains:

- a border (which is blue if the list is not active),

- drop-down autofilter lists on each column (filters are covered in more detail later in this chapter),

- *an insert row is added under the last row in the list, and this contains an asterisk.*

*You may also see the **List** toolbar (if not, you can display it with **View - Toolbars - List**).*

- To display or hide a row of totals, click the ![Σ Toggle Total Row] button on the **List** toolbar.

When the total row is displayed, it appears after the insert row.

- To deactivate a list, click a cell, a row or a column outside the list.

- To convert a list into a normal range of cells, open the drop-down list on the **List** button on the **List** toolbar then click the **Convert to Range** option. Click **Yes** to confirm the conversion.

Opening the data form

A data form helps you to enter records and makes looking for records easier in a list.

- For a list, activate the list; for a normal range, click in that range.

- **Data - Form**

This form is made up of the following elements:

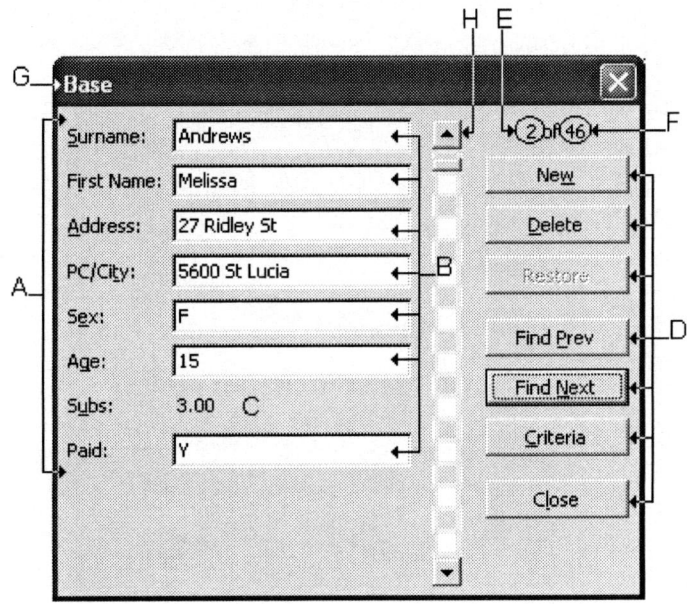

A   Field names

B   Edit boxes for entering field contents

C   Data form fields containing calculated fields

D   Command buttons

E   The number of the current record

F   The total number of records

G   Title bar

H   Vertical scroll bar

Adding records

▪ To start adding a new record, click the **New** button.

▪ Fill in each new record as follows:

- press <kbd>Tab</kbd> to move to the next box, except after the last one (or <kbd>Shift</kbd><kbd>Tab</kbd> if you want to go back to the previous box).

- to confirm the data entered, press ⏎ after the last piece of information is entered; you will go immediately into a new record.

Moving from record to record

▪ Use the scroll bar or the arrow keys, as shown below:

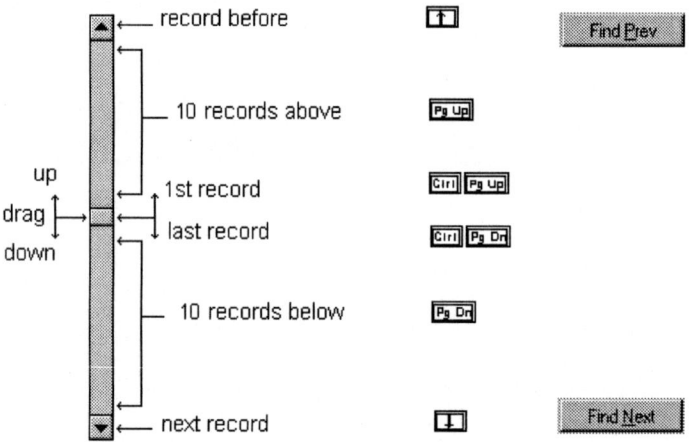

The last form displayed is always a new form ready to be filled in.

Finding a particular record

▪ Go into either the first or last record.

▪ Click the **Criteria** button.

The record number indicator is replaced by the word **Criteria**, the calculated fields become text boxes and the **Criteria** button is replaced by a **Form** button.

■ Set your search conditions as if you were filling in a record but do not press ↵. For example:

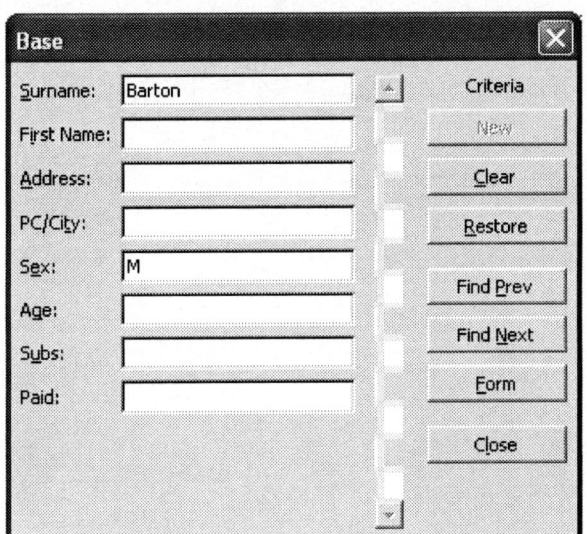

These criteria will find all the records with Barton as the surname field and M (male) in the sex field.

■ If you started from the first record, click the **Find Next** button to begin searching. If you started at the last record, start searching with the **Find Prev** button.

■ Continue your search using the **Find Next** or **Find Prev** buttons.

Modifying a record

■ Go to the record you want to modify.

■ Make your corrections then press ↵ to confirm them.

If you change your mind about the changes you make, click the **Restore** button (before pressing ↵) to go back to the previous values.

Deleting a record

- Go to the record you want to delete.

- Click the **Delete** button.

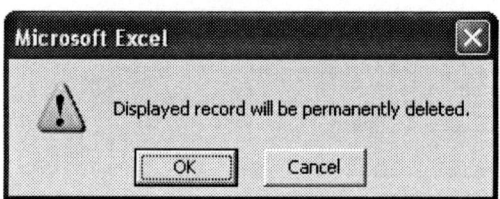

- Confirm the deletion with **OK**.

Leaving the data form

- Click the **Close** button.

2 ▪ Creating and using a simple filter

A filter selects records that meet a set criterion.

- To insert drop-down autofilter lists on a range of cells, activate one of the cells concerned and use **Data - Filter - AutoFilter**.

- To see the drop-down autofilter lists in a list, click one of the cells in it.

Filtering by one of the values listed

- Open the list associated with the field concerned:

Each list includes all the values in the field.

- Click the value that interests you.

   Only the records that correspond to the filter value can now be seen on the screen, those that do not correspond are hidden. The row numbers of the records displayed change colour.

- To show all the records again, open the list on the field you have filtered and click the **All** option at the top of the list.

Filtering by a specific criterion

- Open the list associated with the required field.

- Choose the **Custom** option.

- In the first list box, select an operator of comparison.

- Activate the text box next to it and enter the compare value.

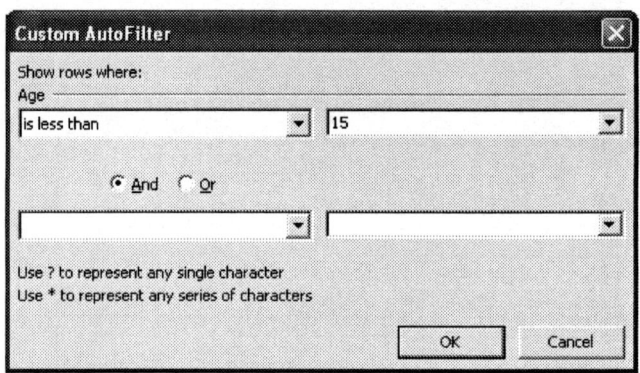

This criterion filters all the records for people aged under 15.

- Click **OK**.

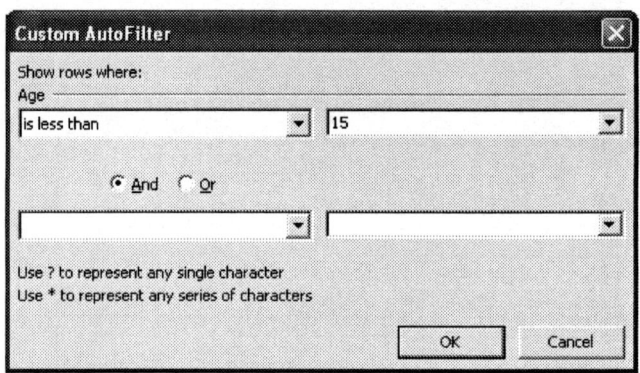 ▪ **Filtering by several criteria**

Two criteria for the same field

- Activate the **AutoFilter** with **Data - Filter - AutoFilter** in a range of cells or, for a list, activate the list.

- Open the list for the field concerned.

- Click the **Custom** option.

- Define the first filter criterion.

- Indicate how the two criteria are to be combined:

  - if both must be satisfied together, choose **And**,

  - if either one or the other must be satisfied, choose **Or**.

- Enter your second condition.

- Click **OK**.

Criteria concerning several fields, combined with "and"

- Activate **AutoFilter**.
- Set the conditions in each field concerned.

4 ▪ Creating an advanced filter

Creating a criteria range

- You first need to locate an empty space of a few columns and a few rows on the sheet (typically next to the list of data).
- In one of the empty rows, enter the field names you want to use to filter the list.
- In the rows below, enter the criteria that should be met, paying attention to the following rules:

Combination	Method
OR	the criteria are entered in several rows.
AND	the criteria are entered in several columns.
OR and AND	the criteria are entered in several rows and several columns.

Look at these examples to better understand the use of AND and OR when setting criteria:

Requirements	Criteria ranges	
Records for members named: BARNETT **OR** SANDERS **OR** KELSEY	NAME	
	BARNETT	
	SANDERS	
	KELSEY	
Records for 18-year-old girls: 18 **AND** F	AGE	SEX
	18	F

Requirements	Criteria ranges	
Records for boys aged 13 **OR** 15	SEX	AGE
	M	13
	M	15

Using a criteria range

* Click the list or the range of cells.

* **Data - Filter - Advanced Filter**

  The ***Filter the list, in-place*** option is active by default.

* Click the **Criteria range** box, use the [icon] to collapse the dialog box and select the criteria range previously created on the worksheet. Click [icon] to restore the dialog box:

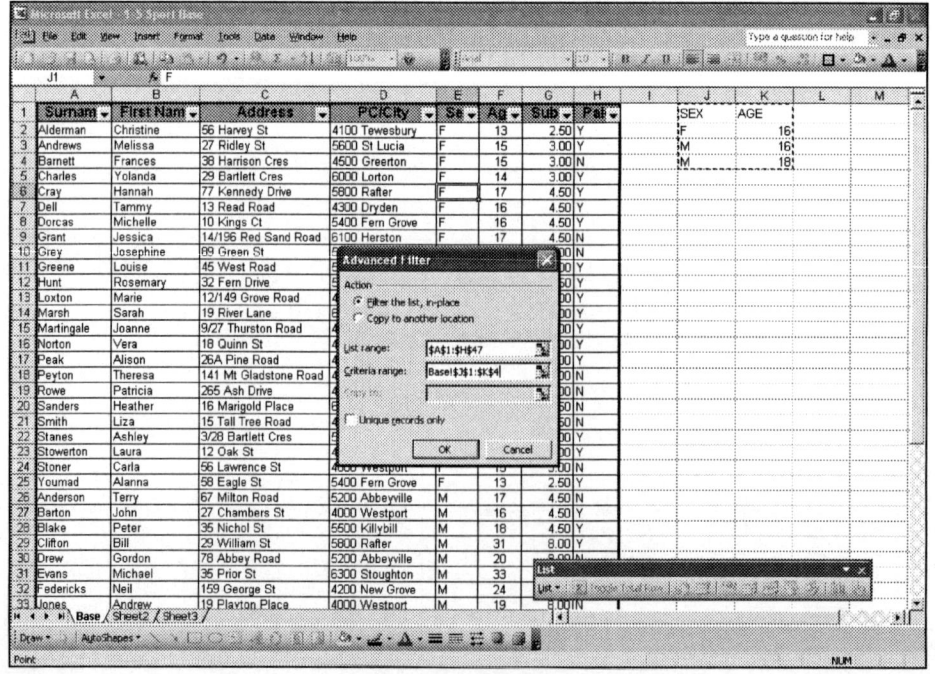

- If necessary, activate the **Unique records only** option to filter out any duplicate records.

- Click **OK**.

  Only the records that meet the criteria are displayed.

- To see all the records again, use **Data – Filter – Show All**.

   *Excel automatically gives the name **Criteria** to the cells in the criteria range.*

5 ▪ Showing all the records again

- If only one filter is active, open the drop-down list on the field that is filtered and click the **All** option.

- If several filters are active, use the **Data - Filter - Show All** command.

6 ▪ Copying records that meet filter criteria

- In another place on the sheet, enter a row of the field headings whose contents you wish to filter and extract.

- Create a criteria range.

- Click in the list.

- **Data - Filter - Advanced Filter**

- In the **Action** frame, activate the **Copy to another location** option.

  *The **Copy to** box becomes available.*

- In the **Criteria range** box, if necessary, indicate where the criteria range can be found.

- Activate the **Copy to** box and select the row of names you have just typed in the sheet.

- If necessary, activate the **Unique records only** option.
- Click **OK**.

📄 *If you change the criteria range, run the filter again.*

7 ▪ Defining authorised data for specific cells

By defining validation criteria, you can limit what information users can enter in given cells.

- Select the cells concerned.
- **Data - Validation - Settings** tab
- Open the **Allow** list and choose an option appropriate to the type of data you wish to allow in the cell(s):

Any value	no restrictions.
Whole number	the cell must contain an integer.
Decimal	the cell must contain a number or a fraction.
List	this option allows you to list cell references containing authorised data.
Date	the cell must contain a date.
Time	the cell must contain a time.
Text length	this option allows you to specify the number of characters authorised in the cell.
Custom	this option allows you to enter a formula to limit the data that the cell will accept.

- If you select **Whole number**, **Decimal**, **Date**, or **Time**, choose an operator from the **Data** list and give values for comparison appropriate to the operator.

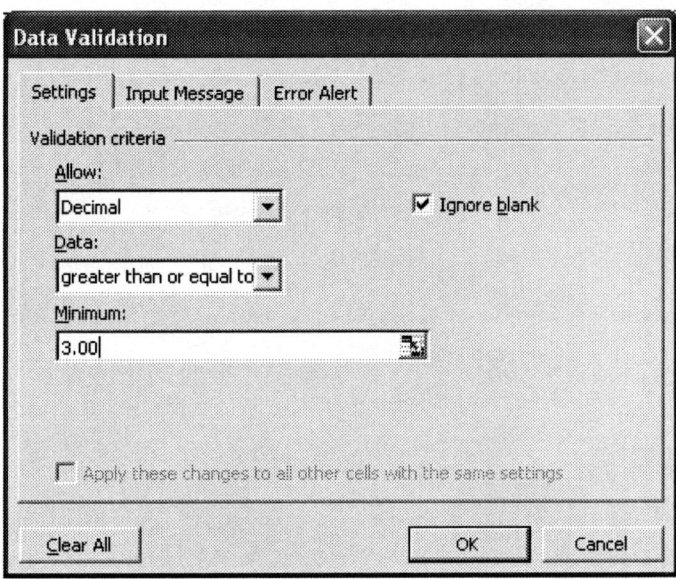

These criteria allow the user to enter only a decimal or integer with a value greater than or equal to 3.00.

- If you choose **Text length**, select the **equal to** operator, then give the authorised number of characters in the **Length** box.

- If you choose **List**, enter the references of the cells containing authorised data in the **Source** box. Activate the **In-cell dropdown** option if you want to add a drop-down list of authorised data to the cell(s) concerned.

*In the **Source** option, you can give a named range of cells, preceded by an = sign (e.g. =stafflist).*

- If you select **Custom**, use the **Formula** box to enter a calculation formula beginning with an equal sign (=). This should be a logical type formula that returns TRUE or FALSE.

- Whatever the type of data specified, activate **Ignore blank** if you authorise the cell to remain empty.

- Click the **Error Alert** tab to enter a message that Excel will display when the data entered do not meet the validation criteria.

- Leave the **Show error alert after invalid data is entered** option active and set the following options:

Style	the symbol that will appear in the error message dialog box and the degree of tolerance shown to unauthorised data.
Stop	the user is limited to only what has been authorised.
Warning	the user can force through an unauthorised entry.
Information	the user is simply warned that an unauthorised value is being entered.
Title	the title of the error message dialog box.
Error message	the text of the error message.

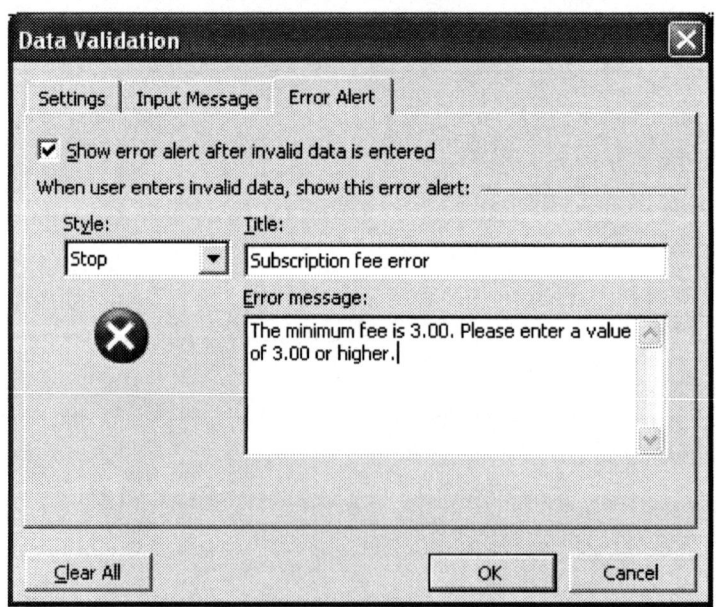

- Click **OK**.

Any entry that does not correspond to the validation criteria will cause an error message to appear:

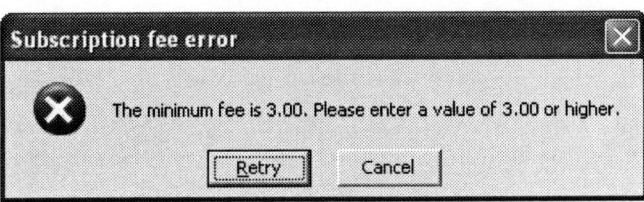

*The buttons that appear on the error message differ depending on the **Style** used for the **Error Alert**. These may or may not allow you to force unauthorised data.*

 Data entered before the criteria were set are not tested. There is however, an option in Excel that will find any data that do not meet the criteria (cf. lesson 2.1.3 - Finding errors and invalid data).

*The options on the **Input Message** page of the **Data Validation** dialog box make it possible to display a message in a ScreenTip when the mouse pointer is on the cell.*

8 ▪ Calculating statistics with database functions

These functions can calculate statistics from the records whose values meet criteria entered in a criteria range.

▪ Create the appropriate criteria range.

▪ Use the following functions:

=DCOUNT(database,field,criteria)	counts the cells
=DSUM(database,field,criteria)	totals the field's values
=DAVERAGE(database,field,criteria)	calculates the field's average value
=DMAX(database,field,criteria)	extracts the highest value in the field
=DMIN(database,field,criteria)	extracts the lowest value in the field

- To fill in the arguments of each function, replace:

  - **database** with the references of your defined list (including the column headings),

  - **field** with the column heading (this is the field's name),

  - **criteria** with the references of the cells containing the criteria range: if you have created a complex filter, you can enter the range name "criteria".

   As soon as you change anything in the criteria range, the statistics are automatically updated.

Below, you can see **Practice Exercise 1.5**. This exercise is made up of 8 steps. If you do not know how to do one of the steps, go back to the title that corresponds to that particular lesson. When you have finished, you can check your work by reading the **Solution** that follows.

Steps in the exercise that are likely to be tested on the exam are preceded by this symbol: ▦. However, it is a good idea to complete all the steps in the exercise, to ensure that you have understood all the points discussed in the lesson.

☞ Practice Exercise 1.5

To work on practice exercise 1.5, open the **1-5 Sport Base.xls** workbook in the **MOS Excel 2003 Expert** folder.

▦ 1. Define the table as a list (A1:H47) then using the data form, look for the record for club member called **John BARTON** and correct his address, which should read **27 Chambers St** instead of **37 Chambers St**.

2. Filter the records in the list for members aged under **15** years then display all the records again (use an AutoFilter).

▦ 3. Using an AutoFilter with several criteria, show all the members who have paid a subscription fee (sub) of **4.50**. Show all the records again.

▦ 4. Show a list of the **females** aged **16** as well as the **males** aged **16 AND 18** by using an advanced filter.

▦ 5. In one action, delete all the filter criteria and show all the records in the list again.

6. Copy the records extracted with the filter used in step 4 (records for **females** aged **16** and **males** aged **16** and **18**), and insert them starting from cell **L8**. Only the **Surname**, **First Name** and **Address** fields corresponding to the filter should be copied.

7. Set a validation condition to the subscription fee cells, because the latest subscription fees should all exceed **3.00**.

8. In cell **J6**, enter a label for **Total females under 17** and in **J7** enter a DCOUNTA function that will count the females under 17 in the club. To do this, you will need to alter the criteria range in **J1** as shown here:

J	K
SEX	AGE
F	<17

If you would like to practise these features more, on another document, you should work through Summary Exercise 1, on MANAGING DATA. You will find the summary exercises at the end of the book.

It is often possible to perform a task in several different ways, but here, only the easiest solution is presented. You can go back to the corresponding lesson if you want to see other techniques you could use.

Solution to Exercise 1.5

 1. To define the table on the worksheet as a list, select the cells from A1 to H47 then use the **Data - List - Create List** command.
Make sure the **My list has headers** option is active then click **OK**.
To display the data form, activate one of the cells in the list then use the **Data - Form** command.
To look for the record concerning **John Barton**, go to the first record in the list (use the vertical scroll bar if necessary) then click the **Criteria** button.
Click the text box for the **Surname** field, in which you want to search and enter the name you are looking for: **Barton**. Use the ⌞Tab⌟ key to go to the text box for the **First Name** field and enter **John**.
Click the **Find Next** button to start searching.
To modify the contents of the **Address** field, click the corresponding text box then edit the street number, changing it from **37** to **27** and confirm by clicking the **Close** button.

2. To filter for members under 15, activate one of the cells in the list then use the **Data - Filter - AutoFilter** command.
Open the list associated with the **Age** field then click the **Custom** option.

Fill in the dialog box, following the example below:

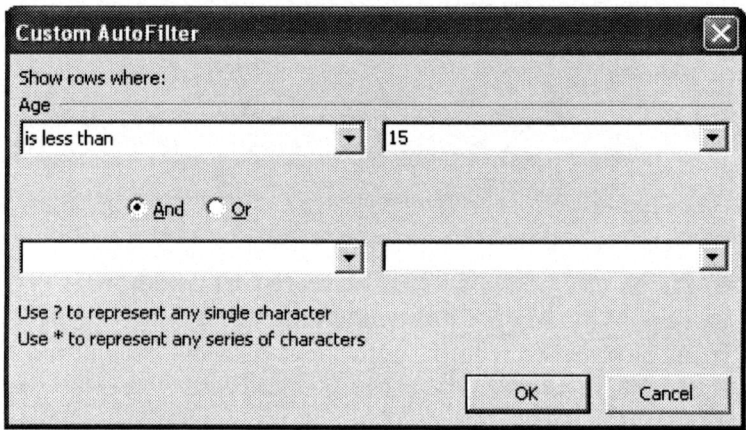

Confirm by clicking **OK**.

To show all the records again, use the **Data - Filter - Show All** command.

3. To filter the members who have paid fees of 4.50, click the list to see the **AutoFilter**.
   Open the list associated with the **Subs** column (Subscription fee) and click the required value: **4.50**, which corresponds to the first criterion; then open the second list on the **Paid** field and click **Y** (for Yes) which is the second criterion.
   Show all the records again with the **Data - Filter - Show All** command.

4. To show a list of all the female club members aged 16 and all the males aged 16 and 18, you should determine the fields and values on which the filters will be run, so your criteria range will resemble the example below:

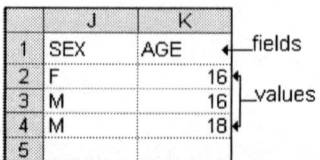

	J	K
1	SEX	AGE	← fields
2	F	16
3	M	16	← values
4	M	18
5		

Click any cell in the data list then run an advanced filter with the **Data - Filter - Advanced Filter** command.
Activate the **Filter the list, in-place** option and fill in the **List range** and **Criteria range** boxes then confirm with **OK**.

You should obtain this result:

E6	▼	ƒx	Surname				

	A	B	C	D	E	F	G	H
1	Surname	First Name	Address	PC/City	Sex	Age	Subs	Paid
7	Dell	Tammy	13 Read Road	4300 Dryden	F	16	4.50	Y
8	Dorcas	Michelle	10 Kings Ct	5400 Fern Grove	F	16	4.50	Y
27	Barton	John	27 Chambers St	4000 Westport	M	16	4.50	Y
28	Blake	Peter	35 Nichol St	5500 Killybill	M	18	4.50	Y
49								

5. To show all the records again, deleting all the filter criteria, use the **Data - Filter - Show All** command.

6. To copy the records returned by the filter set up in step 4, use the criteria range you created previously and enter the field names that you want copying, as shown below:

	A	B	C
52			
53	Surname	First Name	Address
54			

Click in the list.

Run the advanced filter by using the **Data - Filter - Advanced Filter** command. Activate the **Copy to another location** option, check the **List range** and **Criteria range** references and fill in the **Copy to** box with the references of the destination cells (here, A53:C53).

Confirm with **OK**.

7. To set validation criteria in the subscription fee cells, start by selecting all the cells in the **Subs** column and use the **Data - Validation** command then click the **Settings** tab.

   Open the **Allow** list and choose the **Decimal** option. In the **Data** list, choose **greater than or equal to** as the operator. In the **Minimum** box, enter a value of **3.00**. Confirm your entry by clicking **OK**.

8. To use a database function to count the number of females under 17 in the club, start by changing the criteria range that starts from cells **J1** and **K1**. Delete the contents of cells **J2** to **K4** and enter **F** in cell **J2** and **<17** in **K2**.

   In cell **J6**, enter the following label: **Total females under 17**.

   In cell **J7**, enter this formula **=DCOUNTA(A1:H47,F1,J1:K2)**.

   This function counts the nonblank cells in one of the fields (Age, which starts in F1) in the list (A1 to H47), according to the criteria set in a criteria range (J1 to K2).

   Confirm the formula with ⏎.

MANAGING DATA
Lesson 1.6: Excel and XML

🪟1 ▪ Opening an XML file in Excel

XML and Excel

▪ XML stands for eXtensible Markup Language and is the language likely to supersede HTML on the World Wide Web. Like HTML (HyperText Markup Language), XML uses markup which means that information is presented in the form of tags. Whereas HTML uses tags to describe how the information in them should be formatted (what is a title, a table, an image, a link and so on), XML is a meta-language, which means you can invent your own tags. These tags delimit the main information and its derivatives in your Web document (items such as references, names, ID numbers and so on) in a way that can be understood by a variety of applications.

▪ XML is a method that places structured data into a text file, following a standard set of guidelines so that data can be read and interpreted by numerous different applications. This structured data can be shared, meaning that all types of applications (word processors, databases etc.) can interact with Web sites.

▪ What matters in an XML document is its content; the formatting is handled by a stylesheet, associated with the XML document by a tag. This is one of the major differences between XML and HTML, as presentation is separate from content. This means that different formatting can be applied to the same content. This makes the XML document adaptable to a variety of uses (tables, charts etc.)

▪ XML features are available only in Microsoft Office 2003 professional Edition and Microsoft Office Excel 2003 (except for saving files in XML Spreadsheet format).

▪ Excel 2003 provides you with two ways of saving data in XML format. You can save the whole document as an XML file including its formatting. The file created in this way is bigger than the original xls format file. The second way of saving is to save only the data, which produces a "clean" XML file that can be used in other applications if required.

Opening XML files

When you open an XML file in Excel, Excel looks for a tag that refers to the XML stylesheet (in XSL format) that it should apply to present the data correctly. If it finds the tag, Excel will ask you to confirm that it should apply this stylesheet (or to choose one if several are referenced). If there is no XML tag, or if you do not want to apply the XSL file, the item's first tag will be used as a heading and be placed in cell A1. Then Excel will present the data according to its structure (data sets, duplicate fields, etc.).

- **File - Open**
- Open the **Files of type** list and choose **XML Files (*.xml)**.
- Use the **Look in** list or the places bar to find the folder in which the required file is located.
- Click the file's icon and click **Open** or simply double-click the file icon.

If the XML file was created with Excel, using the XMLSS format, it will open straight away, as it contains its own presentation tags and does not need an XSL stylesheet. However if the XML file refers to one or more stylesheets, Excel will display this message:

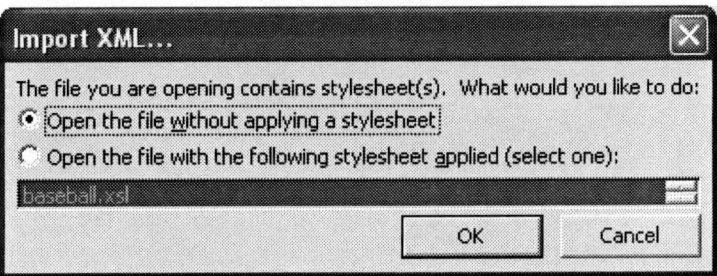

- Activate the **Open the file without applying a stylesheet** option if you want Excel to display the data without taking a stylesheet into account, or activate **Open the file with the following stylesheet applied (select one)** and choose a stylesheet from the drop-down list.
- If you choose to **Open the file without applying a stylesheet**, Excel will ask how you wish to open the file.

* In the **Open XML** dialog box, choose one of the options proposed:

As an XML list   Excel imports the file contents into a new workbook and then into an XML list (which has been mapped to one or more XML elements). If the XML data file does not point to a schema, Microsoft Excel will create a schema based on the XML source's data.

As a read-only workbook   The XML data file is opened as a workbook in read-only mode and the file's structure is flattened.

Use the XML Source task pane   This displays the XML data file's schema in the **XML Source** task pane and you can then drag elements from the schema onto the worksheet in order to map them. If the XML data file does not point to a schema, Microsoft Excel will create a schema based on the XML source's data.

* Click **OK** in the **Open XML** dialog box.

☐2 ▪ Using XML maps

Information can only be easily communicated if everything occurs in the same language. XML works in the same way; you must use the same tags to describe the same information. With this in mind, you can use an **XML schema**. This could be imagined as a sample, that describes the contents of an XML document, giving the names of the tags that can or should be used in an XML document and the child elements it can contain. You can also specify what types of data elements can contain: numbers, text, alphanumerical data and so on.

When you add an XML schema to a workbook, Excel creates an object called an **XML map**. XML maps are used to create mapped ranges and manage the relationships between the ranges and mapped elements in the XML schema. These maps are also used when you import or export XML information, to connect the contents of a mapped range and the schema elements.

Below, you will see how to add maps to a workbook then how to create mapped ranges in which you can import XML data.

Creating an XML map

▪ **Data - XML - XML Source**

*This opens the **XML Source** task pane.*

▪ Click the **XML Maps** button at the bottom of the task pane.

▪ Click the **Add** button in the **XML Maps** window.

▪ Open the folder and/or server where the file concerned is located, using the places bar and/or the **Look in** list.

▪ Click the name of the XML file concerned then click the **Open** button.

If the XML data file does not point to a schema, Microsoft Excel will create a schema based on the XML source's data:

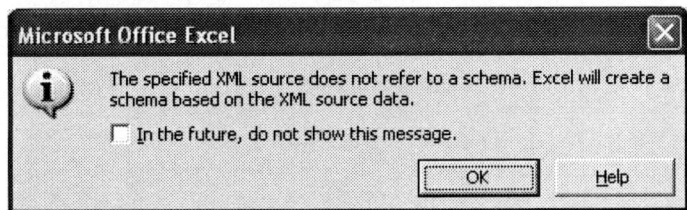

▪ If this occurs, click **OK**.

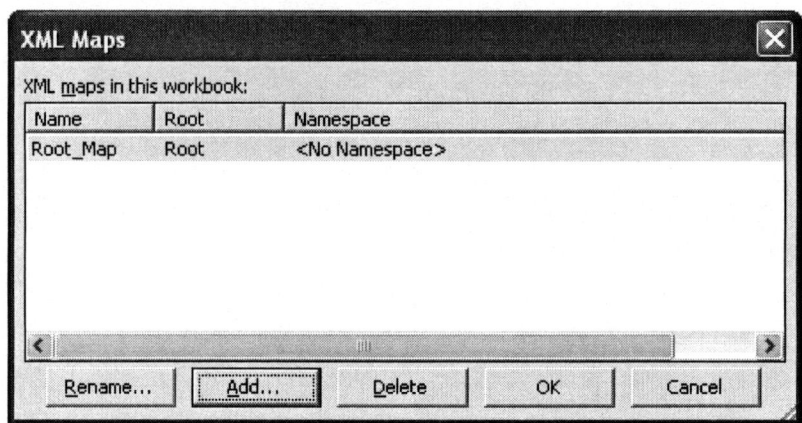

■ Click **OK** on the **XML Maps** dialog box to confirm and close the window.

If you create or edit a map, the XML map appears in the **XML Source** task pane. Here it contains a group of **Meta** identifiers (such as names, global dates or other information that will appear once) and repeating elements, under the **ExpenseItem** heading.

The icon varies depending on the type of element it refers to:

Icon	Element Type
	Parent Element
	Required parent element
	Repeating parent element
	Required repeating parent element
	Child element
	Required child element
	Repeating child element
	Required repeating child element
	Attribute
	Required attribute
	Simple content in a complex structure

Renaming an XML map

- In the **XML Maps** dialog box, click the **Name** of the map to select it.
- Click the **Rename** button.
- Replace the map's old name with the new one.
- Press the ⏎ key to confirm the name.

Deleting an XML map

- In the **XML Maps** dialog box, click the **Name** of the map to select it.
- Click the **Delete** button.
- In the warning message that appears, click **OK** to confirm the deletion.

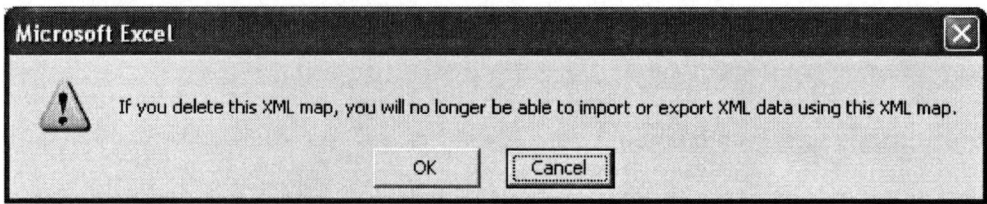

Mapping XML elements to a workbook

Once you have added a map, you can define the structure of the XML file, into which you will import XML data, by placing the map elements at the correct places on the worksheet.

■ If necessary, use **Data - XML - XML Source** to open the **XML Source** task pane.

The hierarchical list of elements in the XML map appears in the main part of the XML Source task pane.

■ Select the element(s) that you want to map in the **XML Source** task pane and drag your selection into the required location on the worksheet.

To select several nonadjacent items, click the first, hold down the ⌨Ctrl *key and click the others.*

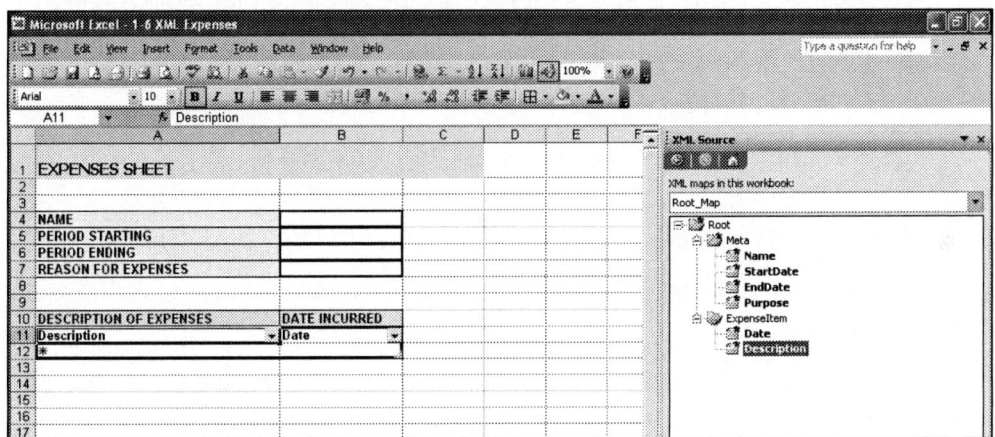

*The four **Meta** elements have been dragged respectively into cells B4 to B7. The two **ExpenseItem** elements have been placed in cells A11 and B11. When you import XML data, the data with **Name**, **StartDate**, **EndDate** and **Purpose** tags will migrate automatically to cells B4 to B7. The data enclosed within the **ExpenseItem** element will fill one or more rows beneath cells A11 and B11, depending on the number of these repeating **Date** and **Description** items in the XML data file.*

Mapped ranges appear with a coloured border and the fields are shown in bold type in the task pane.

 *To remove a mapped range from the worksheet, right-click the field name in the **XML Source Data** task pane and choose **Remove element**.*

⊞3 ▪ Importing XML data into a mapped worksheet

Once you have inserted the maps into the appropriate places on your worksheet, you need to import the XML data that will appear in the mapped ranges.

▪ Activate the worksheet on which you wish to insert the XML data.

▪ **Data - XML - Import**

▪ Use the **Look in** list or the places bar to locate the folder where the XML data file is stored.

▪ Click the file's name and click the **Import** button.

Excel imports the XML data and places it in the ranges where you have mapped the XML elements on the worksheet.

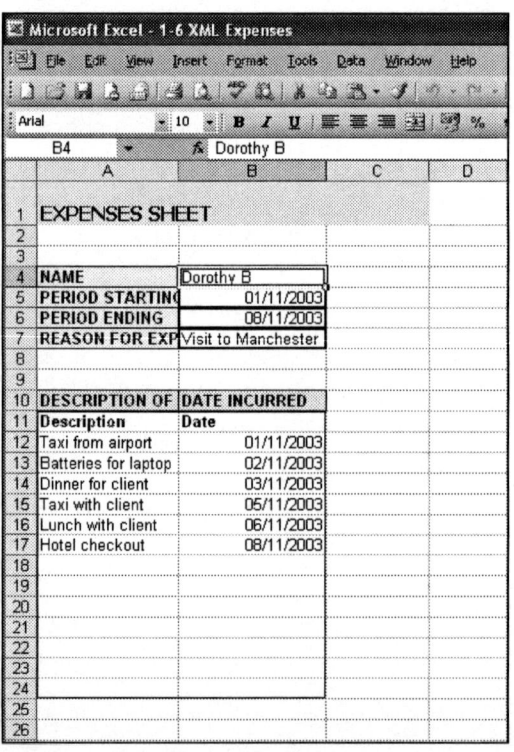

Once data is imported into the workbook, you can format the workbook and the mapped ranges as a normal workbook (such as applying font attributes, colours, column and row sizes and so on).

*The worksheet data is linked to the XML source data. To update the worksheet data if you make changes to the XML source, click the tool button on the **List** toolbar.*

4 ▪ Using the XML Source task pane

▪ If it is not displayed on the screen, use **Data - XML - XML Source** to see the **XML Source** task pane.

*The **XML maps in this workbook** drop-down list can be used to select one of the maps added to the workbook.*

▪ To see the task pane options, click the **Options** button.

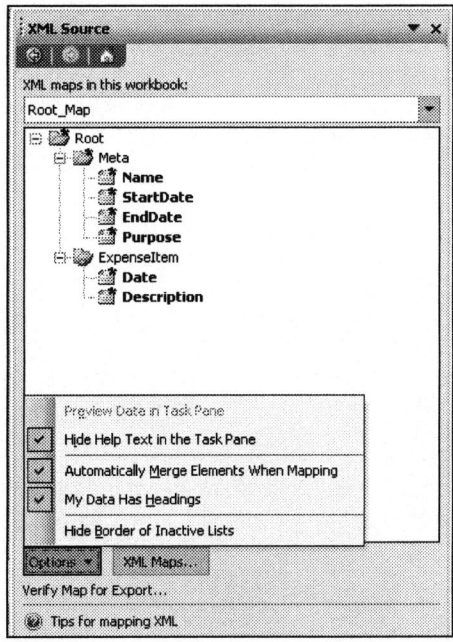

■ Activate or deactivate the following options:

Preview Data in Task Pane — Activate this to see examples of data in the list of elements, if you have imported XML data connected with the XML map during this Excel work session.

Hide Help Text in the Task Pane — When this is active, you will no longer see the help text that appears below the list of elements.

Automatically Merge Elements When Mapping — When this is active, an XML list will be enlarged automatically if you drag an element into a cell adjacent to it.

My Data Has Headings — Activate this to specify that there are existing labels that can be used as column headers when repeating elements are mapped to the worksheet.

Hide Border of Inactive Lists — If this is active, you will no longer see the border of a list, XML list or single-mapped cell once you select a cell outside of the list.

■ To close the **Options**, click outside the task pane.

📄 *Once you have finished working with the **XML Source** task pane, you can close it by clicking its* ☒ *button.*

🖥5 ▪ Saving/exporting XML data

Saving a workbook as an XML spreadsheet

When Excel saves a workbook in XML Spreadsheet format, it uses its own XML Spreadsheet schema (XMLSS). XMLSS preserves the following items of workbook content: data and formulas contained in cells, cell formats and worksheet and workbook parameters.

XML Spreadsheet format retains many Excel features, but not all. Here are some items that cannot be retrieved from an XML workbook: charts, OLE objects, drawings and autoshapes, VBA projects and outline settings.

To see the complete list of available features and format limitations for XML Spreadsheet format, press F1 *on your keyboard to display the* ***Excel Help*** *task pane and type* ***xml spreadsheet limitations*** *in the* ***Search for*** *text box. Start the search then choose the* ***Features and limitations of XML Spreadsheet format*** *topic.*

* Create or open the workbook that you want to save in XML Spreadsheet format.

* **File - Save As**

* Choose the **XML Spreadsheet** file type from the **Save as type** list.

* Enter a **File name** for your file.

* Choose the local or server folder in which you want to save the file. To do this, use the **Look in** list and/or the places bar (which gives you quick access to **My Network Places**).

* Click the **Save** button.

Remember that when you save a workbook in XML Spreadsheet format, some of its features may become unavailable. Excel may display a message to remind you which items it cannot save :

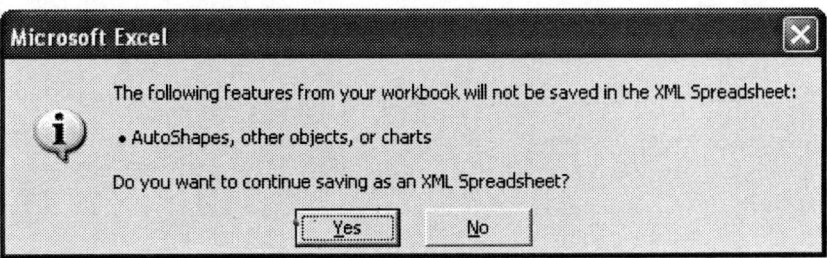

Microsoft Excel

The following features from your workbook will not be saved in the XML Spreadsheet:

• AutoShapes, other objects, or charts

Do you want to continue saving as an XML Spreadsheet?

    Yes   No

* Click **Yes** to confirm the message.

Saving a mapped range in XML data file format

■ **File - Save As**

■ Choose the folder in which you want to save the file.

■ Enter a **File name** for the XML data file.

■ Choose the **XML Data** file type from the **Save as type** list.

■ Click the **Save** button.

■ On the message warning you that some features may no longer work once you save in XML format, click the **Continue** button.

*If you have added more than one map to the workbook, the **Export XML** dialog box may appear. If so, click the XML map that you wish to use and confirm with **OK**.*

Exporting a mapped range to an XML data file

■ If the **List** toolbar does not appear on the screen, display it by right-clicking any toolbar and choosing the **List** option.

■ Click the **Export XML Data** tool button on the **List** toolbar.

■ If you have added more than one map to the workbook, the **Export XML** dialog box may appear. If so, click the XML map that you wish to use and confirm with **OK**.

■ Give a **File name** for the XML data file.

■ Click the **Export** button.

Below, you can see **Practice Exercise 1.6**. This exercise is made up of 5 steps. If you do not know how to do one of the steps, go back to the title that corresponds to that particular lesson. When you have finished, you can check your work by reading the **Solution** that follows.

All the steps of this exercise are likely to be tested in the Microsoft Office Specialist exam.

☞ Practice Exercise 1.6

1. Open the **1-6 Baseball.xml** file in the **MOS Excel 2003 Expert** folder; choose to not use a stylesheet and to open it as an XML list. Look at the contents then close this file without saving it.

2. Create a new workbook and enter the following data and formatting into it:

	A	B	C	D
1	EXPENSES SHEET			
2				
3	NAME			
4	PERIOD STARTING			
5	PERIOD ENDING			
6	REASON FOR EXPENSES			
7				
8	DESCRIPTION OF EXPENSES	DATE INCURRED		
9				
10				
11				

Add an XML map to this workbook using the XML schema file called **ENIExpenses.xsd** which is in the **MOS Excel 2003 Expert** folder. Drag the XML elements onto the worksheet, following these guidelines:

- **Name** element to **B3**

- **StartDate** element to **B4**

- **EndDate** element to **B5**

- **Purpose** element to **B6**

- **Description** element to **A9**

- **Date** element to **B9**

3. Import the XML data contained in the **ENIExpenses.xml** file into the active sheet in the **Open** workbook. Apply bold type to the mapped cells **B3** to **B6** and align the contents on the right of the cells and widen columns **A** and **B** to see the data clearly.

4. In the **XML Source** view options, choose to hide the help text in the task pane and to stop displaying a border around inactive lists.

5. Save the active workbook in the **MOS Excel 2003 Expert** folder in **XML Spreadsheet** format. Call it **1-6 XML Expenses**. Close this workbook.

If you would like to practise these features more, on another document, you should work through Summary Exercise 1, on MANAGING DATA. You will find the summary exercises at the end of the book.

It is often possible to perform a task in several different ways, but here, only the easiest solution is presented. You can go back to the corresponding lesson if you want to see other techniques you could use.

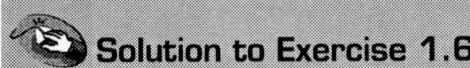

Solution to Exercise 1.6

1. To open the XML file called 1-6 Baseball.xml, use the **File - Open** command. If necessary, browse the hierarchy to find the **MOS Excel 2003 Expert** folder and open it. Double-click the **1-6 Baseball.xml** file icon. If prompted to choose a stylesheet for the file, activate the **Open the file without applying a stylesheet** option and click **OK**.
   In the **Open XML** dialog box, choose the **As an XML list** option and click **OK**.
   If you see another error message, click **OK**.
   Read the contents of the file, which appears in a defined list in a new workbook, then use **File - Close** to close it. Click **No** when prompted to save it.

2. To create a new workbook, use the ⬜ tool button on the **Standard** toolbar.
   Enter the data and cell formatting as shown in the illustration in step 2.

   To add maps to this new workbook, activate this file if necessary by clicking its button on the Windows taskbar.
   Display the **XML Source** task pane using the **Data - XML - XML Source** command.
   Click the **XML Maps** button at the bottom of the task pane then click the **Add** button on the dialog box.
   In the **Select XML Source** dialog box, browse the hierarchy to find the **MOS Excel 2003 Expert** folder and open it. Select the **ENIExpenses.xsd** file (pay special attention to the file type) and click the **Open** button.
   Click **OK** to confirm and close the **XML Maps** dialog box.

To add mapped ranges to the worksheet, drag each element from the **XML Source** task pane onto the cells as described below:

- Drag the **Name** element to cell **B3**.
- Drag the **StartDate** element to cell **B4**.
- Drag the **EndDate** element to cell **B5**.
- Drag the **Purpose** element to cell **B6**.
- Drag the **Description** element to cell **A9**.
- Drag the **Date** element to cell **B9**.

3. To import the data from the ENIExpenses.xml file, use the **Data - XML - Import** command.
In the **Import XML** dialog box, browse to find the **MOS Excel 2003 Expert** folder and open it. Select the **ENIExpenses.xml** file (pay special attention to the file type) then click the **Import** button.

Once the data appears in the worksheet, select cells **B3** to **B6** and click the ▣ tool button to apply bold type. While the cells are still selected, click the ▣ tool button to right-align the cell contents. To widen columns A and B, double-click the right side of each column header.

4. To change the XML Source view options, click the **Options** button on the **XML Source** task pane. Activate the **Hide Help Text in the Task Pane** and **Hide Border of Inactive Lists** options then click the worksheet to close the list.

5. To save the workbook in XML Spreadsheet format, use the **File - Save** command. If necessary, browse the hierarchy to find the **MOS Excel 2003 Expert** folder and open it. In the **File name** text box, type **1-6 XML Expenses**.
Open the **Save as type** list and choose the **XML Spreadsheet** format. Click the **Save** button to confirm. If Excel reminds you about limitations of the format, click **OK** on the message.

ANALYSIS TOOLS
Lesson 2.1: Auditing

ANALYSIS TOOLS
Lesson 2.1: Auditing

1 ▪ Showing/hiding the Formula Auditing toolbar

The **Formula Auditing** toolbar contains tools to help you find and correct errors in your worksheets.

▪ **Tools - Formula Auditing - Show Formula Auditing Toolbar**

This activates or deactivates the **Formula Auditing Toolbar;** a tick next to the toolbar name indicates that it is currently on display.

⊞2 ▪ Tracing the relationships between formulas and cells

Showing precedent cells

These are the cells which are linked to the calculation formula: they can be picked out with auditing arrows.

▪ Activate the cell containing the formula.

▪ **Tools - Formula Auditing - Trace Precedents** or click the **Trace Precedents** tool button on the **Formula Auditing** toolbar.

	A	B	C	D
1				
2	Reference	Price	Quantity	Total
3	QY125	10.5	2	12.5
4	RC457	18.95	1	19.95
5	OP215	25.84	1	26.84
6	MP001	14.75	10	24.75
7	TH158	33	1	34
8			Total due	118.04
9				
10			Total number of products	15
11				

Here the command was used three times, to show the precedents for cells D8, D3 and D4.

▪ To clear the precedent arrows, click the **Remove Precedent Arrows** tool button.

To clear the auditing arrows, use the **Tools - Formula Auditing - Remove All Arrows** command or the tool button on the **Formula Auditing** toolbar.

Showing dependent cells

Dependent cells are those that contain formulas that refer to your selected cell. Like precedents, they can be highlighted with arrows.

- Activate the cell whose dependent formulas you wish to trace.

- **Tools - Formula Auditing - Trace Dependents**

or click the **Trace Dependents** tool button on the **Formula Auditing** toolbar.

	A	B	C	D
1				
2	**Reference**	**Price**	**Quantity**	**Total**
3	QY125	10.5	2	12.5
4	RC457	18.95	1	19.95
5	OP215	25.84	1	26.84
6	MP001	14.75	10	24.75
7	TH158	33	1	34
8			**Total due**	118.04
9				
10			Total number of products	15
11				

This example shows that cell C3 is involved in the formulas that are in D3 and D10.

- To hide the dependent arrows, click the **Remove Dependent Arrows** tool button.

Highlighting cells involved in errors

When a formula result appears in a cell as an error value (such as "#NAME?" or "#VALUE!"), Excel can find all the cells that have supplied data for that formula.

■ Activate the cell containing the error (cells containing errors have a coloured triangle in their top left corner).

■ Click the **Trace Error** ⊡ tool button on the **Formula Auditing** toolbar or use the **Trace Error** command in the **Tools - Formula Auditing** menu.

CURRENT YEAR	HI FI	VIDEO	COMPUTER	TOTAL	AVERAGE TURNOVER	PERCENTAGE OF TURNOVER	OBJECTIVE	COMMISSION
January	1,000.00	2,500.00	5,000.00	8,500.00	2,833.33	7%	Below	425
February	1,500.00	2,000.00	6,000.00	9,500.00	3,16.7	#DIV/0!	Below	475
March	1,000.00	1,000.00	6,500.00	8,500.00	2,833.33	7%	Below	425
April	1,200.00	5,000.00	7,000.00	13,200.00	4,400.00	11%	Above	1,320
May	2,000.00	4,000.00	4,500.00	10,500.00	3,500.00	9%	Above	1,050
June	1,500.00	1,500.00	7,000.00	10,000.00	3,333.33	9%	Below	500
July	1,000.00	5,000.00	5,000.00	11,000.00	3,666.67	9%	Above	1,100
August	800.00	1,500.00	2,000.00	4,300.00	1,433.33	4%	Below	215
September	1,500.00	2,000.00	5,000.00	8,500.00	2,833.33	7%	Below	425
October	2,000.00	3,000.00	4,500.00	9,500.00	3,166.67	8%	Below	475
November	2,500.00	3,500.00	4,200.00	10,200.00	3,400.00	9%	Above	1,020
December	1,600.00	4,000.00	8,000.00	13,600.00	4,533.33	12%	Above	1,360
TOTAL	17,600.00	35,000.00	64,700.00	117,300.00		#DIV/0!		8,790

Auditing arrows appear on the screen. Red arrows link the cell that produced the error to those to which it refers while the blue arrows show the precedents of the cell that caused the error initially.

■ To clear the auditing arrows, click the ⊡ tool button on the **Formula Auditing** toolbar.

🖥 3 ▪ Finding errors and invalid data

Tracing unauthorised data

This is a technique to find cells containing data that do not meet the validation criteria you have set subsequently. Cells containing invalid data will be circled in red:

	A	B	C	D	E	F	G	H
1	**Surname**	**First Name**	**Address**	**PC/City**	**Sex**	**Age**	**Subs**	**Paid**
2	Alderman	Christine	56 Harvey St	4100 Tewesbury	F	13	2.50	Y
3	Andrews	Melissa	27 Ridley St	5600 St Lucia	F	15	3.00	Y
4	Barnett	Frances	38 Harrison Cres	4500 Greerton	F	15	3.00	N
5	Charles	Yolanda	29 Bartlett Cres	6000 Lorton	F	14	3.00	Y
6	Cray	Hannah	77 Kennedy Drive	5800 Rafter	F	17	4.50	Y
7	Dell	Tammy	13 Read Road	4300 Dryden	F	16	4.50	Y
8	Dorcas	Michelle	10 Kings Ct	5400 Fern Grove	F	16	4.50	Y
9	Grant	Jessica	14/196 Red Sand Road	6100 Herston	F	17	4.50	N
10	Grey	Josephine	89 Green St	5500 Killybill	F	22	8.00	N
11	Gree	*Formula Auditing*			St Lucia	F	25	8.00	Y
12	Hunt				Gunston	F	18	4.50	Y
13	Loxton	Marie	12/149 Grove Road	4400 Mt Gladstone	F	22	8.00	Y
14	Marsh	Sarah	19 River Lane	6000 Lorton	F	19	8.00	Y
15	Martingale	Joanne	9/27 Thurston Road	4500 Greerton	F	19	8.00	Y
16	Norton	Vera	18 Quinn St	4100 Tewesbury	F	24	8.00	Y
17	Peak	Alison	26A Pine Road	4200 New Grove	F	21	8.00	Y
18	Peyton	Theresa	141 Mt Gladstone Road	4400 Mt Gladstone	F	25	8.00	N
19	Rowe	Patricia	265 Ash Drive	4400 Mt Gladstone	F	15	3.00	N
20	Sanders	Heather	16 Marigold Place	6100 Herston	F	12	2.50	N
21	Smith	Liza	15 Tall Tree Road	4500 Greerton	F	12	2.50	N
22	Stanes	Ashley	3/28 Bartlett Cres	5200 Abbeyville	F	15	3.00	Y
23	Stowerton	Laura	12 Oak St	4200 New Grove	F	12	3.00	Y
24	Stoner	Carla	56 Lawrence St	4000 Westport	F	15	3.00	N
25	Youmad	Alanna	58 Eagle St	5400 Fern Grove	F	13	2.50	Y
26	Anderson	Terry	67 Milton Road	5200 Abbeyville	M	17	4.50	N
27	Barton	John	37 Chambers St	4000 Westport	M	16	4.50	Y
28	Blake	Peter	35 Nichol St	5500 Killybill	M	18	4.50	Y

In this example, subscription fees of less than 3.50 are circled in red.

▪ On the **Formula Audting** toolbar, click the ⊞ tool button then click the worksheet.

▪ To remove the red circles, click the 🗗 tool button.

Analysing errors in one formula

■ In the **Options** dialog box (**Tools - Options - Error Checking** tab), check that the **Enable background error checking** option is active and if necessary, change the type of errors that Excel should find by activating or deactivating the various **Rules**.

■ Activate the cell containing the error, indicated by a coloured triangle (green by default) in the upper left corner of the cell.

■ Click the ⟨⊕⟩ button that appears to the left of the active cell.

A list of options appears, the first being a description of the type of error Excel has found.

	E	F	G	H	I
5					
6					
7	TOTAL	AVERAGE TURNOVER	PERCENTAGE OF TURNOVER	OBJECTIVE	COMMISSION
8	8,500.00	2,833.33	7%	Below	425
9	9,500.00	3,16⟨⊕⟩ ▾	#DIV/0!	Below	475
10	8,500.00	2,83	7%	Below	425
11	13,200.00	4,40	Divide by Zero Error		1,320
12	10,500.00	3,50			1,050
13	10,000.00	3,33	Help on this error		500
14	11,000.00	3,66	Show Calculation Steps...		1,100
15	4,300.00	1,43			215
16	8,500.00	2,83	Ignore Error		425
17	9,500.00	3,16	Edit in Formula Bar		475
18	10,200.00	3,40			1,020
19	13,600.00	4,53	Error Checking Options...		1,360
20	117,300.00		Show Formula Auditing Toolbar		8,790
21					

■ Click the option of your choice:

Help on this error	displays the help window.
Show Calculation Steps	shows the **Evaluate Formula** dialog box (cf. the Evaluating formulas section).
Ignore Error	deactivates the error indicator: both the coloured triangle and the tag disappear.

Edit in Formula Bar	places the insertion point in the formula bar so you can modify the formula.
Error Checking Options	Shows the **Options** dialog box so you can choose which **Rules** Excel uses for **Error Checking**.
Show Formula Auditing Toolbar	displays the **Formula Auditing** toolbar.

Depending on the type of error, other options may appear.

■ If none of these options interest you, activate another cell to close this options menu.

Analysing the errors in all formulas

■ In the **Options** dialog box (**Tools - Options - Error Checking** tab), check and, if necessary, change the type of errors that Excel should find by activating or deactivating the various **Rules**.

■ Activate the worksheet you wish to check for errors.

■ **Tools - Error Checking** or click the 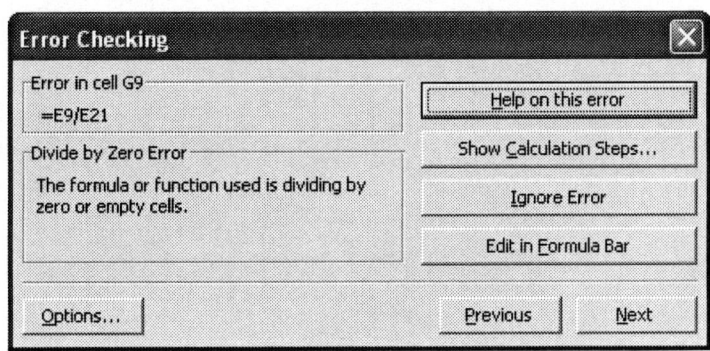 tool button on the **Formula Auditing** toolbar.

*Excel selects the first cell containing a mistake and, in the **Error Checking** dialog box, shows the formula and the error in detail.*

You can choose to get **Help on this error,** to **Show Calculation Steps,** to **Ignore Error** or to **Edit in Formula Bar** (these options are explained under the previous heading) by clicking the appropriate button.

The buttons on the **Error Checking** dialog box may differ depending on the type of error.

Depending on the option you choose, the **Restart** button may appear in the **Error Checking** dialog box which enables you to continue checking the worksheet.

* If you wish to go on to the next or previous error without working on the current one, click the **Next** or **Previous** button.

The **Reset Ignored Errors** button (**Tools - Options - Error Checking** tab) reactivates error indicators in cells where you have chosen the **Ignore Error** option.

4 ▪ Using formula evaluation techniques

Evaluating formulas

This technique can be used to see the result of each part of a nested formula.

* Select the cell you wish to evaluate.

* **Tools - Formula Auditing - Evaluate Formula** or click the 🔳 tool button on the **Formula Auditing** toolbar.

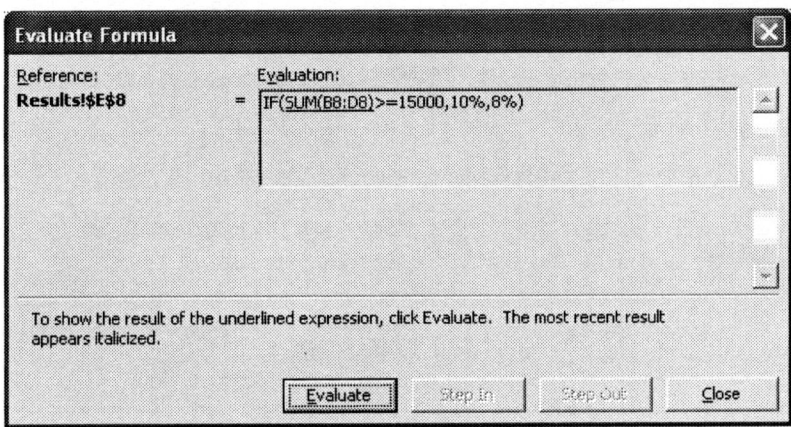

- Click **Evaluate** to see the result of the expression underlined in the **Evaluation** box. The result appears within the formula in italics.

- Click **Evaluate** again to see the result of the next underlined section and so on.

- When you have evaluated the whole formula, click the **Close** button to end the evaluation or the **Restart** button (that replaces the **Evaluate** button) to perform the evaluation again.

  *If the formula you are evaluating contains a reference to another formula, the **Step In** button shows the detail of that formula, when it is underlined, in a new part of the evaluation box. The **Step Out** button returns to the initial formula.*

Using the Watch Window

The Watch Window allows you to see cell contents and details of formulas, without those cells being necessarily on the screen.

- Select the cells you wish to examine.

- **Tools - Formula Auditing - Show Watch Window** or click the **Show Watch Window** tool button on the **Formula Auditing** toolbar.

ANALYSIS TOOLS
Lesson 2.1: Auditing

If the Watch Window appears on the worksheet, you can dock it like an ordinary toolbar by double-clicking its title bar.

* Click **Add Watch**.

* If necessary, modify the selection and click the **Add** button.

   As long as the Watch Window is displayed, you can select a new cell (or range) at any time and add it to the list of watched items.

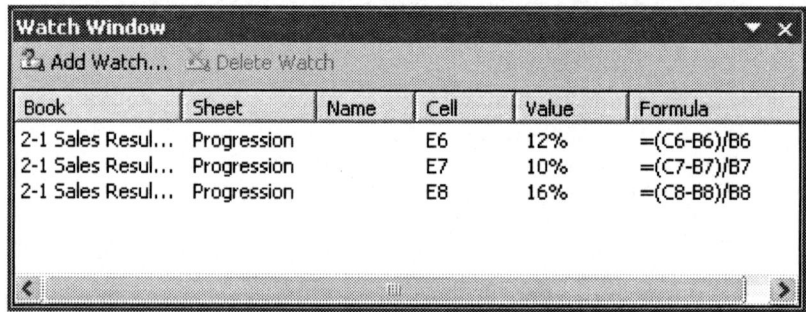

* You can change the column widths on the **Watch Window** by dragging the vertical line between the column headers.

* To go rapidly to a cell listed in the **Watch Window**, double-click that cell's row in the list.

* To select all the cells containing formulas in order to add them to the **Watch Window**, use the **Edit - Go To** command, click the **Special** button and choose **Formulas**.

* When you no longer need the **Watch Window**, close it by clicking the ⊠ button on its title bar.

Below, you can see **Practice Exercise 2.1**. This exercise is made up of 4 steps. If you do not know how to do one of the steps, go back to the title that corresponds to that particular lesson. When you have finished, you can check your work by reading the **Solution** that follows.

Steps in the exercise that are likely to be tested on the exam are preceded by this symbol: 🏢. However, it is a good idea to complete all the steps in the exercise, to ensure that you have understood all the points discussed in the lesson.

☞ Practice Exercise 2.1

*To work on practice exercise 2.1, open the **2-1 HiFi.xls** workbook in the **MOS Excel 2003 Expert** folder and activate the **Williams** worksheet.*

1. Display the **Formula Auditing** toolbar on the screen.

🏢 2. Using the auditing arrows, show the dependent cells for **E8** and the precedent cells for **F8**.
Next, trace the cells that have supplied data for the formula in cell **G9** then clear the auditing arrows.

🏢 3. Analyse the errors on the **Williams** worksheet and correct the formula in cell **G9** by replacing the value **E21** by **E20**: this should make the #DIV/0! error values disappear. Save and close the **2-1 HiFi.xls** workbook.

🏢 4. Open the **2-1 Sales Results.xls** workbook in the **MOS Excel 2003 Expert** folder. Evaluate the formula that is in cell **E8** on the **Results** worksheet then close the **Evaluate Formula** dialog box.

Next, activate the **Progression** workbook and select cells **E6** to **E8** and display them in the **Watch Window**. Move over on the worksheet and enter these figures in cells **P6** to **Q8:**

MAY	JUNE
4867	4883
4714	4906
4600	4817

Then, compare the progression figures in the Watch Window with the table for May/June. Close the Watch Window then save and close the **2-1 Sales Results.xls** workbook.

If you want to put what you have learnt into practice on a real document, you can work on Summary Exercise 2 for the ANALYSIS TOOLS section. The summary exercises are at the end of this book.

It is often possible to perform a task in several different ways, but here, only the easiest solution is presented. You can go back to the corresponding lesson if you want to see other techniques you could use.

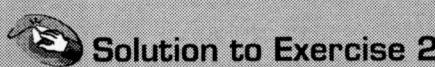 **Solution to Exercise 2.1**

1. To display the Formula Auditing toolbar, use the **Tools - Formula Auditing** command. Choose the **Show Formula Auditing Toolbar** option.

2. To show the dependents of cell E8 with auditing arrows, click cell **E8** then click the [button] tool button on the **Formula Auditing** toolbar. To show the precedents of cell F8, click cell **F8** then click the [button] tool button on the **Formula Auditing** toolbar.
To trace the cells that have supplied data to the formula in cell G9, click cell **G9** then click the [button] tool button on the **Formula Auditing** toolbar.

   To clear the auditing arrows, click the [button] tool button on the **Formula Auditing** toolbar.

3. To evaluate the formulas on the Williams worksheet, make sure this is the active sheet then use the **Tools - Error Checking** command. When the **Error Checking** dialog box stops at the error in cell G9, click the **Edit in Formula Bar** button. On the formula bar, change the reference **E21** to **E20** then enter. Click the [button] tool button to close the **Error Checking** dialog box.

   To save and close the 2-1 HiFi.xls workbook, click its [button] tool button then use **File - Close**.

4. Open the **2-1 Sales Results.xls** workbook in the **MOS Excel 2003 Expert** folder, using the **File - Open** command. Click the **Results** worksheet tab to activate it.

ANALYSIS TOOLS
Exercise 2.1: Auditing

To evaluate the formula in cell E8, click cell **E8** then use the **Tools - Formula Auditing - Evaluate Formula** command. Click the **Evaluate** button four times, then when it is replaced by the **Restart** button, click the **Close** button to close the **Evaluate Formula** dialog box.

To use the Watch Window in the Progression worksheet, start by clicking the **Progression** worksheet tab to activate it.
If necessary, display the **Formula Auditing** toolbar by right-clicking any toolbar and choosing the **Formula Auditing** option.

Drag to select cells **E6** to **E8**, then click the ▨ tool button on the **Formula Auditing** toolbar to display the Watch Window.
Click the **Add Watch** button to insert the cells into the Watch Window.
Check that cells **E6** to **E8** are selected and click **Add**.
To add the new figures as indicated, scroll through the worksheet until you come to the third table. Enter the new data as follows: in **P6**, type **4867**; in **P7**, type **4714**; in **P8**, type **4600**; in **Q6**, type **4883**; in **Q7**, type **4906** and in **Q8**, type **4817**. This will calculate sales progression percentages in column S.
Move the Watch Window until you can see both sets of figures and compare them. When you have done that, click the ✖ button on the **Watch Window** to close it.

Save and close the **2.1 Sales Results.xls** workbook by clicking its 🖫 tool button then use **File - Close**.

ANALYSIS TOOLS
Lesson 2.2: Scenarios

1 ▪ Creating and editing scenarios

Creating a scenario

▪ Click the **Add** button and enter the **Scenario name** for your new scenario.

▪ In the **Changing cells** box, give the cells whose values should vary in this scenario.

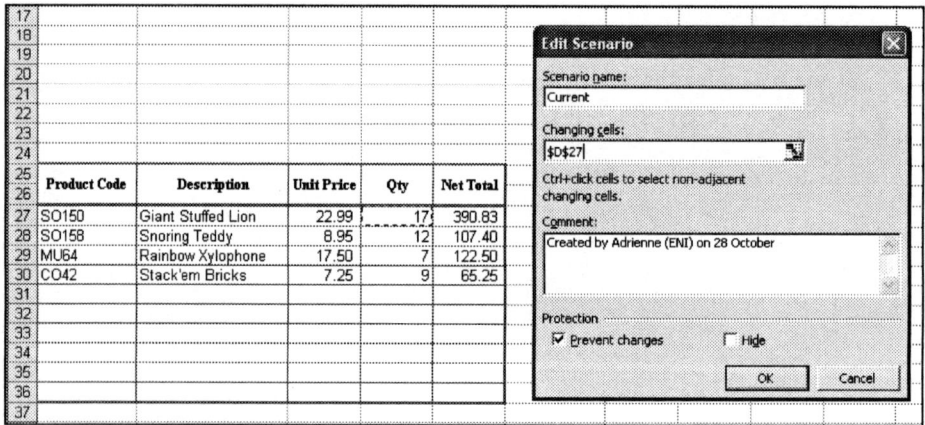

▪ Click **OK** then enter the value for each changing cell according to your hypothesis and confirm.

▪ Create your other scenarios in the same way.

▪ Click **Close** once you have finished.

Editing a scenario

You can apply new changing values to a scenario but keep its original name.

▪ **Tools - Scenarios**

▪ Select the scenario you wish to edit and click the **Edit** button.

▪ If required, enter or select the new changing cell reference in **Changing cells**.

- In the **Scenario Values** dialog box that opens, give any new changing values, then click **OK** to confirm.

📁2 ▪ Using scenarios

Running scenarios

- **Tools - Scenarios**

- If you only want to run one scenario, select it, click **Show** then click the **Close** button. The result replaces the current values on the worksheet (this is why you should start by creating a scenario containing the current values).

  If you want to run a summary report of all the scenarios, click **Summary** then, in the **Result cells** box, enter the cell references (or select the cells) whose results interest you.

- If you clicked the **Summary** button, Excel offers a choice of two reports. In this case, fill in the **Scenario Summary** dialog box and confirm with **OK**.

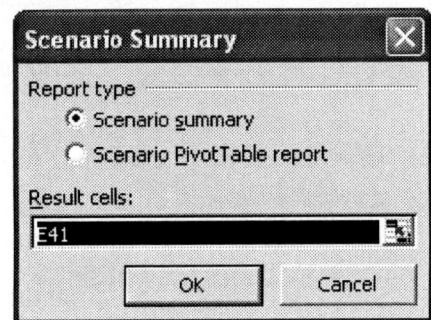

- Click **OK**.

Microsoft Excel - 2-2 Toys

Scenario Summary

	Current Values:	Current	If Lion 18
Changing Cells:			
$D$27	17	17	18
Result Cells:			
$E$39	685.98	685.98	708.97
$E$40	10%	10%	15%
$E$41	617.38	617.38	602.62

Notes: Current Values column represents values of changing cells at time Scenario Summary Report was created. Changing cells for each scenario are highlighted in gray.

The summary is presented as an outline on a separate worksheet.

Scenarios and views can be associated in a report.

Merging scenarios from other worksheets

If your worksheets are laid out in identical ways, you can apply scenarios from another worksheet to the active one. The changing cells on both sheets must correspond.

* Open all the workbooks involved in the scenario merge.
* Make sure the destination worksheet for the merged scenarios is active.
* **Tools - Scenarios**
* Click the **Merge** button.

- In the **Book** list, choose the workbook containing the scenarios you want to merge.

- In the **Sheet** list, click the sheet on which the required scenarios are located.

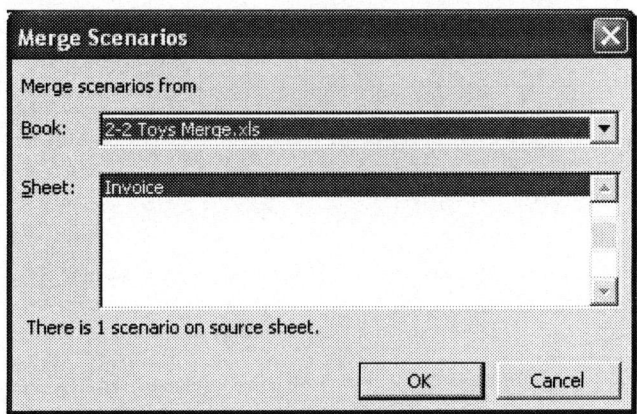

Excel reminds you how many scenarios are on the chosen worksheet.

- Click **OK** to start the merge.

Below, you can see **Practice Exercise 2.2**. This exercise is made up of 2 steps. If you do not know how to do one of the steps, go back to the title that corresponds to that particular lesson. When you have finished, you can check your work by reading the **Solution** that follows.

All the steps of this exercise are likely to be tested in the Microsoft Office Specialist exam.

☞ **Practice Exercise 2.2**

*To work on practice exercise 2.2, open the **2-2 Toys.xls** workbook in the **MOS Excel 2003 Expert** folder.*

1. Create two scenarios from the **Invoice** worksheet in the **2-2 Toys** workbook: save the current scenario, as **Current** and save a second scenario with a quantity of 18 in the Giant Stuffed Lion row called **If Lion 18**.
If the **Total before discount** (E31) is more than 700, the discount accorded is 15%. On this invoice, the client has missed out on the maximum discount because only 17 giant lions were ordered. Using these scenarios, you can see the difference in total price, had 18 of these toys been ordered.

2. Start running the **Current** and **If Lion 18** scenarios, making a summary of their results on a new sheet.

   Next, merge the **If Teddy 14** scenario into the **Invoice** sheet. This scenario is located on the corresponding **Invoice** worksheet in the **2-2 Toys Merge.xls** workbook, stored in the **MOS Excel 2003 Expert** folder.

If you would like to practise these features more, on another document, you should work through Summary Exercise 2, ANALYSIS TOOLS. You will find the summary exercises at the end of the book.

It is often possible to perform a task in several different ways, but here, only the easiest solution is presented. You can go back to the corresponding lesson if you want to see other techniques you could use.

 Solution to Exercise 2.2

1. To create two scenarios from the Invoice worksheet in the 2-2 Toys workbook, make sure the **Invoice** worksheet is active then use the **Tools - Scenarios** command.

   To create a scenario that saves the current data, click the **Add** button and type **Current** in the **Scenario name** text box.
   Click the ▦ button in the **Changing cells** box, click cell **D27** then click the ▦ button.
   Click **OK**, keep **17** in the only text box available, then click **OK**.

   To create a scenario that would show the outcome of ordering 18 giant lions, click the **Add** button then enter **If Lion 18** as the **Scenario name**.
   Keep reference **D27** in the **Changing cells** box then click **OK**.
   Enter **18** in the text box, then click **OK** and finally, click **Close**.

2. To run the Current and If Lion 18 scenarios and create a summary of them on a new sheet, use the **Tools - Scenarios** command, then click the **Summary** button.
   Leave the **Scenario summary** option active, click the ▦ button, select cells **C39** to **C41** and cells **E39** to **E41** then click ▦.
   Click **OK** to confirm.

   To merge the scenario called If Teddy 14, which is located on the Invoice sheet in 2.2 Toys Merge.xls, into the corresponding Invoice sheet in 2.2 Toys.xls, start by opening the **2.2 Toys Merge.xls** workbook, in the **MOS Excel 2003 Expert** folder.

ANALYSIS TOOLS
Exercise 2.2: Scenarios

Make sure the 2.2 Toys workbook is still open and activate its **Invoice** sheet.

Use **Tools - Scenarios** and click the **Merge** button.

In the **Book** list, choose **2.2 Toys Merge**.

In the **Sheet** list, make sure **Invoice** is selected. Click **OK** to confirm. Once the **If Teddy 14** scenario appears in the **Scenario Manager** dialog box, click **Close** to shut the box.

If you wish, use the **File - Save** command to save the changes made to the **2.2 Toys.xls** workbook.

ANALYSIS TOOLS
Lesson 2.3: Pivot table

ANALYSIS TOOLS
Lesson 2.3: Pivot table

🖳1 ▪ Creating a pivot table report

A pivot table allows you to synthesise and analyse data from a list:

	A	B	C	D	E	F
1	Sales ID	(All) ▼				
2						
3	Average of Units Sold	Date ▼				
4	Region ▼	Jan	Feb	Mar	Apr	Grand Total
5	Central	109	128	129	119	119
6	East	130	110	129	139	126
7	North	142	152	111	169	146
8	South	112	129	148	134	130
9	West	136	126	127	117	127
10	Grand Total	123	129	132	132	129
11						

In this example, the pivot table calculates the average unit sales by region and by date.

▪ Click inside the list that you wish to analyse in a pivot table.

▪ **Data - PivotTable and PivotChart Report**

*The **PivotTable and PivotChart Wizard** appears on the screen.*

▪ Under **Where is the data that you want to analyse?**, indicate the location of the pivot table data if the source data is in an Excel database, leave the first option active.

▪ Make sure the **PivotTable** option is active under **What kind of report do you want to create?**

▪ Click **Next**.

▪ Check and, if necessary, select the **Range** of cells containing the data used to fill in the table.

▪ Click the **Next** button.

- Click the **Layout** button then define the table's design by dragging the field buttons from the list into the appropriate areas (ROW, COLUMN, DATA, PAGE).
For example:

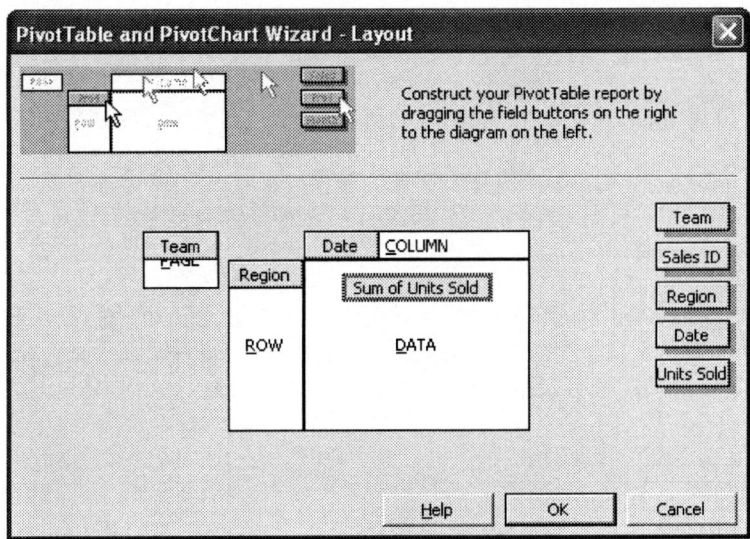

*This pivot table will calculate the sum of Units Sold by Region and Date for each Team listed. The **DATA** area can only contain elements that Excel can calculate.*

- If necessary, customise the fields included in the table by double-clicking the corresponding field button. If for example, you wish to make a calculation other than a sum, double-click the **Sum** button in the DATA area then choose another function.

- Click **OK** on the **Wizard** dialog box.

- Under **Where do you want to put the PivotTable**, indicate whether you want to create it on a **New worksheet** or on an **Existing worksheet**.

- Click the **Finish** button.

*The pivot table, the **PivotTable** toolbar and the **PivotTable Field List** all appear on the screen.*

*You can also define pivot table elements directly in the worksheet. To do this, go to the third step in the **PivotTable and PivotChart Wizard** but do not click the **Layout** button, select the location for the pivot table then click the **Finish** button. Back on the worksheet, drag each field from the **PivotTable Field List** onto the labelled areas in the empty pivot table. If you cannot see the **PivotTable Field List** window, display it by clicking the **Show Field List** tool button on the **PivotTable** toolbar.*

Although a pivot table is still linked to its source data, it is not updated automatically; you must refresh the data yourself.

If you double-click one of the result values in the data area of a pivot table, Excel displays the detail of the source data used to make that calculation in a new sheet.

2 ▪ Modifying a pivot table report

Modifying fields

▪ Click in the pivot table.

▪ **Data - PivotTable and PivotChart Report** or click the **PivotTable** button on the **PivotTable** toolbar and choose the **PivotTable Wizard** option.

▪ Click the **Layout** button.

▪ Redefine the contents of the table, as you did when it was created. To delete a field, drag the field concerned out of the area containing it.

 *A field can also be added by dragging the corresponding field from the **PivotTable Field List** window onto the table. To delete a field, drag it off the pivot table.*

Modifying the data used for the calculation

■ Click the down arrow that appears to the right of each field name.

click here to open the list of groups
that Excel generated
then activate or deactivate
the appropriate option(s).

	A	B	C	D	E	F
1	Sales ID	(All) ▼				
2						
3	Average of Units Sold	Date ▼				
4	Region ▼	Jan	Feb	Mar	Apr	Grand Total
5	Central	109	128	129	119	119
6	East	130	110	129	139	126
7	North	142	152	111	169	146
8	South	112	129	148	134	130
9	West	136	126	127	117	127
10	Grand Total	123	129	132	132	129
11						

■ Activate (or deactivate) the values you wish to include in (or remove from) the table.

■ Click **OK**.

Recalculating values

If the source data have been modified, you should refresh the pivot table to update the values it displays.

■ **Data - Refresh Data** or 🏆 on the **PivotTable** toolbar

Modifying its presentation

■ The cells on a pivot table can be formatted in the same way as those on an ordinary table. You can also apply an AutoFormat to the entire table, using the **Format - AutoFormat** command (see below).

3 ▪ Applying an AutoFormat to a pivot table

▪ Click a cell in the pivot table.

▪ **Format - AutoFormat** or click the **Format Report** 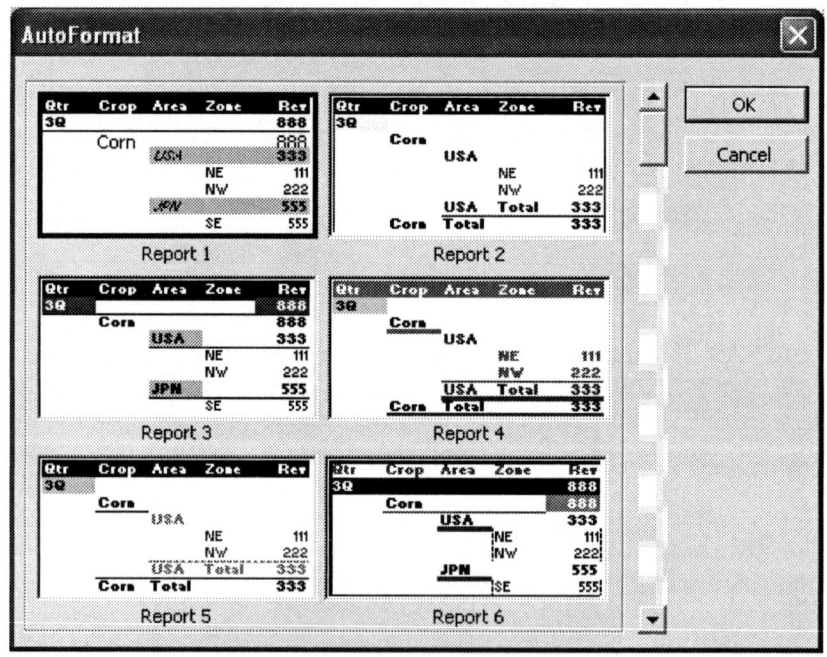 tool button on the **Pivot Table** toolbar.

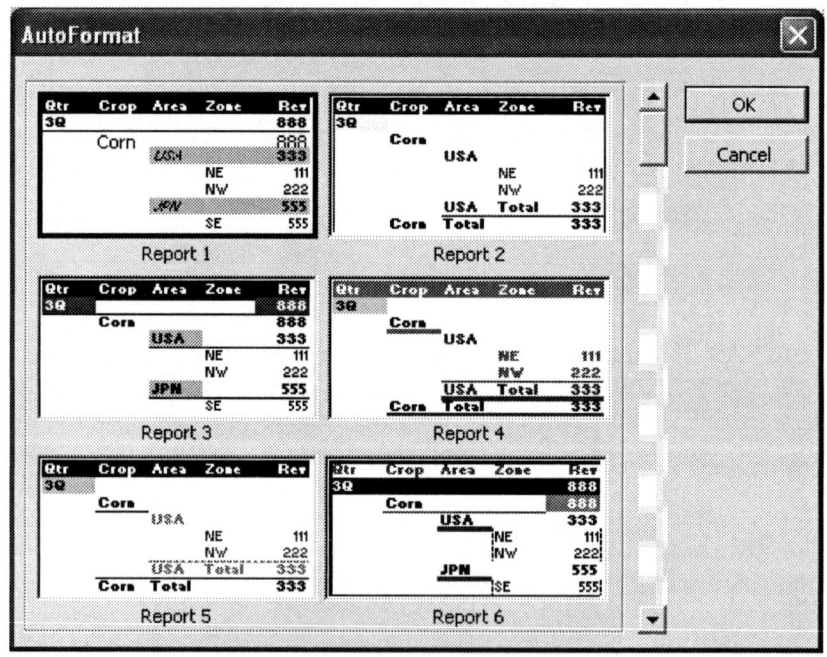

▪ From the range of models shown, choose the one that suits you best.

*The **None** model, which is at the end of the list, deletes all formatting from the cells in the table, but keeps the arrangement of rows and columns as defined in the last AutoFormat applied.*

▪ Confirm by clicking **OK** then click outside the pivot table to view the result.

4 • Grouping fields in a pivot table

*This function allows you to group a **Dates** field by month, for example.*

- Click the name of the field whose data you intend to group.
- **Data - Group and Outline - Group**
- Indicate how the data should be grouped by activating the appropriate options.

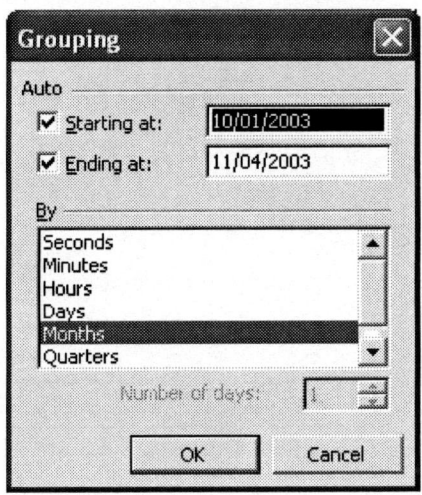

The dates here will be grouped together by month.

- Click **OK**.
- To cancel the grouping, use the command **Data - Group and Outline - Ungroup**.

Below, you can see **Practice Exercise 2.3**. This exercise is made up of 4 steps. If you do not know how to do one of the steps, go back to the title that corresponds to that particular lesson. When you have finished, you can check your work by reading the **Solution** that follows.

Steps in the exercise that are likely to be tested on the exam are preceded by this symbol: ▦. However, it is a good idea to complete the whole exercise to ensure you have understood everything covered in the lesson.

☞ Practice Exercise 2.3

To work on practice exercise 2.3, open the **2-3 Team Sales.xls** workbook in the **MOS Excel 2003 Expert** folder.

▦ 1. Create the pivot table shown below, on a new worksheet, using the data from the **2-3 Team sales.xls** workbook.

	A	B	C	D	E	F	G	H	I	J	K	L	M	N	O	P
1	Team	(All)														
2																
3	Sum of Units Sold	Date														
4	Region	10/01/2003	17/01/2003	24/01/2003	31/01/2003	07/02/2003	14/02/2003	21/02/2003	28/02/2003	06/03/2003	13/03/2003	20/03/2003	27/03/2003	03/04/2003	10/04/2003	Grand Total
5	Central	153	168	274	165	155	162	99	225			261	126	116	478	2362
6	East	142	135	159	82	136	131	89	85	134	114	98	297	163	255	2020
7	North	232	68	125	142	145	178	124	161		102		119	185	323	1904
8	South	127	102	183	260	156	231		130	294	175		270	253	264	2465
9	West	158	254	308	96	89	160	254	128	152		205	152	392	192	2540
10	Grand Total	812	727	1049	745	681	862	566	729	580	391	564	964	1109	1532	11311
11																

This pivot table shows the sum of the sales for each sales team, by region and by date.

▦ 2. Modify the pivot table so you have a report which can be produced for each **Sales ID** instead of for each **Team** and that the results shown are an **Average** and not a **Sum**. Also, display the results without any decimal places.

3. Apply the AutoFormat called **Table 4** to your pivot table report.

4. Show the sales averages by **month**.

If you would like to practise these features more, on another document, you should work through Summary Exercise 2, on ANALYSIS TOOLS. You will find the summary exercises at the end of the book.

It is often possible to perform a task in several different ways, but here, only the easiest solution is presented. You can go back to the corresponding lesson if you want to see other techniques you could use.

Solution to Exercise 2.3

 1. To make a pivot table report like the one shown in the exercise, click one of the cells in the list of data in the **2-3 Team Sales** workbook (**Vendors** sheet).

Use the **Data - PivotTable and PivotChart Report** command.

If necessary, activate the **Microsoft Office Excel list or database** and **PivotTable** options before clicking the **Next** button.

Make sure the cell range listed as the data source is: **$A$1:$E$89** then click **Next**.

If necessary, activate the **New worksheet** option then click the **Layout** button.

Drag the names of the **Date**, **Team**, **Region** and **Units Sold** fields onto the appropriate areas, referring to the model below:

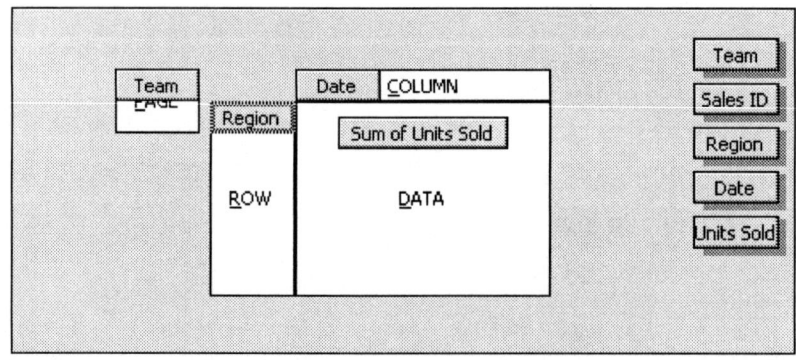

The Sum function is the default function attributed to the DATA field.

Click **OK** on the **Layout** dialog box.

Click **Finish** to create the pivot table report, on a new worksheet.

2. To replace the Team field with the Sales ID field, activate a cell in the pivot table then click the **PivotTable** button on the **PivotTable** toolbar and choose the **PivotTable Wizard** option (with the [icon] icon). Click the **Layout** button then drag the **Team** field from the PAGE area and replace it with the **Sales ID** field.

To change the **Sum** function on the **Units Sold** field, double-click the **Sum of Units Sold** field button, choose the **Average** function under **Summarize by** then click **OK**.
Confirm the changes made in the **Layout** dialog box by clicking **OK**.

Close the Wizard, confirming your work, by clicking the **Finish** button.

To change the format of cells on a pivot table, use the same features as for an ordinary table. Start by selecting all the result cells (from **B5** to **P10**), then use the **Format - Cells** command.
Click **Number** in the **Category** list (**Number** tab) and set the **Decimal places** option to **0** then confirm with **OK**.

3. To apply an AutoFormat to the Pivot Table report, activate one of the cells in the pivot table then use the **Format - AutoFormat** command.
Using the vertical scroll bar, scroll through the models then click the **Table 4** model.
Click **OK** to confirm your choice.

4. To show the average sales per month, click the heading of the **Date** field on the pivot table then use the **Data - Group and Outline - Group** command.
Choose the **Months** option in the **By** list then click **OK**.

ANALYSIS TOOLS
Lesson 2.4: Pivot chart

ANALYSIS TOOLS
Lesson 2.4: Pivot chart

▥1 ▪ Creating a pivot chart

A pivot chart is always associated with a pivot table. Any changes made to the pivot table are carried over into the pivot chart and vice versa.

Several different methods exist for creating pivot charts, which vary depending on the source of the data you are using. It is possible to create a pivot chart from a range of Excel cells and to generate, at the same time, a corresponding pivot table. In this lesson, the pivot chart will be created directly from an existing pivot table.

▪ Go to the pivot table that is your data source.

▪ Click the **Chart Wizard** ▥ tool button on the **PivotTable** toolbar.

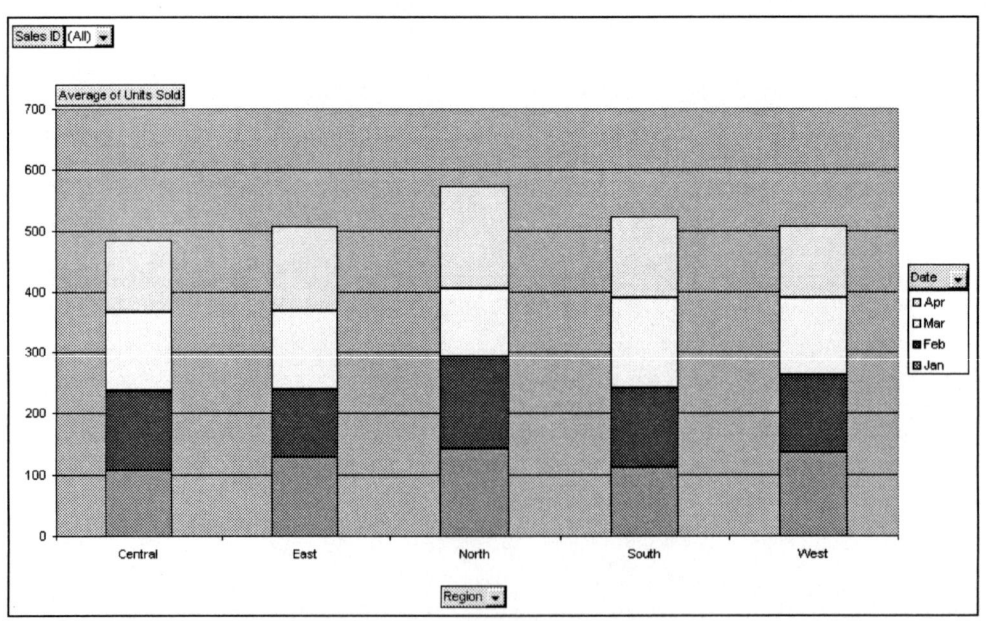

A stacked column chart (which is the default type) is created automatically on a chart sheet. The data on the rows of the pivot table become the chart categories and the data from the pivot table columns become the chart series.

*The **PivotChart report (with PivotTable report)** option you see when you use the **Data - PivotTable and PivotChart Report** command can be used to create a pivot chart with, as its source, an Excel, Access or OLAP database, or a simple range of Excel cells. In all these cases, a pivot table will be generated at the same time as the pivot chart.*

*To move a pivot chart's legend, choose one of the options in **Chart - Chart Options - Legend** tab. The legend cannot be moved or resized with the mouse.*

The titles on a pivot chart and its axes cannot be moved, but you can change their size by changing the font or font size of the characters.

2 ▪ Displaying/hiding chart data

Displaying/hiding certain values

▪ Open the list corresponding to the field concerned and deactivate or activate the option that corresponds to the data you want to hide or display.

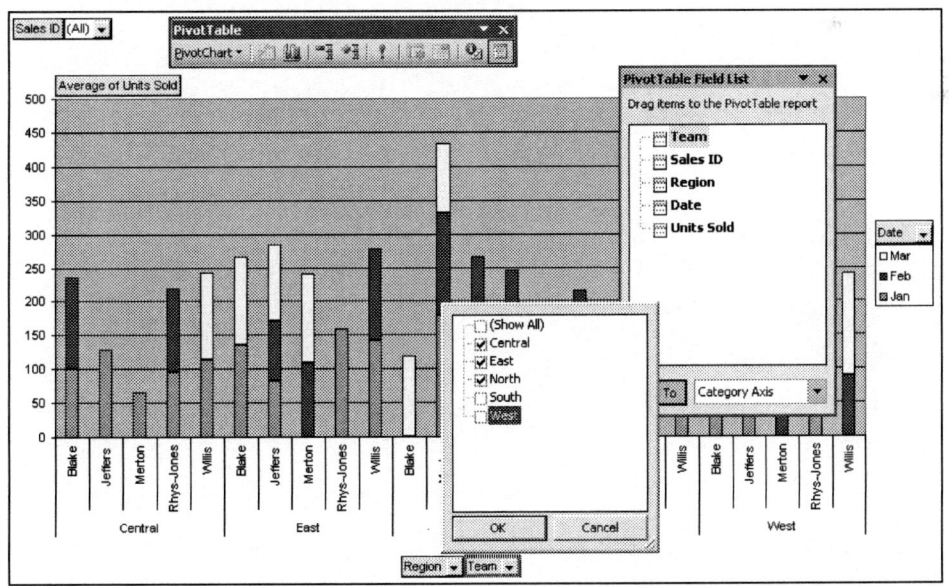

In this example, the data concerning three regions, instead of five, will be displayed simultaneously in the pivot chart and the corresponding pivot table.

❊ Click **OK**.

Adding/deleting a pivot chart field

❊ To add a field, drag it from the **Pivot Table Field List** window onto the chart. If this window cannot be seen, click the **Show Field List** 🔲 tool button on the **PivotTable** toolbar to display it.

❊ To delete a field, drag the field button off the chart.

🖳3 ▪ Changing the pivot chart type

❊ Select the chart area.

❊ **Chart - Chart Type**

❊ Select a type then a **Chart sub-type**.

❊ Click **OK**.

📄 *The **Scatter**, **Bubble** and **Stock** chart types cannot be used on pivot charts.*

4 ▪ Moving a pivot chart to an existing sheet

❊ Activate the chart sheet and select the pivot chart.

❊ **Chart - Location**

❊ Click the **As object in** option and give the name of the sheet to which you want to move the chart.

❊ Click **OK**.

By default, the pivot chart is selected and is placed in the centre of the screen.

- To move the chart on the sheet, make sure it is still selected and drag it to the required position.

- To resize the chart, make sure it is selected then drag one of the selection handles (the black squares around its edge) until the chart reaches the required size.

When a pivot chart is moved, it may lose some of its formatting. The original chart sheet is deleted.

Below, you can see **Practice Exercise 2.4**. This exercise is made up of 4 steps. If you do not know how to do one of the steps, go back to the title that corresponds to that particular lesson. When you have finished, you can check your work by reading the **Solution** that follows.

Steps in the exercise that are likely to be tested on the exam are preceded by this symbol: ⊞. However, it is a good idea to complete all the steps in the exercise, to ensure you have understood all the points discussed in the lesson.

☞ Practice Exercise 2.4

To work on practice exercise 2.4, open the **2-4 Chart.xls** workbook in the **MOS Excel 2003 Expert** folder.

⊞ 1. On a new sheet in the **2-4 Chart.xls** workbook, create a pivot chart based on the model below:

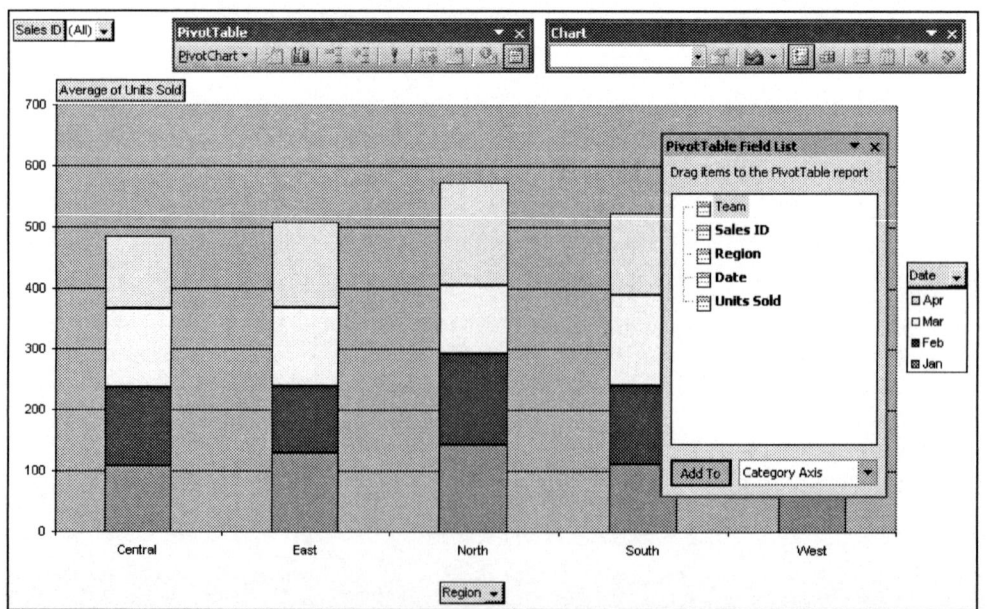

2. Show the average sales for the first quarter only then add the **Team** field to the category axis, obtaining the result below:

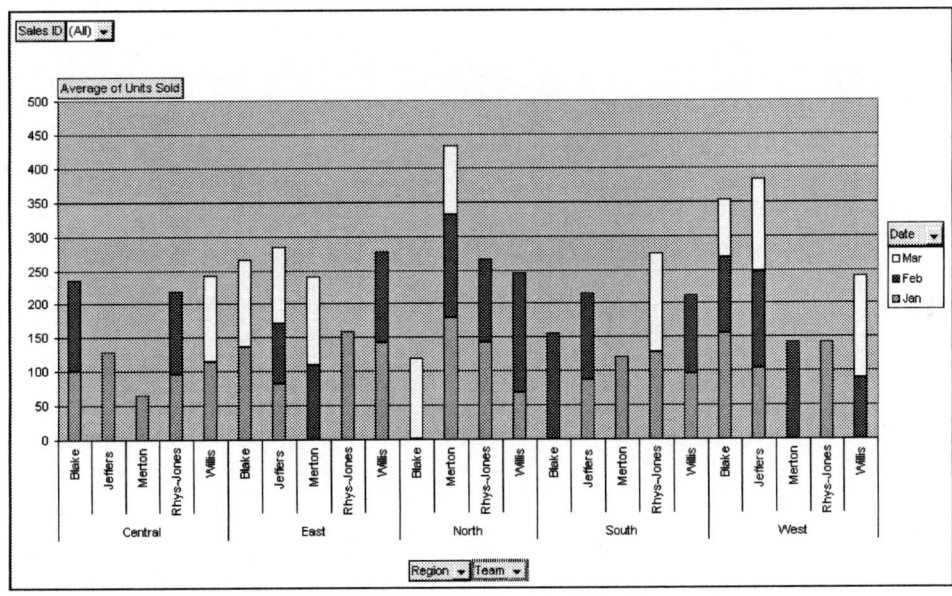

3. Change the pivot chart type to a **Clustered Column** type.

4. Move the pivot chart to the right of the pivot table located on the **PivotTable** worksheet, then change the object size so the chart can be seen clearly.

If you would like to practise these features more, on another document, you should work through Summary Exercise 2, on ANALYSIS TOOLS. You will find the summary exercises at the end of the book.

It is often possible to perform a task in several different ways, but here, only the easiest solution is presented. You can go back to the corresponding lesson if you want to see other techniques you could use.

 Solution to Exercise 2.4

1. To create a pivot chart from the pivot table in the 2-4 Chart.xls workbook, click the **PivotTable** sheet tab to activate it then if the **PivotTable** toolbar does not appear, display it with the **View - Toolbars - PivotTable** command.

   Activate one of the cells in the pivot table then click the 🔲 tool button on the **PivotTable** toolbar.

   *A new sheet (**Chart1**) is created and in it appears a stacked column pivot chart.*

2. To show only the average sales for the first quarter, open the drop-down list on the **Date** field, then deactivate the **Apr** (April) option and click **OK**.

   To add the **Team** field to the right of the **Region** field on the category axis, make sure the **PivotTable Field List** is on the screen (if not, click the 🔲 tool button on the **PivotTable** toolbar).
   Drag the **Team** field onto the pivot chart, to the right of the **Region** field, releasing the mouse button when this symbol ▓▓ appears to the right of the **Region** field.

3. To change the chart type used to a Clustered Column type, make sure the chart is selected and use the **Chart - Chart Type** command.
   Leave the **Chart type** as **Column** then click the first sub-type, called **Clustered Column**.
   Click **OK**.

4. To move the pivot chart onto the **PivotTable** worksheet, select the pivot chart then use the **Chart - Location** command.
Activate the **As object in** option and select **PivotTable** from the list attached to this option.
Click **OK** then move the chart object to the right of the pivot table.

To change the object's size, click the chart object, then drag the appropriate selection handles (the small black squares around its edges) until you can see the chart correctly.

ANALYSIS TOOLS
Lesson 2.5: What-If analysis/Projections

ANALYSIS TOOLS
Lesson 2.5: What-If analysis/Projections

▦1 ▪ Creating one- or two-input data tables

The objective of a data table is to see what might happen to a result if you modify certain values in a formula. It is a way of seeing several possibilities arising from variations of a single formula.

Creating a two-input data table

▪ Enter the initial data for the calculation you want to make, for example, here, the interest rate, the loan duration and the amount being borrowed.

▪ Enter the table's column and row headers, which will be the variables.

Make sure that the table which will display the results is not attached to the initial input data. The variables must be laid out correctly; the row headers must be one row above the column headers and the column headers must be one column to the left of the first row header. There should be a blank cell at the intersection of the two sets of headers.

	A	B	C	D	E	F	G	H	I
1									
2									
3		Capital borrowed		£ 15,000.00					
4		Interest rate		10%					
5		Loan duration in months		12					
6									
7									
8									
9		What are all the possible monthly repayments?							
10		2 years	3 years	4 years	5 years	6 years	7 years	8 years	10 years
11		24 months	36 months	48 months	60 months	72 months	84 months	96 months	120 months
12	9.00%								
13	9.25%								
14	9.50%								
15	9.75%								
16	10.00%								
17									

▪ In the blank cell at the headers' intersection, enter the calculation formula then confirm.

- Select the range of cells from the calculation formula down to the last cell in the results table.

- **Data - Table**

- In the **Row input cell** box, give the cell reference used in your formula that matches the variables in the first row of the data table.

  For example, if the loan durations are in the row, give the cell that corresponds to the initial loan duration in the calculation formula.

- Enter the **Column input cell** with the appropriate cell reference.

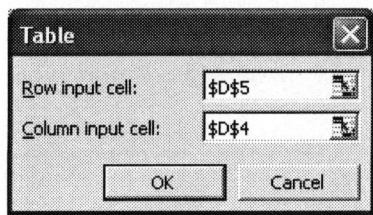

- Click **OK**.

	A11	▼	fx	=ABS(PMT(D4/12,D5,D3))					
	A	B	C	D	E	F	G	H	I
1									
2									
3		Capital borrowed		£ 15,000.00					
4		Interest rate		10%					
5		Loan duration in months		12					
6									
7									
8									
9		What are all the possible monthly repayments?							
10		2 years	3 years	4 years	5 years	6 years	7 years	8 years	10 years
11	£ 1,318.74	24 months	36 months	48 months	60 months	72 months	84 months	96 months	120 months
12	9.00%	£ 685.27	£ 477.00	£ 373.28	£ 311.38	£ 270.38	£ 241.34	£ 219.75	£ 190.01
13	9.25%	£ 686.99	£ 478.74	£ 375.06	£ 313.20	£ 272.25	£ 243.24	£ 221.70	£ 192.05
14	9.50%	£ 688.72	£ 480.49	£ 376.85	£ 315.03	£ 274.12	£ 245.16	£ 223.66	£ 194.10
15	9.75%	£ 690.44	£ 482.25	£ 378.64	£ 316.86	£ 276.00	£ 247.08	£ 225.63	£ 196.16
16	10.00%	£ 692.17	£ 484.01	£ 380.44	£ 318.71	£ 277.89	£ 249.02	£ 227.61	£ 198.23
17									

Excel repeats the calculation for each set of variables and fills in the results table.

Creating a one-input data table

- To create a one-input data table, follow the same guidelines as for a two-input table, with these differences in mind:

  - The variables need be entered only in a row or a column, depending on how you set out your table.

  - If the variables are in a column, type the formula one row above and one cell to the right of the first value in the column. If the variables are in a row, type the formula one column to the left and one cell below the first value in the row.

  - In the **Table** dialog box, type in the cell reference for column-oriented data in the **Column input cell** box or for row-oriented data in the **Row input cell** box.

B8	▼	ƒₓ =ABS(FV(D4,D3,D2,,1))		
	A	B	C	D
1				
2		Yearly investment		£ 1,000.00
3		Investment duration in years		3
4		Annual interest rate offered		4%
5				
6				
7	Final investment return			
8		£3,246.46		
9	3.50% £	3,214.94		
10	3.75% £	3,230.68		
11	4.25% £	3,262.30		
12	4.50% £	3,278.19		
13				

*Here, we want to see what the final return would be on our investment plan with a different rate of interest. The **Column input cell** was D4.*

🖳 2 ▪ Finding a goal value

This feature helps you solve the problem of knowing what value one cell must contain to obtain a given value in another cell.

- Activate the cell that needs to obtain a specific value; check that this cell contains a calculation formula.

- If possible, show the cell you want to modify on the screen at the same time.

- **Tools - Goal Seek**

- Check that the **Set cell** box refers to the cell (or cell name) for which you want to find the goal value (remember this must contain a calculation).

- In the **To value** box, enter the required goal value.

- In the **By changing cell** box, enter or choose the cell reference or name that should be adjusted in order to find the goal value.

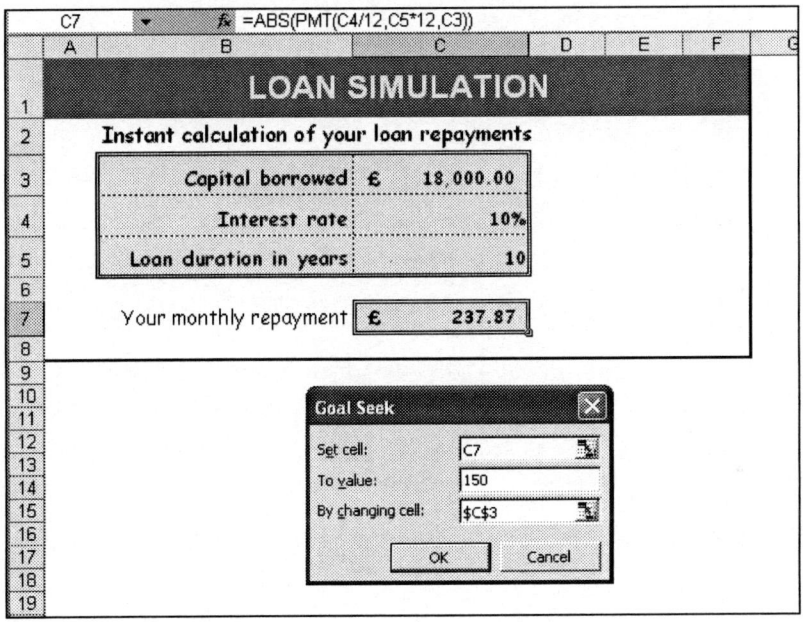

If the lender can repay £150 each month, how much money can he borrow?

- Click **OK** to start the search.

ANALYSIS TOOLS
Lesson 2.5: What-If analysis/Projections

Once Excel has found a solution, it stops and displays its conclusions on the worksheet:

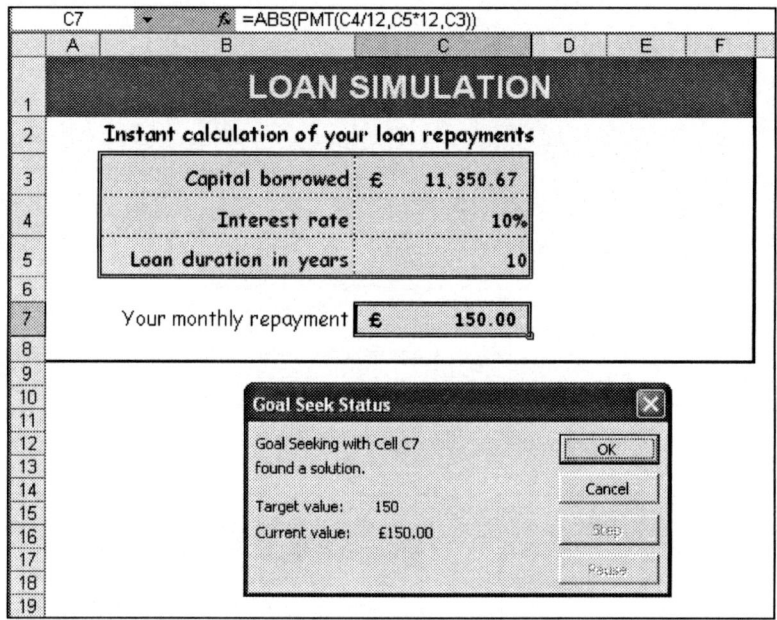

* If the proposed solution is satisfactory, click **OK** to keep it in the worksheet. If you want to return to the original values, click the **Cancel** button.

3 ▪ Using the Solver to resolve problems

To find the answer to a problem with several unknowns and constraints, you can use an analysis tool called the Solver. It can find results for many "what if?" types of problem, such as finding a minimal or maximal value that would result from other cells being modified.

Setting the problem's parameters

* **Tools - Solver**

■ If the **Solver** option does not appear in the **Tools** menu, you will have to load the Solver add-in (**Tools - Add-Ins -** tick the **Solver Add-In** box and **OK**).

■ Indicate which cell you wish to define in the **Set Target Cell** box.

■ Specify what the target cell should be **Equal To**: a maximum value (**Max**), a minimum (**Min**) or a precise amount (**Value of**).

■ In the **By Changing Cells** box, tell the Solver which cells it can change in attempting to reach its target value.

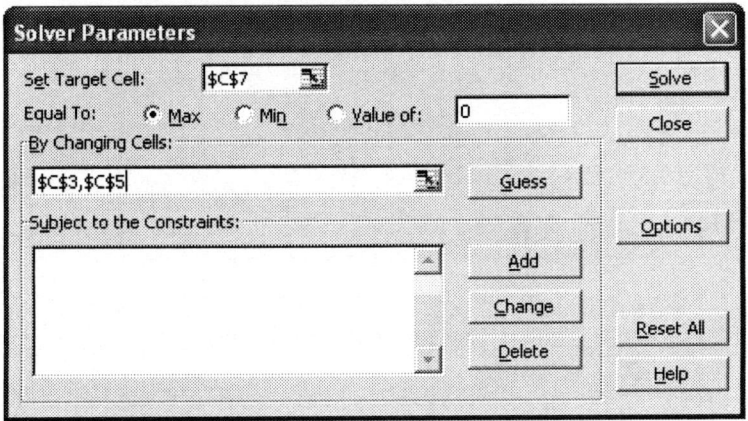

Managing constraints

■ To create an initial constraint, click the **Add** button in the **Solver Parameters** dialog box.
Give the **Cell Reference** for the cell concerned by the constraint, then define the **Constraint**, not forgetting the operator such as equals (=), less than (<) and so on.

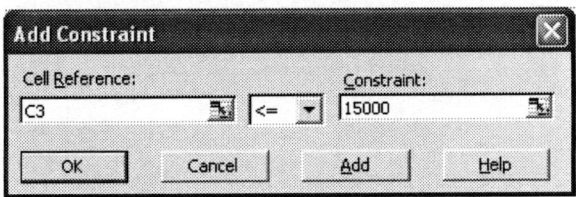

- To create additional constraints, click the **Add** button on the **Add Constraint** dialog box and define any other constraints in the same way as the first.

- When you have created all the constraints, confirming each one with **Add**, click **Cancel** on the dialog box.

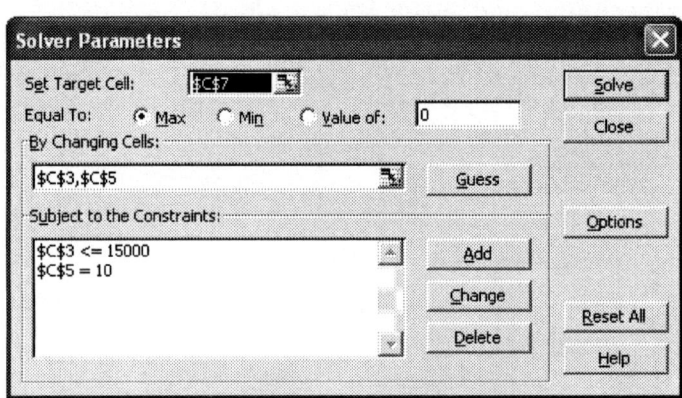

*You can edit or remove a constraint by selecting it and clicking the **Change** or **Delete** button.*

Running the problem through the Solver

- Click the **Solve** button on the **Solver Parameters** dialog box.

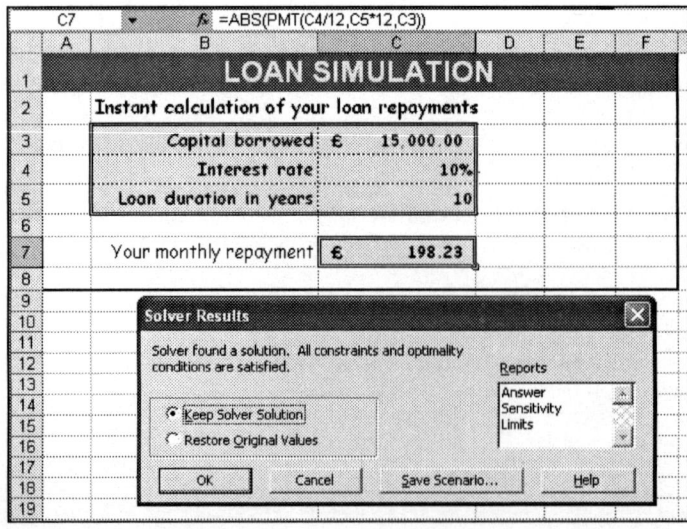

Excel displays several messages on the status bar then, once it finds a solution, it enters the solution values on the work-sheet. Here for example, to meet the constraints applied, the loan value must be £15 000, at 10% interest, over 10 years.

■ If you are satisfied with the Solver's solution, choose the **Keep Solver Solution** option; otherwise, you can **Restore Original Values**.

■ Click **OK** to confirm.

 *In some cases, a problem may take a long time to solve; if this occurs, Excel pauses the process and asks if you want to **Continue** or if you prefer to **Stop**.*

Cancelling all a problem's parameters

■ **Tools - Solver**

■ Click the **Reset All** button.

■ Click **OK** to confirm then click the **Close** button.

Saving a Solver problem model

■ Activate a cell on the worksheet; this will be the first data entry cell that Excel will use to note the model.

■ **Tools - Solver**

■ If it is not already defined, set out the problem's parameters.

■ Click the **Options** button then click the **Save Model** button.

■ Click **OK** twice then click **Close**.

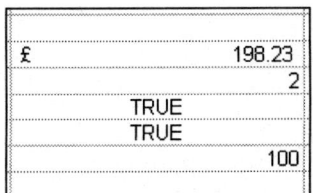

A problem model is a set of logical values.

Loading a saved Solver problem model

- **Tools - Solver**

- Click the **Options** button then click the **Load Model** button.

- Select a data entry area for the problem model.

- Click **OK**.

- Close the options window by clicking **OK**.

  This retrieves all the problem's constraints and parameters, except for the target cell.

Saving Solver solutions

- Run Solver to find a solution to the problem.

- Once Excel has found a solution, click the **Save Scenario** button, then enter a **Scenario Name**.

- Click **OK**.

- Close the **Solver Results** dialog box.

  📄 *Once you have saved a Solver scenario, you can run it like any other scenario using the **Tools - Scenarios** command.*

🪟4 ▪ Using complex analysis tools

Excel 2003 provides you with a set of specific tools for more complicated calculations in finance, engineering, statistics and so on. This is called the Analysis ToolPak and it is an add-in that does not appear in Excel by default. As these tools provide an extensive array of statistical commands, we cannot explore all of them here; however we can look at two useful types of analyses, trendlines and linear regression.

Installing the Analysis ToolPak

■ **Tools - Add-Ins**

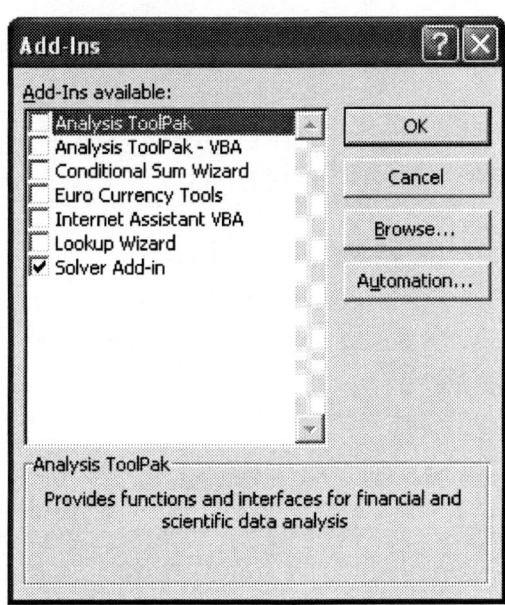

■ Tick the **Analysis ToolPak** check box in the **Add-Ins available** list and click **OK**.

Excel may need to install this add-in from your installation CD-ROM; if this is the case, insert your Excel or Office CD-ROM in the drive and follow the instructions.

■ Once you have installed the add-in, the command **Data Analysis** appears in the **Tools** menu.

Using data analysis commands

■ Open the workbook in which you wish to make a statistical analysis.

■ **Tools - Data Analysis**

ANALYSIS TOOLS
Lesson 2.5: What-If analysis/Projections

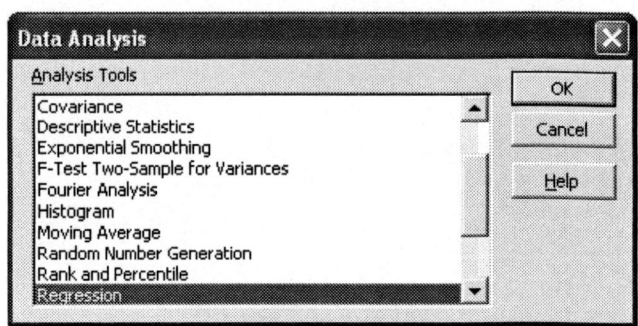

In the dialog box, each name corresponds to a type of analysis.

- Click the required type of analysis to open a dialog box in which you can specify the data for that particular function.

- If you wish to see a detailed description of one of the commands, click its name then click the **Help** button on the dialog box.

Making a linear regression analysis

*Here we will use the example of the **Regression** function. This calculates using a method called "least squares" to determine how a line could be drawn through a group of given observations, to see how one dependent variable may change according to the values of other variables. This example shows how manufacturing times may change for trailers depending on their size and shape.*

- **Tools - Data Analysis**

- Click the **Regression** function then click **OK**.

  This calculation is in the form $Y = a_1x_1 + a_2x_2 + \ldots + a_nx_n + b$ where Y is the manufacturing time, x_1, x_2 to x_n are the variables required during assembly, a_1, a_2 to a_n are the coefficients of these variables and b is the constant.

- In the **Input Y Range** box, specify which is the dependent variable range (here this is C3 to C16).

- In the **Input X Range** box, specify which is the independent variable field (or fields). Here, this is D3 to H16 which give all the factors such as width, height etc. that affect assembly time.

  You can use up to 16 independent variables.

- Tick the **Labels** option if the first row/column or your input range(s) contains field headers.

- A 95% confidence level is applied by default, but you can enter an additional level by ticking **Confidence Level** and entering a percentage.

- Under **Output options**, specify where you want Excel to put the calculation results. By default, this will be copied onto a new worksheet in the same workbook (**Worksheet Ply**) You can also specify the upper left cell of an **Output Range** of your choice or choose to create a **New Workbook**. In this example we will put the results under the input range.

- Choose to include **Residuals** or **Standardized Residuals** in the residuals output table.

- Tick **Residual Plots** to create a chart comparing independent variables and the residuals.

- Tick **Line Fit Plots** to create a chart comparing predictions and observations.

- You can also create a chart of **Normal Probability Plots** by ticking the corresponding option.

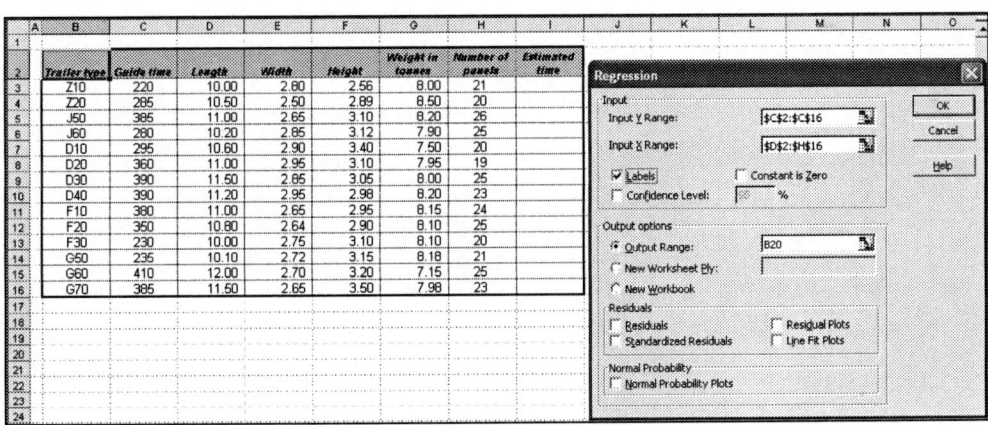

- Click **OK** to start calculating.

Excel displays its calculation results in the location indicated in the **Output options**:

Trailer type	Guide time	Length	Width	Height	Weight in tonnes	Number of panels	Estimated time
Z10	220	10.00	2.80	2.56	8.00	21	
Z20	285	10.50	2.50	2.89	8.50	20	
J50	385	11.00	2.65	3.10	8.20	26	
J60	280	10.20	2.85	3.12	7.90	25	
D10	295	10.60	2.90	3.40	7.50	20	
D20	360	11.00	2.95	3.10	7.95	19	
D30	390	11.50	2.85	3.05	8.00	25	
D40	390	11.20	2.95	2.98	8.20	23	
F10	380	11.00	2.65	2.95	8.15	24	
F20	350	10.80	2.64	2.90	8.10	25	
F30	230	10.00	2.75	3.10	8.10	20	
G50	235	10.10	2.72	3.15	8.18	21	
G60	410	12.00	2.70	3.20	7.15	25	
G70	385	11.50	2.65	3.50	7.98	23	

SUMMARY OUTPUT

Regression Statistics

Multiple R	0.971573957
R Square	0.943955953
Adjusted R Sc	0.908928424
Standard Erro	20.54980279
Observations	14

ANOVA

	df	SS	MS	F	Significance F
Regression	5	56902.00198	11380.4004	26.94897336	8.31041E-05
Residual	8	3378.355159	422.2943949		
Total	13	60280.35714			

	Coefficients	Standard Error	t Stat	P-value	Lower 95%	Upper 95%	Lower 95.0%	Upper 95.0%
Intercept	-1539.55952	329.3177337	-4.6749973	0.001592167	-2298.96757	-780.151461	-2298.96757	-780.151461
Length	103.1914013	12.16326006	8.483860473	2.85459E-05	75.14287328	131.2399292	75.14287328	131.2399292
Width	66.29143553	46.89328738	1.413665777	0.195170792	-41.844679	174.4275501	-41.844679	174.4275501
Height	11.9182986	29.22506201	0.407810892	0.694108176	-55.4748152	79.3114124	-55.4748152	79.3114124
Weight in tonn	51.69540184	21.66876866	2.385710173	0.04415044	1.72713174	101.6636719	1.72713174	101.6636719
Number of par	5.273621643	2.853401586	1.848187675	0.101759258	-1.30633421	11.85357749	-1.30633421	11.85357749

 In each command's dialog box there is a **Help** button: click it to see an explanation of each option in the dialog box.

Adding a trendline to a chart

The main objective of a trendline is to predict future results of existing data by showing, graphically, how the current situation or result is likely to proceed. This type of statistical analysis (which is also known as a regression analysis) enables you to extend a trendline from an existing data series in a chart, to obtain an idea of that series' potential future values.

Certain types of chart can manage trendlines added to their data series; these types are unstacked 2D area charts, bar, column, line, stock, scatter (xy) and bubble charts. Stacked, 3D, radar, pie, surface or doughnut charts cannot use trendlines.

▪ Create or open the chart to which you wish to add the trendline.

▪ Click the data series you want the trendline to analyse.

▪ **Chart - Add Trendline**

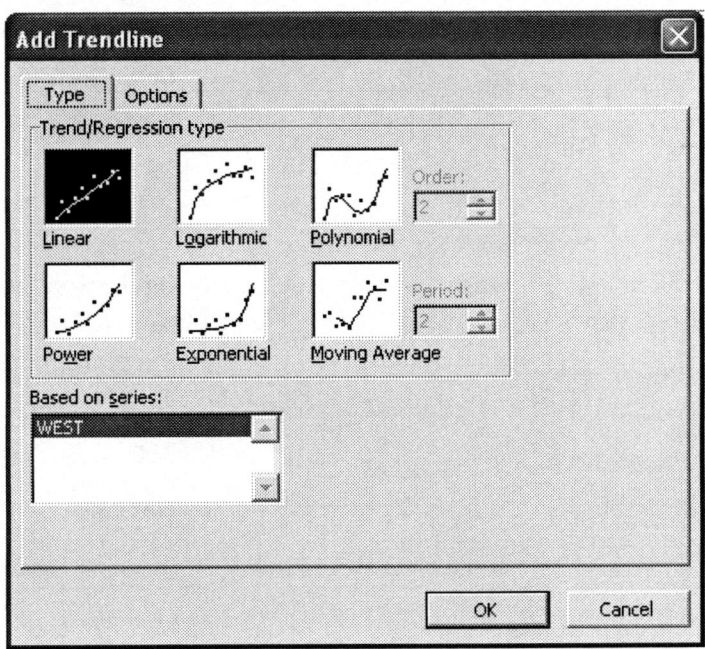

ANALYSIS TOOLS
Lesson 2.5: What-If analysis/Projections

* Click the **Type** tab then choose the required type of regression trendline or moving average from those in the **Trend/Regression type** frame:

Linear	generally represents a regular increase or decrease by a weighted straight line.
Logarithmic	a logarithmic trendline that uses positive and/or negative values is used when there is a rapid increase or decrease in the rate of change of data.
Polynomial	represents fluctuations in data. Either the number of fluctuations in the data or the number of bends in the curve can determine the order of the polynomial curve. For example, an order 2 polynomial curve has either one "hill" or one "valley".
Power	is used to compare sets of measurements that increase at a specific rate.
Exponential	analyses values that increase or decrease exponentially (that is, more and more rapidly).
Moving Average	smoothes data fluctuations to show trends or patterns more clearly.

* If you chose the **Polynomial** type, click the **Order** box and type the highest power for the independent variable.

* If you chose the **Moving Average** type, click the **Period** box and enter the number of periods required to calculate the moving average.

* The **Based on series** box lists all the data series in the chart to which you could add a trendline. You can add the trendline to the series of your choice.

* Click the **Options** tab.

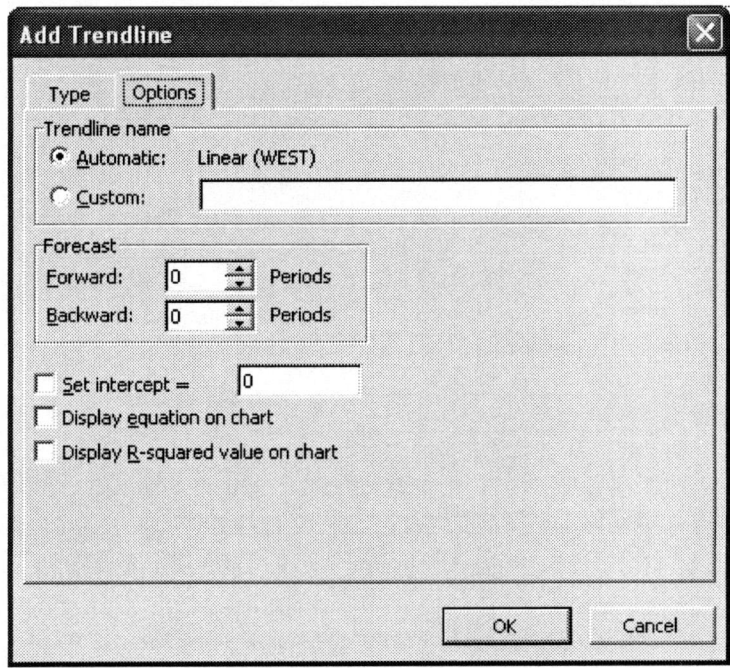

By default, Excel names the trendline automatically, taking the type of curve used, followed by the name of the data series to which you are adding the trendline.

■ To customise the name of the trendline, activate the **Custom** option, click its text box and enter your chosen name (this will appear in the chart legend).

■ You can determine the intersecting point between the trendline and the Y-axis. To do this, tick the **Set intercept =** check box then enter the value of the intersection point in the corresponding text box.

■ To **Display equation on chart** (in the trendline label), tick the corresponding check box.

■ To **Display R-squared value on chart** (in the trendline label), tick the corresponding check box (cf. below).

■ Click **OK** to confirm creating the trendline.

The trendline appears on the chart.

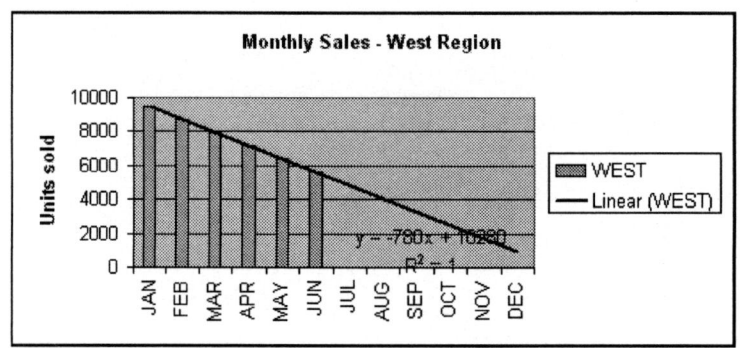

The example above shows a linear trendline. The equation and R-squared value have been displayed on this chart.

The R-squared value is the indicator (between 0 and 1) that indicates to what degree the estimated trend values correspond to the real chart data. The closer this value is to 1, the more the trend values are reliable.

If you did not choose to display the R-squared value as you create the trendline, you can add it later; you can also hide the value if it is already displayed.

- To display or hide the R-squared value on an existing trendline, click the trendline concerned and use **Format - Selected Trendline**.

- Click the **Options** tab.

- Tick the **Display R-squared value on chart** option to show the value or deactivate the check box to hide it.

 It is not possible to display the R-squared value of a moving average.

*You can use the settings under the **Patterns** tab on the tab on the **Format Trendline** dialog box to change the appearance of the trendline, if you wish.*

To delete a trendline, select it then press the Del *key on the keyboard.*

Below, you can see **Practice Exercise 2.5**. This exercise is made up of 4 steps. If you do not know how to do one of the steps, go back to the title that corresponds to that particular lesson. When you have finished, you can check your work by reading the **Solution** that follows.

All the steps of this exercise are likely to be tested on the Microsoft Office Specialist exam.

☞ Practice Exercise 2.5

*To work on practice exercise 2.5, open the **2-5 Loans.xls** workbook in the **MOS Excel 2003 Expert** folder.*

1. On the worksheet called **Data tables**, calculate the possible repayments using the data table set out for you. The input data is as follows: a capital of £15 000 (cell D3), a 10% interest rate (cell D4) and a 12-month loan duration (cell D5). Loan repayments are calculated with a PMT function, possibly nested within an ABS function, which gives the absolute value of the result.

2. On the worksheet called **Goal seek**, find what amount could be borrowed for a monthly repayment of **£150**, on a **10-year loan** at **10% interest**. Display your result in **C7**. Keep the solution offered by Excel if it is suitable.

3. On the worksheet called **Solver**, determine what the maximum monthly repayment could be, if the loan parameters were subject to these constraints: the borrower can only borrow up to **£15 000** and the loan duration must be **ten years**. The problem result should appear in cell C7. Keep Solver's suggested solution.
   Save this problem model, displaying its variables in the cells from B13 onwards.
   Save the **2-5 Loans.xls** workbook then close it.

4. Open the workbook called **2-5 Trendline.xls**, in the **MOS Excel 2003 Expert** folder. Add a linear trendline to the WEST data series and call it **Linear trend**. Display the R-squared value and the equation on the linear trendline. Save and close the workbook.

If you would like to practise these features more, on another document, you should work through Summary Exercise 2, on ANALYSIS TOOLS. You will find the summary exercises at the end of the book.

It is often possible to perform a task in several different ways, but here, only the easiest solution is presented. You can go back to the corresponding lesson if you want to see other techniques you could use.

Solution to Exercise 2.5

1. To calculate the possible repayments in the data table in the Data tables worksheet, click the **Data tables** sheet tab to activate it, if necessary. In cell **A11**, enter the calculation formula: **=ABS(PMT(D4/12,D5,D3))**. This calculates the absolute value of the repayments obtained by the yearly interest rate divided by the quantity of months (D4/12), the length of the loan (D5) and the capital (D3).
Select the range of cells from **A11** to **I16**.

   Use the **Data - Table** command. In the dialog box, click the ▣ button on the **Row input cell** box and click **D5** on the worksheet then click ▣ to restore the dialog box.

   Next, click the ▣ button on the **Column input cell** box and click **D4** on the worksheet then click ▣ to restore the dialog box. Click **OK** to confirm.

2. To find the amount that could be borrowed for a monthly repayment of £150, on a 10-year loan at 10% interest in the table in the Goal seek worksheet, start by clicking the **Goal seek** sheet tab to activate it. Click cell **C7** then use the **Tools - Goal Seek** command.
Check that **C7** appears in the **Set cell** box.
In the **To value** box, enter your target amount, which is **150**.
In the **By changing cell** box, click the ▣ button and click **C3** on the worksheet (this is the cell that Goal Seek can vary to find the target) then click ▣ to restore the dialog box. Click **OK** to confirm.
As the Excel solution is suitable, click **OK** to keep it in the worksheet.

3. To determine what the maximum monthly repayment could be on a loan of up to £15 000, with a duration of 10 years, in cell **C7** on the **Solver** worksheet, start by clicking the **Solver** sheet tab to activate it.
Click cell **C7** to select it.
Use **Tools - Solver** and check that cell **C7** (the repayment instalment) appears in the **Set Target Cell** box (otherwise type it in).
Activate the **Max** option under **Equal to**.
In the **By Changing Cells** box, enter **C3,C5** (these are the cells that can be modified).

To apply the constraints given, click the **Add** button. In the **Cell Reference** box, enter **C3**, choose **<=** as the operator then enter **15000** in the **Constraint** box. Click **Add**.
In the **Cell Reference** box, enter **C5**, choose **=** as the operator then enter **10** in the **Constraint** box. Click **Add** then the **Cancel** button to close the **Add Constraint** dialog box.

To run the problem, click the **Solve** button. When Solver has found a solution, make sure the **Keep Solver Solution** option is active then click **OK**.

To save this problem model, activate cell **B13** on the **Solver** worksheet and use **Tools - Solver**. The problem's parameters are still in the dialog box. Click the **Options** button then the **Save Model** button. Click **OK** once, click **OK** again on the **Solver Options** dialog box then click **Close** to close the Solver.

To save the **2-5 Loans.xls** workbook, click the [icon] tool button then use **File - Close**.

4. Open the 2-5 Trendline.xls workbook: use the **File - Open** command, choose the **MOS Excel 2003 Expert** folder and double-click the **2-5 Trendline.xls** file icon.

To add a linear trendline to the WEST data series, select the WEST data series by clicking one its value on the chart.
Use the **Chart - Add Trendline** command then click **Linear** as the **Trend/Regression type** in the dialog box.

To change the trendline's name, click the **Options** tab and activate the **Custom** option. The insertion point places itself in the text box automatically, so type **Linear trend** and confirm by clicking **OK**.

To display the R-squared value and the equation on the linear trendline, click anywhere on the curve to select it and use the **Format - Selected Trendline** command.
Click the **Options** tab, tick the **Display R-squared value on chart** and **Display equation on chart** options then confirm with **OK**.

Click to save the workbook then use **File - Close** to close it.

TEMPLATES, WORKBOOKS AND WORKGROUPS
Lesson 3.1: Templates

TEMPLATES, WORKBOOKS AND WORKGROUPS
Lesson 3.1: Templates

1 ▪ Creating a custom template

A **template** *is a document that contains presentations, data and other elements that can be used when you create new workbooks.*

▪ Set up the template workbook, adding any elements you want workbooks created from this template to have. If required, activate worksheet or cell protection.

▪ **File - Save As**

▪ Open the **Save as type** list and click the **Template** option.

▪ Indicate the name of the template in the **File name** box.

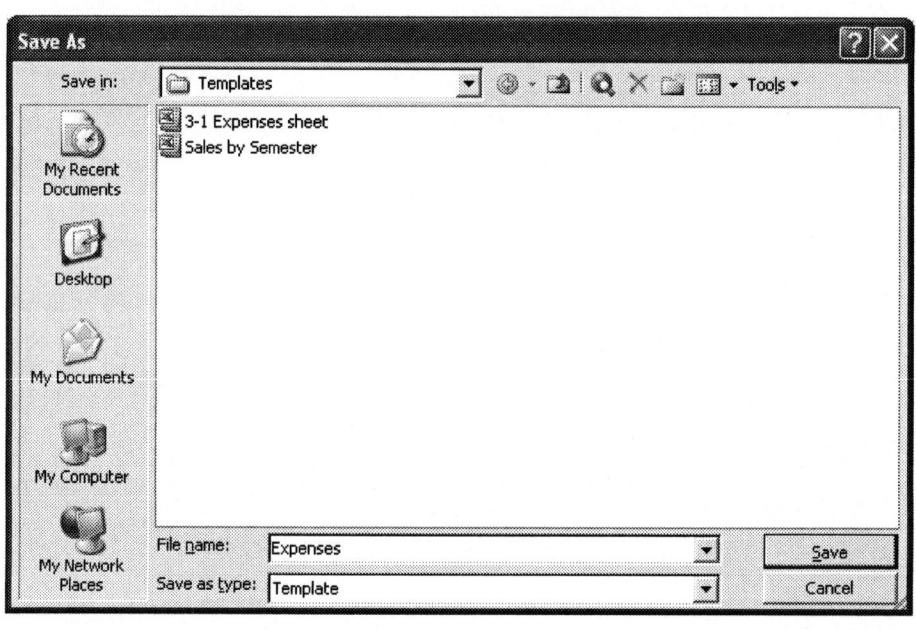

*By default, Excel offers to save the template in the **Templates** folder on your hard disk. If you use Windows XP, you will find it at **C:\Documents and Settings\user_name\Application Data\Microsoft\Templates**. You 'should save your custom templates in this folder or you will not be able to use them as templates, you will merely be able to open it.*

*If you cannot see the **Application Data** folder in the **Save in** list, you may have to activate the **Show hidden files and folders** option (in the Windows Explorer, **Tools - Folder Options - View** tab).*

■ If you want to save your template in the **My Web Sites on MSN** folder, click the **My Network Places** shortcut in the dialog box then double-click the **My Web Sites on MSN** link. If you do this, the folder in which these templates are stored in generally **My Web Documents/Documents**.

The first time you access My Web Sites on MSN, you need to identify yourself with a Microsoft.NET passport. Fill in the information required in the wizard:

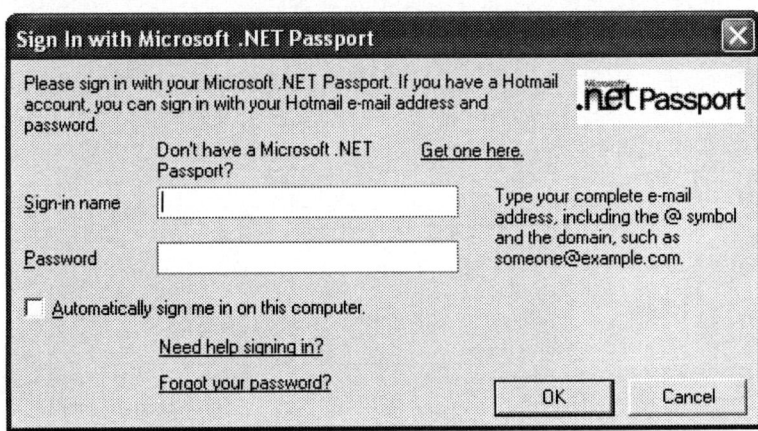

■ Once you have chosen the required folder, click the **Save** button to save the template.

Template files have an .xlt extension, but depending on your Windows settings, this extension may not be visible.

📖 2 • Modifying a custom template

To modify a template, you must first open it.

- **File - Open** or 📂 or ⌊Ctrl⌋ **O**

- Open the **Files of type** drop-down list and click the **Templates** option.

- Choose the folder in which you saved the template.

This could be the Templates folder (C:\Documents and Settings\user_name\ Application Data\Microsoft\Templates) or, if you saved them in My Web Sites on MSN, My Network Places\My Web Sites on MSN\My Web Documents\ Documents.

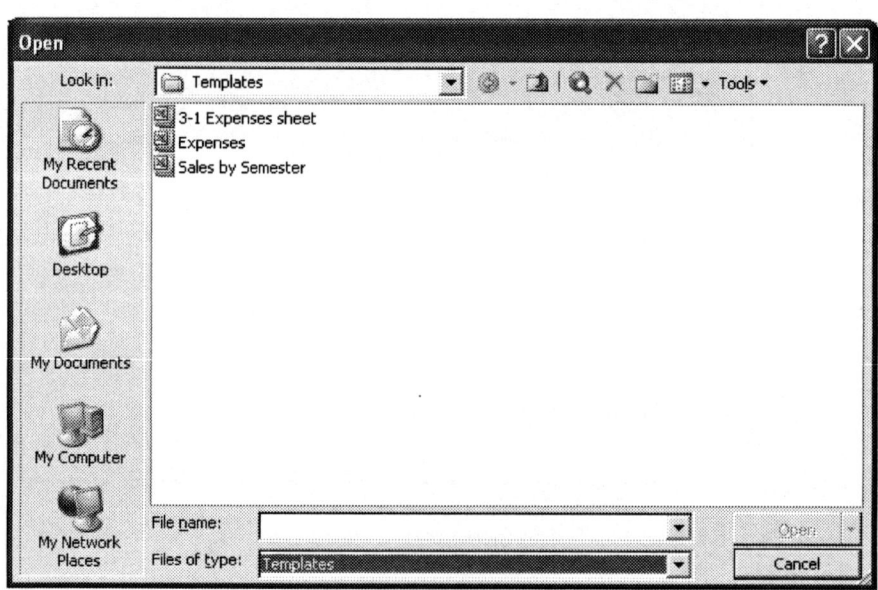

*Only templates are now visible in the **Open** dialog box.*

- Double-click the name of the template you want to open, or select it then click the **Open** button.

- Make the changes you require in the template, then click the 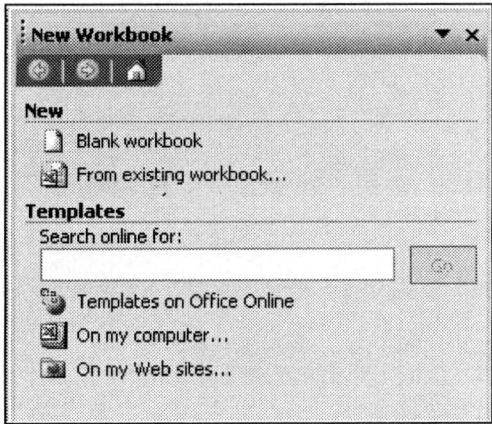 tool button or use **File - Save** to save them.

- Close the template.

3 • Creating a workbook based on a template

- If necessary, use the **File - New** command to display the **New Workbook** task pane.

How you access the template depends on where it is stored.

Using a template saved on your computer

- Click the **On my computer** link in the **New Workbook** task pane.

  *The templates stored in your **Templates** folder on your hard disk appear on the **General** page.*

- If necessary, click the tab that corresponds to the folder containing the template.

- Double-click the template's name.

When you open a template in this way, Excel copies its contents into a new workbook, then it gives the workbook the same name as the template, followed by a number.

▪ Enter your data into the new workbook.

▪ Save your workbook as any ordinary workbook, using the **File - Save** command, and choosing the correct folder; make sure that **Microsoft Office Excel Workbook** appears in the **Save as type** box.

 *Once you have used a template to create a workbook, the template's name appears as a link in the **Recently used templates** section of the **New Workbook** task pane. To create another new workbook based on that template, simply click the link.*

Using a template saved on the MSN server

▪ Make sure that your Internet connection is online.

▪ In the **Templates** section of the **New Workbook** task pane, click the **On my Web sites** link.

*By default, Excel opens the **My Network Places** folder in the **New from Templates on my Web Sites** dialog box.*

▪ Go to the site on which the template was saved.

*Remember that Microsoft provides you with a storage space called **My Web Sites on MSN** in which you can save your documents such as templates or pictures. To use this service, you need to have a Microsoft.NET passport.*

▪ Double-click the name of the template you wish to use.

A new workbook based on the chosen template is automatically created in Excel.

▪ Enter your data in the new workbook

▪ Save your workbook as any ordinary workbook, using the **File - Save** command, and choosing the correct folder; make sure that **Microsoft Office Excel Workbook** appears in the **Save as type** box.

Below, you can see **Practice Exercise 3.1**. This exercise is made up of 3 steps. If you do not know how to do one of the steps, go back to the title that corresponds to that particular lesson. When you have finished, you can check your work by reading the **Solution** that follows.

All the steps of this exercise are likely to be tested in the Microsoft Office Specialist exam.

Practice Exercise 3.1

1. Create a template called **Expenses.xlt** in which you should enter and format the following data:

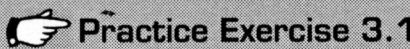

	A	B	C	D	E	F	G	H	I	J
1	**Expenses sheet**									
2										
3										
4	Surname:									
5	Name:									
6	Staff ID:									
7										
8	Week no:									
9										
10	Date submitted:									
11										
12										
13		Mon	Tues	Wed	Thurs	Fri	Sat	Sun	TOTAL	
14	Petrol									
15	Parking									
16	Taxi									
17	Air/Rail									
18	Meals									
19	Hotel									
20	Other									
21	TOTAL									
22		Date:	Place:		Clients visited:			Comments:		
23										
24										
25	Approved by:							To be refunded:		
26	Date:									
27										
28										
29										
30										

Expenses / Sheet2 / Sheet3 /

2. In the **3-1 Expenses sheet.xlt** template, make the following changes:
   - put cells **B4** and **B5** in **bold** type,
   - apply the fill colour **Gray -25%** to cells **I14** to **I21** and cells **B22** to **I22**.
   The **3-1 Expenses sheet.xlt** template can be found in the **Templates** folder.
   Save your changes, then close the **3-1 Expenses sheet.xlt** template.

3. Create a new workbook based on the **3-1 Expenses sheet.xlt** template and complete the top of **Sheet1** as shown below:

	A	B	C	
1	**Expenses sheet**			
2				
3				
4	Surname:	**ANDREWS**		
5	Name:	**Robin**		
6	Staff ID	BAR15		
7				
8				
9	*Week no:*		41	
10				
11	*Date submitted:*		13/10/2003	
12				

Save this new workbook as **3-1 Expenses Andrews 41.xls** in the **MOS Excel 2003 Expert** folder.

If you would like to practise these features more, on another document, you should work through Summary Exercise 3, on TEMPLATES, WORKBOOKS AND WORKGROUPS. You will find the summary exercises at the end of the book.

It is often possible to perform a task in several different ways, but here, only the easiest solution is presented. You can go back to the corresponding lesson if you want to see other techniques you could use.

Solution to Exercise 3.1

1. To create the Expenses.xlt template, create a new workbook by clicking the 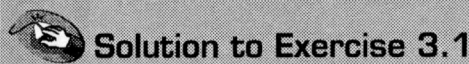 tool button, then enter and format the following information on **Sheet1** of this workbook:

	A	B	C	D	E	F	G	H	I	J
1	Expenses sheet									
2										
3										
4	Surname:									
5	Name:									
6	Staff ID:									
7										
8	Week no:									
9										
10	Date submitted:									
11										
12										
13		Mon	Tues	Wed	Thurs	Fri	Sat	Sun	TOTAL	
14	Petrol									
15	Parking									
16	Taxi									
17	Air/Rail									
18	Meals									
19	Hotel									
20	Other									
21	TOTAL									
22		Date:	Place:		Clients visited:			Comments:		
23										
24										
25	Approved by:							To be refunded:		
26	Date:									
27										
28										
29										
30										

Expenses / Sheet2 / Sheet3 /

Use the **File - Save As** command.
Open the **Save as type** list and click the **Template** option.
Type **Expenses** in the **File name** text box and click the **Save** button.

▦ 2. To edit the 3-1 Expenses sheet.xlt template, which is in the Templates folder, use the **File - Open** command.
The **Templates** folder is probably located in c:\Documents and Settings\ your-user-name\Application Data\Microsoft\Templates.
Open the **Files of type** list and select **Templates (*.xlt)**.
Choose the **3-1 Expenses sheet.xlt** template then click the **Open** button.

To put cells B4 and B5 in bold type, select cells **B4** and **B5**, then click the ⬚ tool button.

To apply the fill colour **Gray -25%** to cells I14 to I21 and cells B22 to I22, select cells **I14** to **I21**, hold down the ⬚ key and select cells **B22** to **I22**.

Open the list on the ⬚ tool button and choose the **Gray -25%** colour (second last colour in the last column of the colour palette).

Click the ⬚ tool button to save the worksheet, then click the ⬚ button on the workbook window to close it.

▦ 3. To create a new workbook based an the 3-1 Expenses sheet template, use the **File - New** command to display the **New workbook** task pane, if it is not on the screen. Click the **On my computer** link then in the **Templates** dialog box, make sure the **General** tab is active.
Double-click the **3-1 Expenses sheet** icon to open a new workbook based on the template.
Complete the top part of **Sheet1** as shown on the illustration in step 3.

To save this new workbook, click the ⬚ tool button.
Open the **MOS Excel 2003 Expert** folder.
Make sure that **Microsoft Office Excel Workbook** appears in the **Save as type** list.
Type **3-1 Expenses Andrews 41** in the **File name** box and click the **Save** button.

TEMPLATES, WORKBOOKS AND WORKGROUPS
Lesson 3.2: Workbooks

TEMPLATES, WORKBOOKS AND WORKGROUPS
Lesson 3.2: Workbooks

1 ▪ Changing the properties of a workbook

▪ Open the workbook concerned then display its properties with the **File - Properties** command.

The **Properties** dialog box may differ slightly if the document is in a document library.

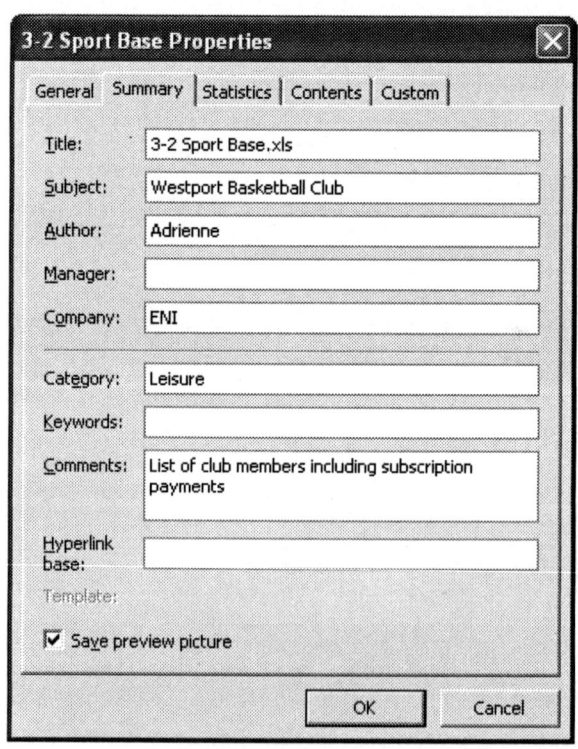

There are five tabs in the **Properties** dialog box, each showing different types of information.

▪ To create custom properties, click the **Custom** tab.

Creating a property linked to the active workbook

- Enter a **Name** for the new property or choose one from the associated list.

- Choose the new property's **Type**.

- Give a **Value** for the property. This must correspond to the property type you specified. If not, the value will be saved as text.

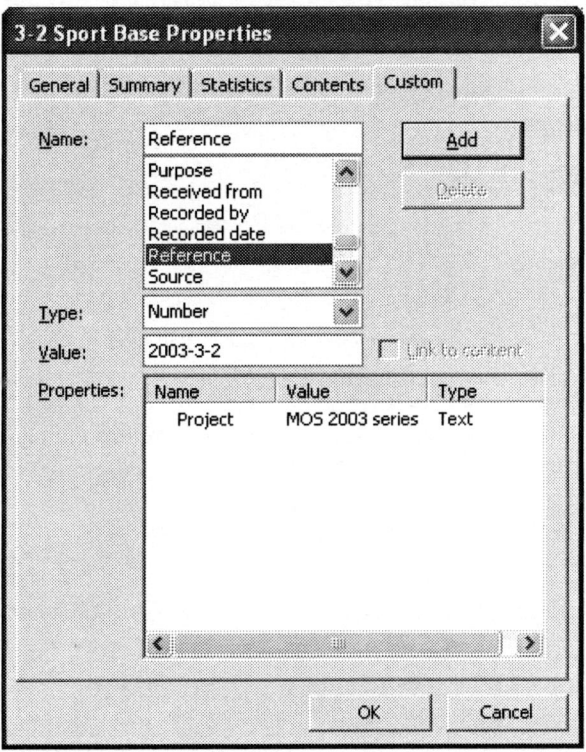

- Click the **Add** button.

- When you have added all the required properties, click **OK** to close the **Properties** box.

Creating a property linked to the active workbook's contents

If you want to link a cell or range of cells to a property, you must have already named that cell or range.

- Enter the **Name** of the new custom property.

- Tick the **Link to content** option.

  This option is only available when the workbook contains at least one named range.

- In the **Source** list which appears, choose the named content to which you wish to link the property.

- Click the **Add** button.

- When you have added all the required properties, click **OK** to close the **Properties** box.

📄 *The **Properties** command is unavailable if the structure of the workbook is protected against changes.*

*If you want the **Properties** dialog box to open automatically when a workbook is saved, use **Tools - Options - General** tab and tick the **Prompt for workbook properties** option.*

 *To change the properties of a workbook that is not open, use **File - Open** and select the file concerned. Click the **Tools** button then the **Properties** option.*

🔲2 • **Working with shared workbooks**

The advantage of sharing a workbook is that several users can work on it simultaneously.

Before sharing a workbook, its author should enter all the necessary data and formatting. This workbook will then be saved as a shared workbook and stored in a network location (not on a Web server) which the appropriate users can access.

Before you share a workbook, be aware that some features become unavailable once sharing is activated. Make sure these features are correctly set up before you share the workbook: merging cells, conditional formatting, data validation rules, charts, pictures, objects, hyperlinks, scenarios, outlines, subtotals, data tables, PivotTables and PivotCharts, workbook/worksheet/macro protection.

Creating a shared workbook

▪ Open the workbook that you want to share.

▪ **Tools - Share Workbook - Editing** tab.

▪ Activate the **Allow changes by more than one user at the same time** option.

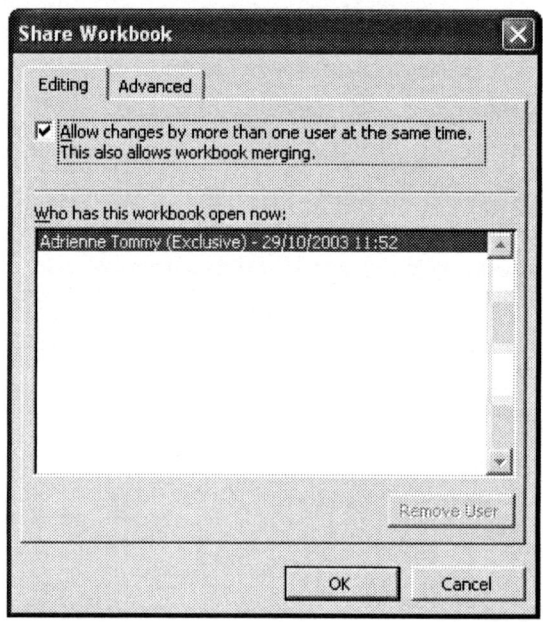

You can see the names of the users who are currently working with the workbook, in addition to the date and time they opened the workbook.

- Click **OK**.

- Excel asks you to save the workbook if you want to continue: click **OK**.

   The name of the workbook appears on the title bar, followed by the word ***Shared***. *You can now place the workbook in a shared location.*

Using a shared workbook

- Go to the network location where the shared workbook is stored and open it.

   *The mention **[shared]** on the title bar reminds you that the workbook is shared.*

- **Tools - Options - General** tab

- Enter your **User name** in the corresponding text box so any changes you make to the workbook can be identified as yours.

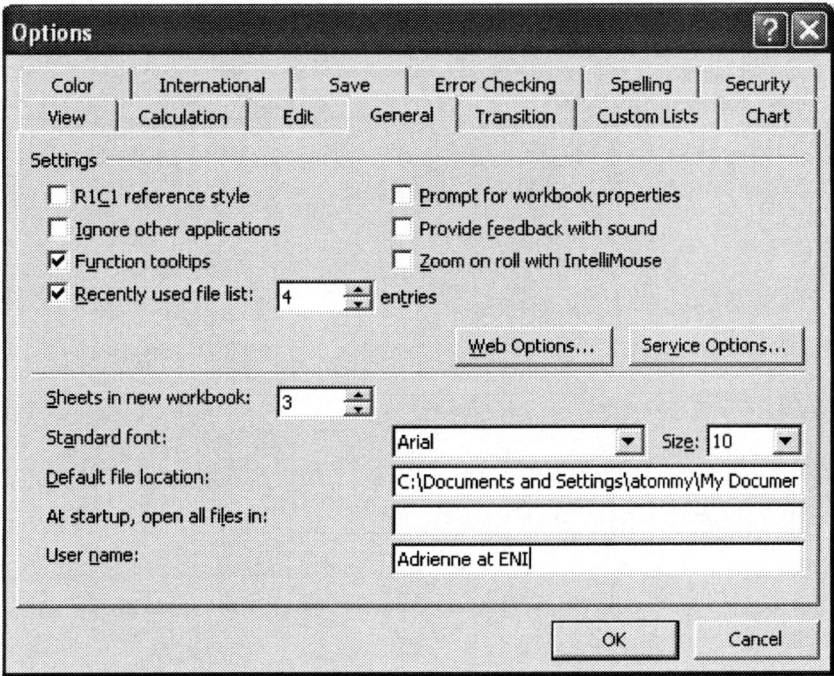

- Click **OK** to confirm.

- Make your changes (enter, edit data and so on).

  Remember that some changes cannot be made in a shared workbook.

- If required, set up your personal filter and print settings. Each user's personal settings will be saved by default.

  *If the original author's filter and print settings should be activated each time the workbook is opened, use **Tools - Share Workbook - Advanced** tab and in the **Include in personal view** frame, deactivate the **Print settings** and **Filter settings** options.*

- Save the shared workbook with **File - Save**; this will update the file with the changes you have just made and display those that other users may have made since the last time you saved.

*If you want user changes to be updated at regular intervals rather than at each save, use **Tools - Share Workbook - Advanced** tab and under **Update changes** tick the **Automatically every** option and give an interval in minutes.*

* If the **Resolve Conflicts** dialog box appears, solve the problems (cf. Chapter 3.3 Solving modification conflicts in a shared workbook).

*To find out who else is currently using the workbook, use **Tools - Share Workbook - Editing** tab.*

Turning off workbook sharing

* Open the workbook that you no longer wish to share.

* **Tools - Share Workbook - Editing** tab

* Make sure you are the only user listed in the **Who has this workbook open now** list. If you turn off sharing while someone else is using the document, any unsaved changes will be lost.

* Deactivate the **Allow changes by more than one user at the same time** option and confirm with **OK**.

3 ▪ **Merging workbooks**

You can make copies of a shared workbook that can be used and changed independently by different users. These copies can be merged in order to recreate a single workbook from the various copies.

Copying a shared workbook

* Before making one or more copies of a shared folder which you intend to merge later, a little preparation is required. To start, use **Tools - Share Workbook**, and click the **Editing** tab.

* If the workbook is not already shared, tick the **Allow changes by more than one user at the same time** option.

* Click the **Advanced** tab.

■ If necessary, activate the **Keep change history for** option in the **Track changes** frame.
In the **days** box, enter the number of days during which users can make changes and add comments to the shared workbook.

Be careful, you will not be able to merge copies of the workbook if this period is not observed. If there is any doubt about the date, enter a very high number of days, such as 1000.

■ Click **OK**.

■ If necessary, confirm saving the workbook.

■ To copy the workbook, use the **File - Save As** command and give a different name to each copy.

Merging workbooks

*The workbooks must be merged before the end of the period during which a history of any changes is kept (revision period). The length of this period is specified on the **Advanced** page of **Tools - Share Workbook**.*

■ Open the shared workbook into which you want to merge changes from another workbook on the disk.

■ **Tools - Compare and Merge Workbooks**

■ If Excel asks you, save the workbook by clicking **OK**.

*The **Select Files to Merge Into Current Workbook** dialog box appears.*

■ Select one or more copies of the shared workbook to be merged.

To select several files, use the Shift *key to select adjacent files, or the* Ctrl *key for non-adjacent files.*

■ Click **OK** to merge the files.

 *If you do not want to merge several copies of the shared workbook at the same time, you can use the **Tools - Compare and Merge Workbooks** command several times.*

4 ▪ Consolidating data

When you consolidate data, you combine and analyse several separate ranges of data.

Consolidation methods

▪ Excel offers three consolidation methods:

With 3-D formulas   A 3-D formula refers to cells located on different worksheets. With this type of consolidation, you create formulas that refer to cells in each range you wish to combine. Unlike other types of consolidation, there is no restriction on the layout of the separate ranges involved.

By position   You can consolidate by position if the data is arranged in an identical location and order in each source range.

By category   You can consolidate by category to summarise a group of sheets with identical column and row headings but which may have the data organised in a different way.

Consolidating by position or by category

▪ Before starting the consolidation, you should check that:

- Each range of data to be consolidated is set out as a list, with a label in the first row, with columns containing similar data, and with no empty rows or columns.

- Each source range must be on a separate worksheet. None of the source ranges must be on the sheet where you wish to consolidate the data.

- If you are consolidating by <u>position</u>, make sure all the ranges are in the same place on each sheet.

- If you are consolidating by <u>category</u>, make sure the row and columns labels you want to associate have the same spelling and character case.

- If you wish, you can name each source range of cells.

■ On the required sheet, activate the first destination cell where you want to display the consolidated data.

■ **Data - Consolidate**

■ Choose the **Function** you wish to use for the calculation.

■ For each range of cells you want to consolidate:

- click the button to collapse the dialog box,

- go to the worksheet then select the cells concerned or enter the name of the source range,

- click the button to display the dialog box again.

- click the **Add** button.

■ Tick the **Create links to source data** option if you want to create a permanent link between the source sheets and the consolidation sheet. If there is a link, the consolidated data will be updated each time the source data is changed.

■ Activate or deactivate the **Use labels in** options accordingly:

- When consolidating by position, deactivate the options as Excel does not copy the row or column headings from the source ranges. If you want headings for the consolidated data, you can copy them manually from one of the source ranges.

- When consolidating by category, tick one or both options to indicate where the labels are located in the source ranges (**Top row** or **Left column**).

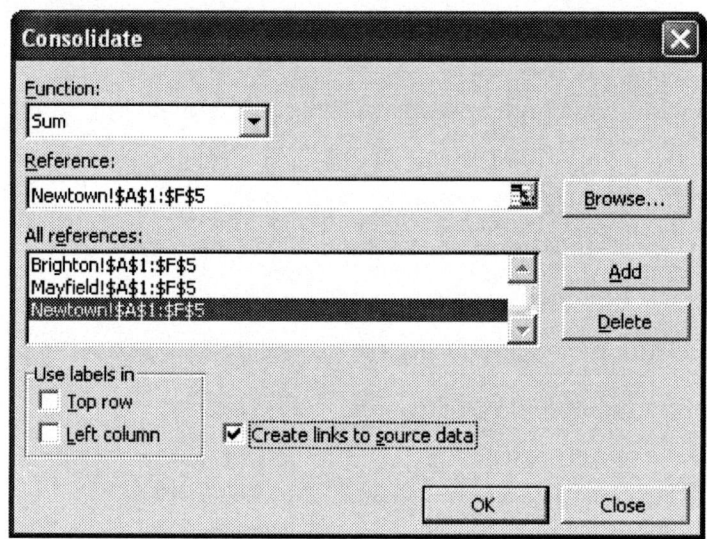

* Click **OK** to confirm.

   If you request a link, Excel produces an outline of the table as well.

   📄 *Remember that a pivot table can also be a way of consolidating data by category.*

Below, you can see **Practice Exercise 3.2**. This exercise is made up of 4 steps. If you do not know how to do one of the steps, go back to the title that corresponds to that particular lesson. When you have finished, you can check your work by reading the **Solution** that follows.

All the steps of this exercise are likely to be tested in the Microsoft Office Specialist exam.

☞ Practice Exercise 3.2

*All the workbooks used here are in the **MOS Excel 2003 Expert** folder.*

1. Create the following custom properties for the **3-2 Sport Base.xls** workbook:

   - Create an **Editor** property, using your own name. This is a Text type property.

   - Create a **Reference** property, using a Number type; the reference to add is **2003-3-2**.

   Close the **Properties** box then save and close the workbook.

2. Create a shared file using the **3-2 Sport base.xls** workbook. Save this shared workbook on a disk drive where other users can access it.

   Sort the data in the list in the **3-2 Sport base.xls** workbook (that you just saved in a shared network folder) in ascending order by the **Surname** column.
   To finish, close and save the workbook.

3. Merge the **3-2 Shared1.xls** and **3-2 Shared2.xls** workbooks into the **3-2 Sport base merge.xls** workbook. The **3-2 Shared1** and **3-2 Shared2** workbooks are copies of **3-2 Sport base merge.xls**. Before you do this merge, you should open **3-2 Shared1.xls** and **3-2 Shared2.xls** to see the changes that have been made to them, notably:
   - in the **3-2 Shared1** workbook, the text in cell **C9** has been changed and the characters in this cell are coloured red.
   - in the **3-2 Shared2** workbook, row 8 has been inserted to enter the information about Clare Brown.

4. Create a new table in the **Total** worksheet of the **3-2 Energy Total.xls** workbook that will consolidate the data contained in the **Brighton**, **Mayfield** and **Newtown** worksheets; this is a consolidation by position.

   This new table should contain the **Sum** of the energy consumption tables on the three worksheets stated and should be linked to the data in those tables.

If you would like to practise these features more, on another document, you should work through Summary Exercise 3, on TEMPLATES, WORKBOOKS AND WORKGROUPS section. You will find the summary exercises at the end of the book.

It is often possible to perform a task in several different ways, but here, only the easiest solution is presented. You can go back to the corresponding lesson if you want to see other techniques you could use.

 Solution to Exercise 3.2

1. To create custom properties in the 3-2 Sport Base.xls file, open the workbook in the **MOS Excel 2003 Expert** folder then use **File - Properties**. Click the **Custom** tab.

   To create an Editor property, click **Editor** in the list of names, In the **Type** list, choose **Text**, then in the **Value** box type your own name. Click the **Add** button.
   To create a Reference property, click **Reference** in the list of names. In the **Type** list choose **Number**. In the **Value** box, type **2003-3-2**. Click **Add** then click **OK** to close the **Properties** box.

   Save the workbook with **File - Save** then close it by clicking the ☒ button on its window.

2. To create a shared file using the 3-2 Sport Base.xls workbook, open, if necessary, **3-2 Sport Base.xls** from the **MOS Excel 2003 Expert** folder.
   Use the **Tools - Share Workbook** command then click the **Editing** tab.
   Activate the **Allow changes by more than one user at the same time** option, click **OK** and then **OK** again.

   Save the shared workbook on a network so that it is available to other users. To do this, use **File - Save As**.
   In the **Save in** list, select a drive on the disk that is accessible via a network connection then, if necessary, the folder in which the shared workbook is to be saved.
   Click the **Save** button.

   To sort the list of data in the 3-2 Sport Base.xls workbook in ascending order by Surname, click cell **A2** then click the ⬇ tool button.

Click the ⊠ button on the shared **3-2 Sport Base.xls** workbook window and click **Yes** on the message that asks you if you want to save the changes you have made.

▦ 3. To merge the workbooks 3-2 Shared1 and 3-2 Shared2 into the shared workbook 3-2 Sport Base merge.xls, open **3-2 Sport Base merge.xls** in the **MOS Excel 2003 Expert** folder and use **Tools - Compare and Merge Workbooks**. Click **OK** to save the workbook.
In the **MOS Excel 2003 Expert** folder, select workbooks **3-2 Shared1** and **3-2 Shared2** and click **OK**.

▦ 4. To create a table in the Consolidate worksheet of the 3-2 Energy Total.xls workbook that would consolidate the data in the tables on the **Brighton**, **Mayfield** and **Newtown** sheets, open the **3-2 Energy Total.xls** worksheet (in the **MOS Excel 2003 Expert** folder). Click the **Total** sheet tab, if necessary then activate cell **B5** and use the **Data - Consolidate** command. In the **Function** list, select **Sum**.

Click the 🔲 button on the **Reference** box then click the **Brighton** sheet tab. Drag from cell **B2** to cell **F5** then click the 🔲 button again and on the dialog box click the **Add** button.

Click the 🔲 button on the **Reference** box then click the **Mayfield** sheet tab. Check that cells **B2** to **F5** are selected, click the 🔲 button then click **Add**.

Click the 🔲 button on the **Reference** box then click the **Newtown** sheet tab. Check that cells **B2** to **F5** are selected, click the 🔲 button then click **Add**.

Tick the **Create links to source data** check box and click **OK**.

TEMPLATES, WORKBOOKS AND WORKGROUPS
Lesson 3.3: Tracking changes

1 ▪ Tracking changes in a shared workbook

In a shared workbook, this action will allow you to choose which changes you want to see and will highlight them.

▪ Open the shared workbook.

▪ **Tools - Track Changes - Highlight Changes**

▪ Activate the **Track changes while editing** option.

*When this option is active, the options in the **Highlight which changes** frame are available and will allow you, if necessary, to specify the type of changes you want to highlight.*

▪ Activate the **When** option to highlight the changes that have been made during the time interval specified in this option's drop-down list:

Since I last saved	highlights only those changes made since the last time the workbook was saved.
All	highlights all the changes made to the workbook.
Not yet reviewed	highlights the changes that have not been accepted or rejected.
Since date...	highlights the changes made since the date entered in the **When** box.

▪ Activate the **Who** option and use the drop-down list to select the users whose changes you want to see.

▪ Activate the **Where** option and select the cell range for which you want to see the changes.

*If none of the options in the **Highlight which changes** frame is active, all the changes made to the shared workbook (yours and those made by other users) will be shown.*

▪ Activate the **Highlight changes on screen** option to highlight the changes in each cell directly.

When you choose this option, Excel highlights the modified areas with a different colour for each user. When you point to a highlighted cell, a comment appears to give more details about the changes made.

■ Activate the **List changes on a new sheet** option if you want to see the changes on a separate sheet.

When you choose this option, Excel lists the changes on a new worksheet called History; this list can be filtered.

■ Click **OK**.

📄 *By default, the history of tracked changes is kept for 30 days. You can change this lapse of time by changing the number of **days** in the **Keep change history for** option (**Tools - Share Workbook - Advanced** tab).*

 2 ▪ Accepting or rejecting changes in a shared workbook

Changes made can be accepted into the shared workbook or rejected. All the users of the shared workbook can do this.

■ Open the shared workbook.

■ **Tools - Track Changes - Accept or Reject Changes**

■ If Excel asks you to save the workbook, click **OK**.

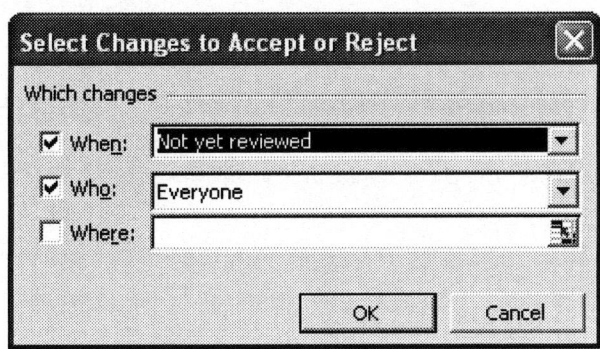

- If you like, change the time interval in the **When** option, to define which changes to review:

  Not yet reviewed selects the changes that you have not yet reviewed.

  Since date... reviews the changes made to the workbook since the date given in the **When** box.

- Activate the **Who** option and use the drop-down list to select the users whose changes you want to review.

- Activate the **Where** option then select the cell range in which you want to review the changes.

  If none of these options are active, all the changes made to the workbook will be reviewed.

- Click **OK**.

  *The **Accept or Reject Changes** dialog box appears and the first change is highlighted in the workbook. You can see the details of the change in the dialog box.*

- For each change, you can choose to **Accept** the change or **Reject** it. Once you have made your choice, Excel goes on to the next change.

  *If several changes appear in the same cell, Excel will ask you to choose one of the values. Click the value you require and click the **Accept** button.*

- You can click the **Accept All** button if you wish to accept all the changes made in the worksheet with a single action, or click **Reject All** to reject all the changes.

3 • Solving modification conflicts in a shared workbook

When several users are working on the same file at the same time, it is possible that conflicts will arise when, for example, they change the contents of the same cell. Excel will display a dialog box so you can choose which changes should be kept.

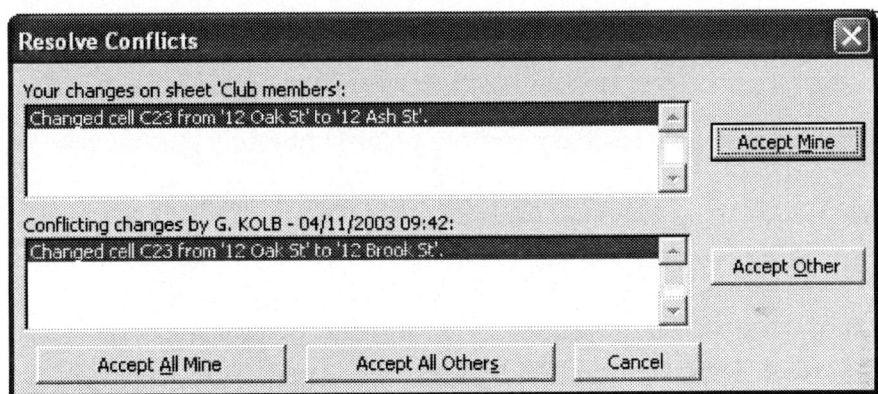

- To work on each conflict separately, click **Accept Mine** or **Accept Other** to accept, respectively, the change you have made, or the change made by the other user and go on to the next modification.

- To accept all your changes or all the changes made by the other user, click respectively **Accept All Mine** or **Accept All Others**.

 *If you want your changes to take priority over the changes made by others, which means that the **Resolve Conflicts** dialog box will no longer appear, use the **Tools - Share Workbook** command, click the **Advanced** tab and in the **Conflicting changes between users** frame, tick the **The changes being saved win** option.*

TEMPLATES, WORKBOOKS AND WORKGROUPS
Exercise 3.3: Tracking changes

Below, you can see **Practice Exercise 3.3**. This exercise is made up of 3 steps. If you do not know how to do one of the steps, go back to the title that corresponds to that particular lesson. When you have finished, you can check your work by reading the **Solution** that follows.

All the steps of this exercise are likely to be tested on the Microsoft Office Specialist exam.

☞ Practice Exercise 3.3

*To work on practice exercise 3.3, open the **3-3 Sport Base.xls** shared workbook in the **MOS Excel 2003 Expert** folder.*

1. Display on the screen all the changes made by the user called **Adrienne**.

2. Accept all the changes that have not yet been reviewed, made by all the users, except the insertion of column **E** made by **Adrienne**.

3. For conflicting changes, replace them with your changes when you save the workbook.

If you would like to practise these features more, on another document, you should work through Summary Exercise 3, on TEMPLATES, WORKBOOKS AND WORKGROUPS section. You will find the summary exercises at the end of the book.

It is often possible to perform a task in several different ways, but here, only the easiest solution is presented. You can go back to the corresponding lesson if you want to see other techniques you could use.

Solution to Exercise 3.3

1. To display on the screen all the changes made by the user called Adrienne, use the **Tools - Track Changes - Highlight Changes** command.
   Open the drop-down list on the **When** option and click the **All** choice.
   Open the drop-down list on the **Who** option and click the **Adrienne Tommy** option.
   Leave the **Highlight changes on screen** option active and click **OK**.

2. To accept the changes made by all users that have not yet been reviewed, except the insertion of column E by user Adrienne, use the **Tools - Track Changes - Accept or Reject Changes** command.
   Leave the **Not yet reviewed** choice selected in the **When** list.
   Open the drop-down list on the **Who** option, click the **Everyone** choice and click **OK**.
   Click **Accept** for all the changes, except the change described as **Inserted column E**, for which you should click **Reject**.

3. To replace conflicting changes with your changes when you save the workbook, use the **Tools - Share Workbook** command and click the **Advanced** tab.
   Activate the **The changes being saved win** option in the **Conflicting changes between users** frame and click **OK**.

TEMPLATES, WORKBOOKS AND WORKGROUPS
Lesson 3.4: Protection

▦1 ▪ Protecting a workbook's structure and/or windows

▪ Open the workbook concerned.

▪ **Tools - Protection - Protect Workbook**

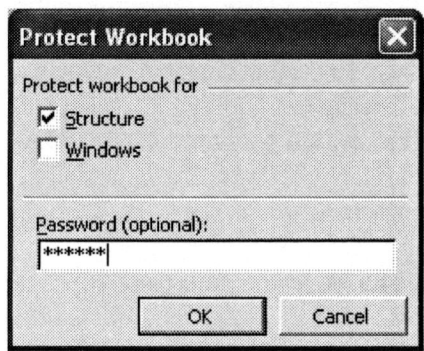

▪ If you tick the **Structure** option, another user will not be able to move, delete, hide, unhide or rename any existing sheets or add any new sheets.

▪ If you tick the **Windows** option, the workbook window cannot be moved, resized, hidden or closed.

▪ If you wish, enter a **Password** (of up to 16 characters) in the appropriate text box.

▪ Click **OK**.

▪ If necessary, confirm the password then click **OK**.

> To remove the protection from the workbook and its sheets, use the **Tools - Protection - Unprotect Workbook** command.

2 ▪ Protecting cells

If you want to authorise data entry in certain cells only, you need to indicate in which cells data entry is authorised (unlocking them) then protect the entire worksheet.

Unlocking cells

▪ Select the cells in which data entry is allowed.

▪ **Format - Cells** or ⌷Ctrl⌷ **1**

▪ Under the **Protection** tab, deactivate the **Locked** option.

▪ Click **OK**.

Activating worksheet protection

▪ **Tools - Protection - Protect Sheet**

▪ Make sure the **Protect worksheet and contents of locked cells** option is active.

▪ In the **Allow all users of this worksheet to** list, choose which actions users will be able to perform by ticking the corresponding options.

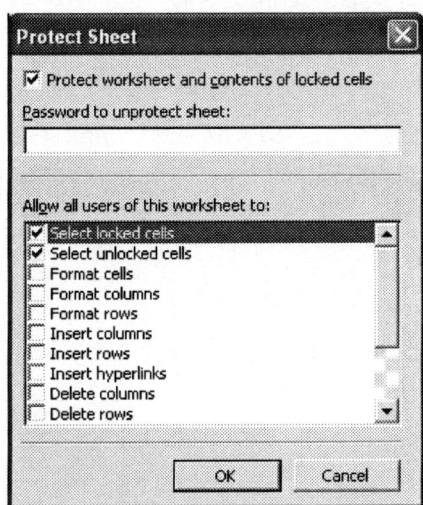

* If you wish, enter a password in the **Password to unprotect sheet** box (if you are not using a password, click **OK** directly).

Be careful, Excel distinguishes between upper and lower case characters and the password characters do not appear explicitly on the screen. You can use up to 255 characters for this password.

* To confirm, enter the password again then click the **OK** button.

If you try to enter data into a protected cell, the warning message below appears:

Microsoft Excel

The cell or chart you are trying to change is protected and therefore read-only.

To modify a protected cell or chart, first remove protection using the Unprotect Sheet command (Tools menu, Protection submenu). You may be prompted for a password.

OK

* Click **OK** to close this dialog box.

*Depending on the actions users are allowed to perform, some of the options in the **Format** menu are not available in a protected worksheet (the corresponding buttons appear grey).*

*To remove protection from a worksheet, use the **Tools - Protection - Unprotect Sheet** command. If necessary, enter the password used to protect the sheet and enter.*

⊞3 ▪ **Authorising cell access to certain users**

With this technique you can protect cells in a worksheet and authorise access to certain cell ranges, using either different passwords or, if you are using Windows 2000 or later, by choosing user names (providing your workstation is in a domain).

▪ **Tools - Protection - Allow Users to Edit Ranges**

This command is available only if the sheet is not protected.

▪ Click the **New** button.

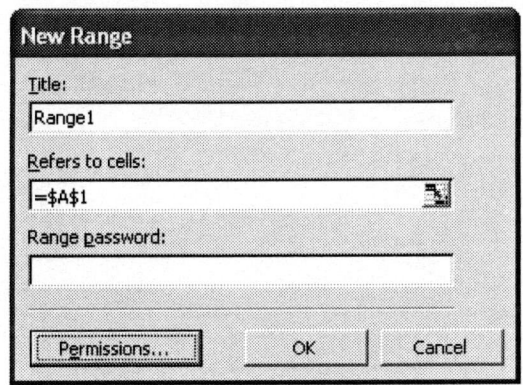

▪ If you wish, change the **Title** for that range of cells.

▪ Click the button in the **Refers to cells** text box, select the cell range concerned in the worksheet then click to display the **New Range** dialog box again.

You can use the Ctrl *-click technique to select non-adjacent cells.*

▪ In the **Range password** text box, type the password that users will have to give to be able to modify that range of cells. Confirm, then enter the password again and confirm.

If you do not give a password, anyone can edit the cells.

■ To define which users can have access rights, click the **Permissions** button then click the **Add** button.

This is available for users in a domain working with Windows 2000 or above.

■ Enter the names of the users/computers/groups concerned, separating each one with a semi-colon.

*If you click the **examples** link, you will see what syntaxes to use.*

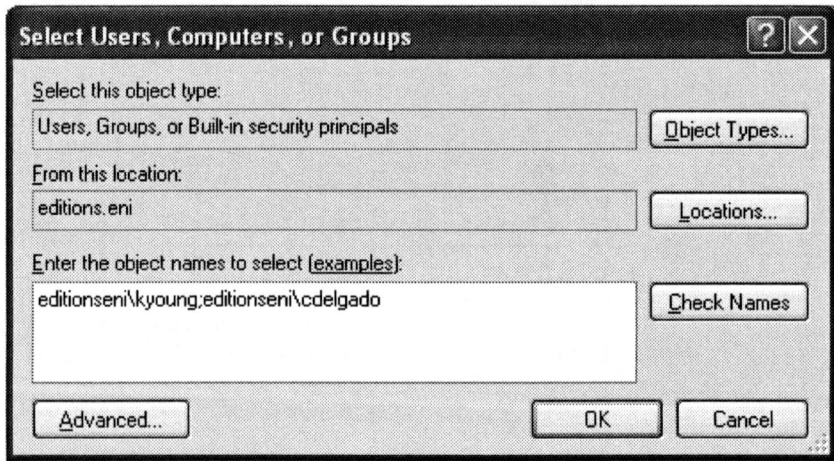

■ Click the **Check Names** button to see whether or not the names you gave can be correctly identified.

■ Once you have entered and checked all the names, click the **OK** button.

■ If you wish to define another password for a different range of cells, click the **New** button again and repeat the same operation for each cell range concerned.

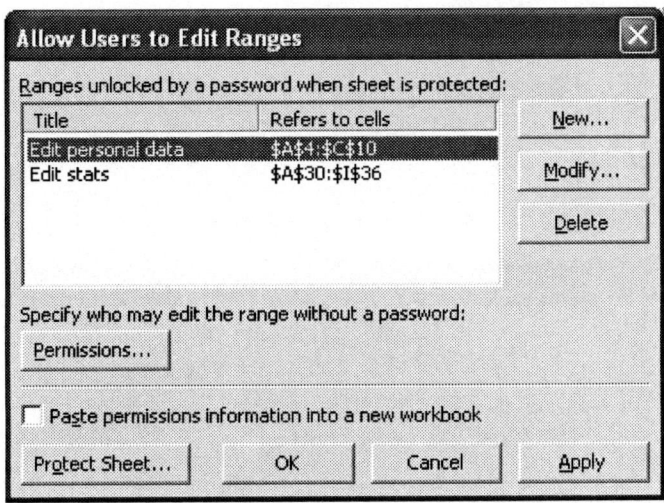

The **Permissions** button is only available if you are working under Windows 2000 or later. It will open the **Permissions** dialog box.

■ Click the **Protect Sheet** button.

■ Make sure the **Protect worksheet and contents of locked cells** option is active and, if necessary, activate or deactivate the options in the **Allow all users of this worksheet to** list to specify the actions that users will be allowed to perform. If required, enter a **Password to Unprotect sheet**.

■ Click **OK** to confirm.

If you are prompted, retype the sheet password to confirm it.

Excel will prompt for a password if you try to enter data in a cell that is in a password-protected range or if you use Windows 2000 or later and you are not one of the users who has permission to modify the cells without a password.

 *The **Paste permissions information into a new workbook** option in the **Allow Users to Edit Ranges** dialog box will make a summary of the user permissions in a new workbook.*

▥4 ▪ Protecting a workbook with a password

▪ **Tools - Options**

▪ Click the **Security** tab.

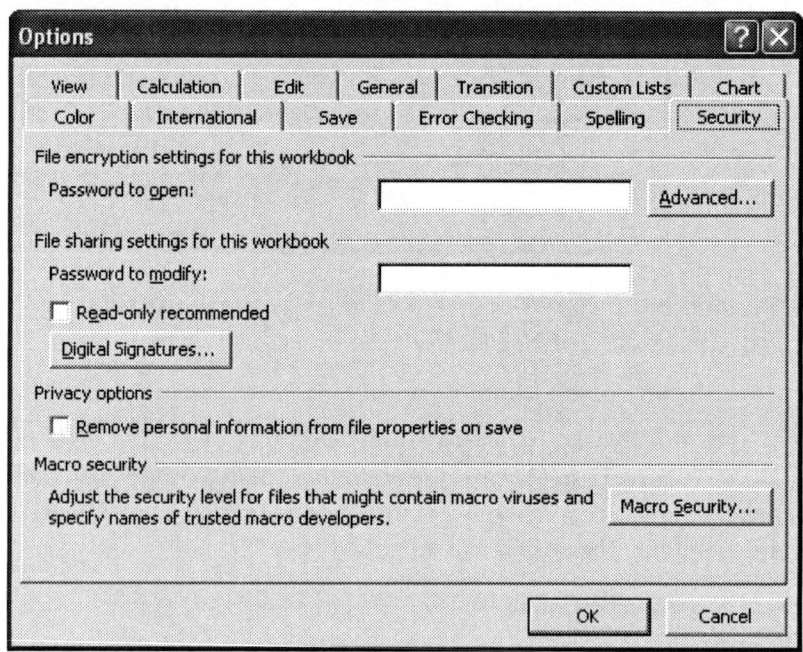

Protecting a workbook from opening

▪ If you want to control who opens the workbook, to prevent unauthorised users seeing its contents, enter a password in the **Password to open** box.

If you do this, Excel encrypts the file to protect its contents. This is a truly effective security measure.

▪ To change the type of encryption used, click the **Advanced** button then select the required type of encryption and click **OK**.

*The default type of encryption used for Excel 2003 workbooks is **Weak Encryption (XOR)**.*

Protecting a workbook from editing

- To prevent any intentional or accidental changes to the workbook, enter a password in the **Password to modify** box.

- To confirm the password, enter it in the **Reenter password to modify** box that then appears in another dialog box.

  This is not a watertight security feature, but a simple protection device as there is no encryption involved. While another user cannot alter the contents of your original file, he/she can make changes to it then save those under another file name.

Setting a workbook to open as read-only

- If you want other users to be able to at least read your file's contents, tick the **Read-only recommended** option in the **File sharing settings for this workbook** frame.

  You can combine this option with a password prompt which will prevent another user saving any changes.

  The way the workbook is opened differs, depending on whether or not a modify password is required.

  If a modify password prompt is requested, Excel will ask for the password when you try to open the workbook:

*If you do not know the password, you can click the **Read Only** button to open the workbook but you will not be able to save any changes you make.*

*If you do enter the password and click **OK**, Excel will ask whether or not the file should be opened in read-only mode:*

*If you want to be able to save any changes made, click the **No** button.*

*You will see this same message for workbooks on which the **Read-only recommended** option has been ticked but which require no modify password.*

 The same workbook can have one password for opening and another password for modifying.

*To remove a password, use **Tools - Options - Security** tab and select the contents of the **Password to open** and/or **Password to modify** fields then press the* Del *key to delete them.*

*You can also enter or edit passwords in the **Save Options** dialog box (accessible with **File - Save As**; click the **Tools** button and choose **General Options**).*

5 ▪ Creating digital signatures

What are digital signatures?

▪ Excel uses **Microsoft Authenticode** technology to enable you to digitally sign a file or macro project with a digital certificate, should you want to send your data to someone or make it available to other users. The digital signature (which is an electronic "stamp of authenticity", encrypted and secured) confirms that the file or macro comes from the signer and that nothing in it has been modified.

If any changes are made to a document once it has been signed, the signature becomes invalid.

- Excel manages two types of signed files: workbooks and macros. There is a subtle difference in the way you sign each type of file and the advantages obtained by the signature in each case. As a general rule, a file is signed to validate its contents and a macro is signed as a guarantee that it does not contain a virus.

- In the USA, the Electronic Signatures in Global and National Commerce Act makes digital signatures legally binding, as real ink signatures on paper; you should still be vigilant when it comes to digitally signing documents or reviewing a file signed by someone else. Remember that the validity of a digital signature is directly linked to the trustworthiness of the person or company using it or the certification authority that issued it. A digital signature can be falsified and its usefulness depends largely on how much you trust the person who signed the file; other factors come into play such as the date and time the file was signed and the type and origin of the signature.

- You can attach several signatures to the same file, which can be useful to indicate that several people have agreed on the final contents of the document.

- To obtain a certificate, you can use a commercial certification authority such as VeriSign Inc., or ask your company's security administrator or other internal IT professional. You can also create a digital signature yourself.

Here we will be describing how to create your own personal certificate.

Creating your own digital certificate

When you create your own digital certificate, since it is not issued by a formal certification authority, it will not be considered as authenticated. If a macro project is signed with this type of certificate and the macro security level is set to Medium or High, a security warning will be displayed.

This features requires you to install the SelfCert.exe program on your computer.

To install the SelftCert.exe component

- Start by closing all open programs.

■ Click the **start** button on the Windows taskbar then **Control Panel**.

■ Click the **Add or Remove Programs** option.

■ Click **Microsoft Office...** or **Microsoft Excel** depending on how you installed Excel (individually or as part of the Office package).

■ Click the **Change** button.

■ Click **Add or Remove Features** then click **Next**.

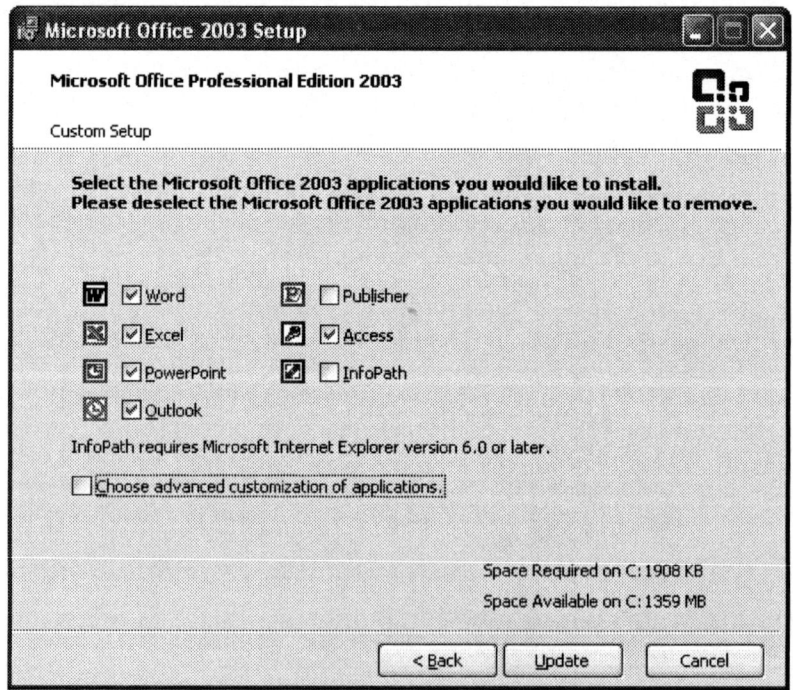

■ Tick the **Choose advanced customization of applications** option then click **Next**.

■ Click the plus sign (+) next to **Office Shared Features**.

■ Click the arrow next to **Digital Signature for VBA Projects** then choose the **Run from My Computer** option.

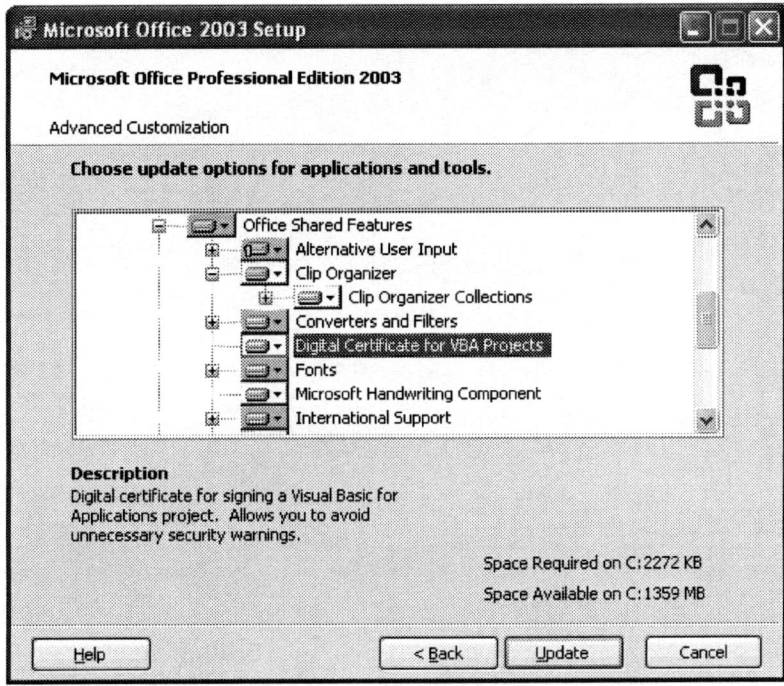

- Click the **Update** button, then click **OK** on the messages telling you that the installation was a success.

- Click the button to close the **Add or Remove Programs** dialog box.

Creating a digital certificate

- Click the **start** button on the Windows taskbar then point to **All Programs**.

- Choose **Microsoft Office - Microsoft Office Tools - Digital Certificate for VBA Projects**.

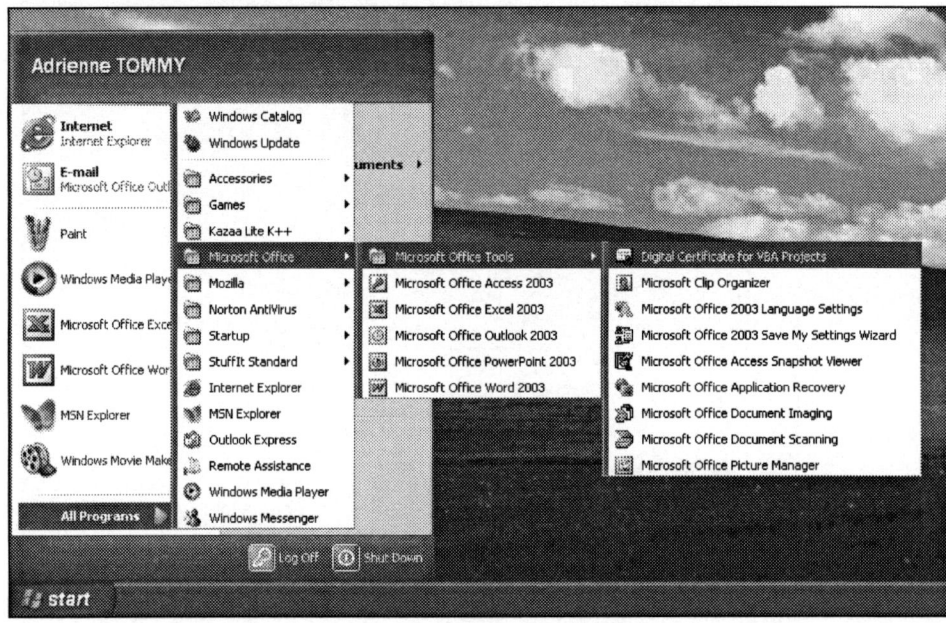

✳ In the dialog box that opens, enter **Your certificate's name** in the corresponding text box.

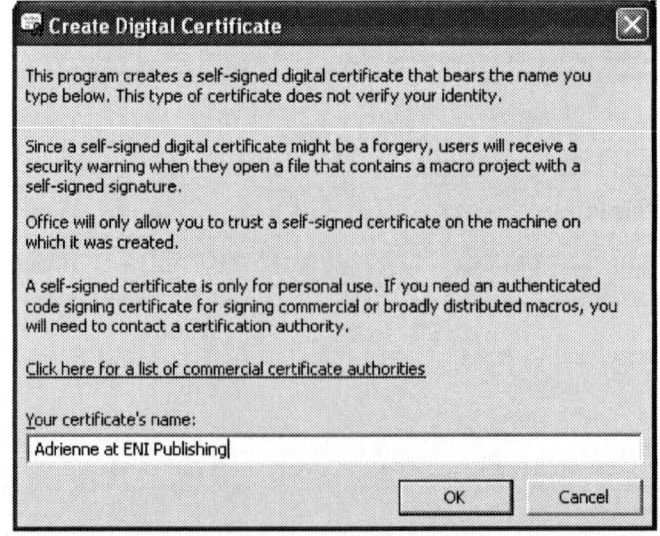

- Confirm what you enter with **OK**.

- Click **OK** on the message telling you that the new certificate was successfully created.

- Open the Excel 2003 program again.

6 ▪ Adding a signature to a file or macro project

Signing a file

- Open the file you want to digitally sign.

- **Tools - Options**

- Click the **Security** tab then the **Digital Signatures** button.

- Click the **Add** button.

- Select the digital certificate you want to use.

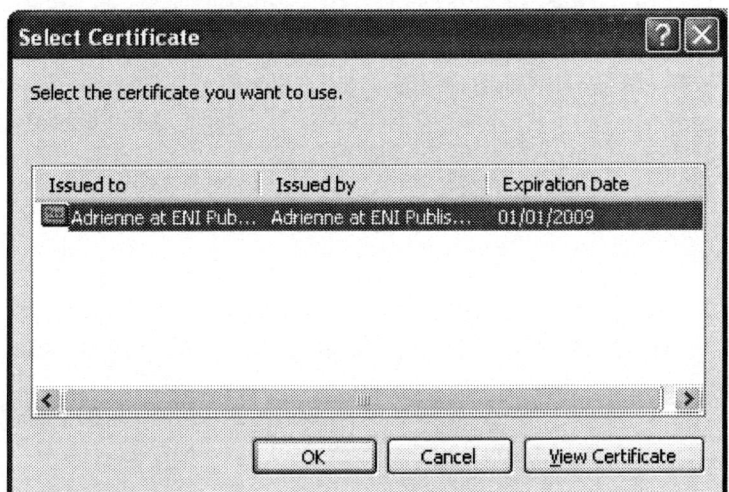

- Click **OK**.

In the **Digital Signature** dialog box, you can now see the signature matching the certificate that you selected previously.

- If you want users of the digitally signed file to be able to see the details of the certificate, tick the **Attach certificates with newly added signatures** option.

- Click **OK** on both dialog boxes.

The next time you open the file, the term **[Signed, unverified]** will appear on the title bar.

If you make changes to the file and try to save them, you will see a message informing you that all the file's digital signatures will be deleted:

Signing a macro project

- Open the file containing the macro project you want to sign.

- **Tools - Macro - Visual Basic Editor** or **Alt F11**

- In the **Project Explorer**, select the project you want to sign.

- **Tools - Digital Signature**.

  If you have not already selected a digital signature, no certificate will be suggested:

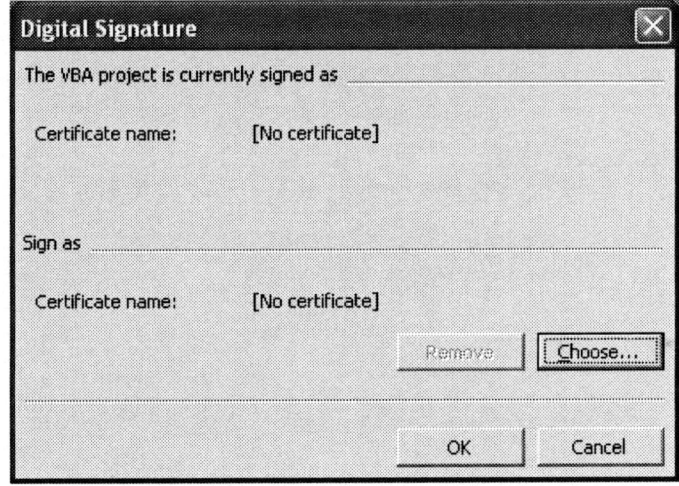

  *Otherwise the name of the last digital signature selected appears in the **Digital Signature** window.*

- Click the **Choose** button to select a certificate (if the suggestion is not suitable for example); click the required certificate and click **OK** to confirm.

- Click **OK** in the **Digital Signature** window to digitally sign the macro project with the selected certificate.

- If you want to close the Microsoft Visual Basic window, use the **File - Close and Return to Microsoft Excel** command or **Alt Q**.

7 ▪ Checking a digital certificate

▪ To find out who signed a digitally signed file, display the **Digital Signature** dialog box by using **Tools - Options - Security** tab - **Digital Signatures** button.

This shows you who signed the file, who issued the certificate and its issuing date.

▪ If several certificates are associated with the file, choose the certificate that interests you then click the **View Certificate** button.

As the certificate was created by the signer (and so is unauthenticated) the **General** page displays a warning that the certificate is not trustworthy.

If the certificate was authenticated, there would be no red cross on the **Certificate Information** icon.

▪ Check the **Issued to** and **Issued by** details to see whether or not you should trust this source.

In our example, the certificate was issued by an individual and not by a certification authority.

▪ Check too the **Valid from/to** dates to see if the certificate is still valid.

▪ Click **OK** three times to close all the dialog boxes.

8 ▪ Checking the macro security level

Depending on Excel's macro security level, you may see warnings when signed or unsigned macros are present; Excel may also suggest actions you should take to protect your files from potentially destructive macros.

▪ **Tools - Options - Security** tab

▪ Click the **Macro Security** button.

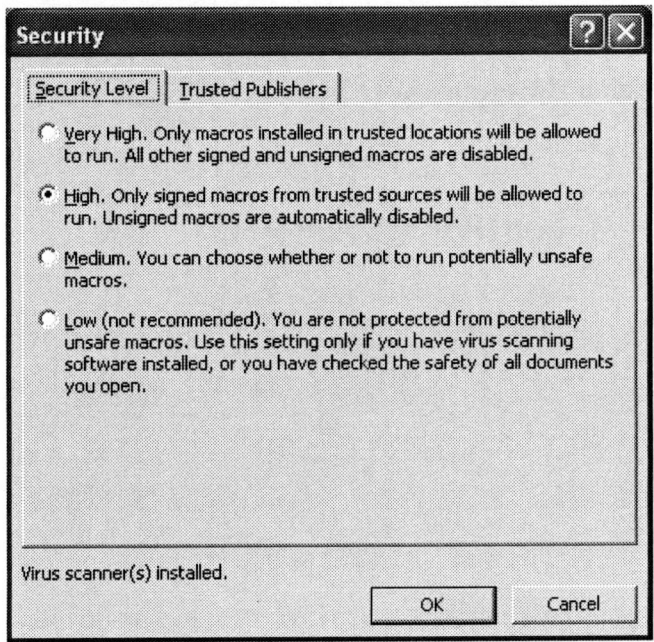

255

* Activate the option for the security level you wish to apply.

* Click **OK** to confirm.

9 ▪ Removing a digital signature

Removing a signature from a file

* **Tools - Options**

* Click the **Security** tab then the **Digital Signatures** button.

* Select the signature you wish to delete then click the **Remove** button.

Removing a signature from a macro project

* Open the file containing the macro project.

* **Tools - Macro - Visual Basic Editor** or [Alt][F11]

* In the **Project Explorer**, select the project whose signature you wish to remove.

* **Tools - Digital Signature**

* Click the **Remove** button.

* If you want to close the Microsoft Visual Basic window, use the **File - Close and Return to Microsoft Excel** command or [Alt] **Q**.

Below, you can see **Practice Exercise 3.4**. This exercise is made up of 9 steps. If you do not know how to do one of the steps, go back to the title that corresponds to that particular lesson. When you have finished, you can check your work by reading the **Solution** that follows.

All the steps of this exercise are likely to be tested in the Microsoft Office Specialist exam.

 **Practice Exercise 3.4**

*The workbooks used in this exercise are in the **MOS Excel 2003 Expert** folder.*

1. Open the **3-4 HiFi.xls** workbook. Protect the structure of the sheets and the workbook, using this password: **34cat** (in lower case letters).

2. Protect all the cells in the **Turnover** worksheet in the **3-4 HiFi.xls** workbook, except cells **B8** to **D19** and cell **B26**, in which data entry can be allowed. Apply the password **34horse** to this protection.

3. Allow other users to edit the range of cells **A2** to **B15** on the **Stats** worksheet in the **3-4 HiFi.xls** workbook (you can give the title **edit stats** to this range). If you have Windows 2000 or later and you are in a domain, you can choose 2 users who can have access to these cells. Protect the other cells on the sheet.

4. Control who can open the **3-4 HiFi.xls** workbook by assigning an open password: use the password **34dog**. Excel should advise users to open the workbook in read-only mode. Save and close the workbook then open it again in read-only mode to check your changes.

5. If necessary, install the **SelfCert.exe** file on your computer then create your own digital certificate, identified by your own first name and surname.

6. Use the digital certificate you just created to add a digital signature to the **3-4 Energy.xls** workbook; attach the certificate to the signature. Close the workbook.

7. Open the **3-4 Energy.xls** workbook and check its digital signature, viewing the certificate if you wish.

8. Check the macro security level currently applied.

9. Remove the digital signature from the **3-4 Energy.xls** workbook then save and close it.

If you would like to practise these features more, on another document, you should work though Summary Exercise 3, on TEMPLATES, WORKBOOKS AND WORKGROUPS. You will find the summary exercises at the end of the book.

It is often possible to perform a task in several different ways, but here, only the easiest solution is presented. You can go back to the corresponding lesson if you want to see other techniques you could use.

Solution to Exercise 3.4

1. Open the **3-4 HiFi.xls** workbook in the **MOS Excel 2003 Expert** folder using **File - Open**. To protect the structure of the sheets and the workbook window, use **Tools - Protection - Protect Workbook**.
   Leave the **Structure** option active then tick the **Windows** option. Enter **34cat** in the **Password** text box then click **OK**.
   Re-enter the password then click **OK**.

2. To protect all the cells in the Turnover worksheet in the 3-4 HiFi.xls workbook, except cells B8 to D19 and cell B26, make sure the **Turnover** sheet tab is active then select cells **B8** to **D19** and cell **B26**. Use the **Format - Cells** command.

   Click the **Protection** tab, deactivate the **Locked** option then click **OK**. Use the **Tools - Protection** command then choose the **Protect Sheet** option.
   Make sure the **Protect worksheet and contents of locked cells** option is active. In the **Allow all users of this worksheet to** list, leave the two options that are already active.
   In the **Password to unprotect sheet** box, enter the password **34horse** (in lower case letters) and click **OK**. Enter **34horse** once more in the **Reenter password to proceed** box and click **OK**.

3. To allow other users to edit the range of cells A2 to B15 on the Stats worksheet in the 3-4 HiFi.xls workbook, start by making sure the **Stats** sheet is the active sheet. Next, use **Tools - Protection - Allow Users to Edit Ranges**.

Click the **New** button. In the **Title** box, enter the title **edit stats**. Click the ⬛ button on the **Refers to cells** text box and select the range **A2:B15** on the **Stats** worksheet. Click ⬛ to restore the dialog box. You do not need to enter a password for this exercise.

- If you have Windows 2000 or later and you are in a domain, you can click the **Permissions** button at this stage. In the **Enter object names to select** box, you can enter the two user names to whom you are giving permission to access the cells (if you are unsure how to enter the names, click the **examples** link for name synatexs). Click the **Check Names** button to verify your syntaxes then when all is correct, click **OK**.

- If you are not using Windows 2000 or later, click **OK** directly, as the **Permissions** button will be unavailable.

To protect the other cells on the sheet, click the **Protect Sheet** button in the **Allow Users to Edit Ranges** dialog box. Check that the **Protect worksheet and contents of locked cells** option is active and leave the default options active in the **Allow all users of this worksheet to** list. Click **OK** to confirm.

⬛ 4. To control who can open the 3-4 HiFi.xls workbook, use **Tools - Options** and click the **Security** tab. In the **Password to open** box, enter the password **34dog**.
Tick the **Read-only recommended** option and click **OK**. Re-type the **34dog** password in the **Reenter password to proceed** text box and press ⏎.

Save the **3-4 HiFi.xls** workbook by clicking the ⬛ tool button then use **File - Close** to close it.

To re-open it in read-only mode, use **File - Open** then double-click the **3-4 HiFi** file icon in the **MOS Excel 2003 Expert** folder.

In the **Password** text box that appears, type **34dog** and click **OK**. Click **Yes** on the message that appears to open the file in read-only mode (you can now close it again, if you wish).

5. If the SelfCert.exe file is not installed on your computer, close all the open applications, put the Office or Excel application CD-ROM in your drive and use **start - Control Panel** on the Windows taskbar.

Click the **Add or Remove Programs** option. Click **Microsoft Office...** or **Microsoft Excel** then click the **Change** button.

Click **Add** or **Remove Features** then click **Next**.

Tick the **Choose advanced customization of applications** option then click **Next**.

Click the plus sign (+) associated with the **Office Shared Features**.

Click the black down arrow on the icon for **Digital Signature for VBA Projects** and choose the **Run from My Computer** option.

Click the **Update** button, then click **OK** on the messages.

Click ⊠ to close the **Add or Remove Programs** dialog box.

To create your own digital certificate using your name and surname, click the **start** button on the Windows taskbar then point to **All Programs - Microsoft Office - Microsoft Office Tools - Digital Certificate for VBA Projects**.

Type your own first name and surname in the **Your certificate's name** text box and click **OK**.

Click **OK** on the message that tells you the new certificate has been created successfully then open the Microsoft Excel 2003 application again.

6. To add your digital signature to the 3-4 Energy workbook, start by opening the **3-4 Energy.xls** file with **File - Open**.

Use the **Tools - Options** command, click the **Security** tab then the **Digital Signatures** button.

Click the **Add** button then select the certificate you want to use and click **OK** to close all the dialog boxes.

To close the 3-4 Energy workbook, use the **File - Close** command.

7. To open the 3-4 Energy workbook, use **File - Open** in the Excel application, choose the **MOS Excel 2003 Expert** folder and double-click the **3-4 Energy.xls** icon.

   To check the workbook's digital signature, use the **Tools - Options** command, click the **Security** tab then the **Digital Signatures** button.
   If you want to see the accompanying certificate, click the **View Certificate** button.

   Once you have viewed all the details, click the ⊠ button to close each dialog box.

8. To check the current macro security level, use **Tools - Options - Security** tab. Click the **Macro Security** button.
   Check the level currently applied (**Medium** or **High** provide better protection against macro viruses) then click **OK** to close the box.
   Close the **Options** dialog box by clicking **OK**.

9. To remove the digital signature from the 3-4 Energy workbook that is currently open, use **Tools - Options - Security** tab then click the **Digital Signatures** button. Select the signature that represents your name then click the **Remove** button. Click **OK** to confirm.

   To save the changes made to the 3-4 Energy workbook, click the 🖫 button then use **File - Close**.

CONFIGURATION
Lesson 4.1: Toolbars/Default settings

CONFIGURATION
Lesson 4.1: Toolbars/Default settings

1 ▪ Showing/hiding a toolbar

▪ **View - Toolbars**

▪ Click the name of the toolbar that you want to show or hide.

An active toolbar has a tick next to its name.

 You can also right-click any toolbar displayed, then click the name of the toolbar you want to show or hide.

*To show or hide several toolbars at once, use **View - Toolbars - Customize**. Click the **Toolbars** tab then activate or deactivate the names of the toolbars you want to show or hide and click the **Close** button.*

2 ▪ Creating/deleting a custom toolbar

▪ To create a new toolbar, use the **View - Toolbars - Customize** command.

*You can see the same dialog box using **Tools - Customize**.*

▪ Click the **Toolbars** tab.

▪ Click the **New** button.

▪ Give the **Toolbar name** in the appropriate text box then click **OK**.

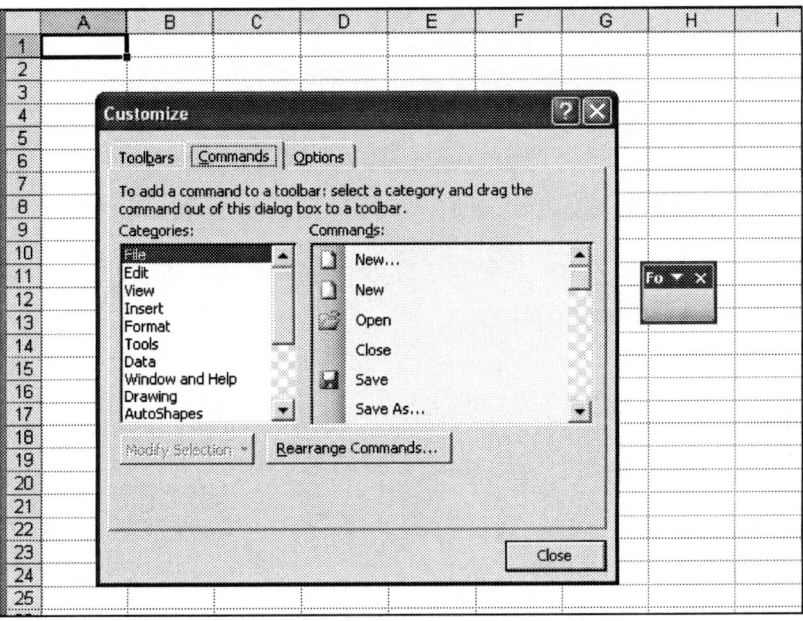

A small floating toolbar appears in the worksheet.

- To add the tools of your choice to the new toolbar, click the **Commands** tab.

- Add a tool to the bar by dragging it from the **Commands** list in the dialog box onto the new bar.

- Once all the tools have been added, click the **Close** button in the **Customize** dialog box.

- To delete a custom toolbar, click the name of the toolbar in the **Customize** dialog box (**Toolbars** tab) and click the **Delete** button.

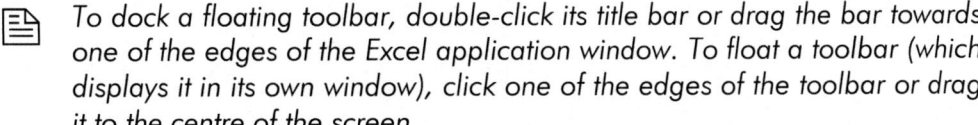 *To dock a floating toolbar, double-click its title bar or drag the bar towards one of the edges of the Excel application window. To float a toolbar (which displays it in its own window), click one of the edges of the toolbar or drag it to the centre of the screen.*

🏳3 ▪ **Managing tools on an open toolbar**

▪ Make sure the required toolbar is displayed on the screen.

▪ **View - Toolbars - Customize** or **Tools - Customize**

Deleting a tool button

▪ Drag the tool you want to delete from the toolbar, clear of any toolbar or menu.

As soon as you have removed the tool from the bar, it disappears.

▪ If necessary, close the **Customize** dialog box by clicking **Close**.

Adding a tool button

▪ Click the **Commands** tab in the **Customize** dialog box.

▪ In the **Categories** list, select the category of the tool you want to add.

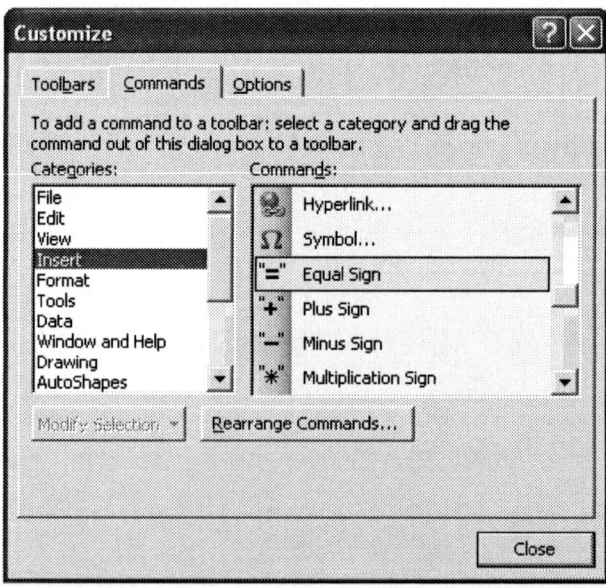

- Drag the tool button or menu from the **Commands** box to the bar in question.

- A black bar indicates the tool's position on the toolbar; when this position is correct, release the mouse button.

- If necessary, click **Close** in the **Customize** dialog box.

> Clicking the ■ symbol at the right end of some toolbars allows you to add or remove buttons.

Moving a tool button

- On the toolbar in the application window, drag the tool button from its current position to the new position you require.

- If necessary, click **Close** to close the **Customize** dialog box.

> After you change a toolbar, you can restore the original bar by clicking the **Reset** button in the **Customize** dialog box (**Toolbars** tab).

4 ▪ Customising menus

- Open the **Customize** dialog box with the **Tools - Customize** command.

Deleting a menu/menu option

- If necessary, click the **Commands** tab in the **Customize** dialog box.

- To delete a menu or an option within a menu, open the menu concerned on the application window. To delete an option, drag that option clear of any menu or toolbar. To delete a menu, drag the menu name clear of the menu bar and any toolbar.

- Click **Close** to close the **Customize** dialog box.

Adding an option to a menu

* If necessary, click the **Commands** tab in the **Customize** dialog box.

* Open the menu concerned on the menu bar in the application window.

* In the **Categories** list, choose the category containing the option you want to add.

* In the **Commands** list, click the option you want to add.

* Drag the option onto the open menu in the Excel window.

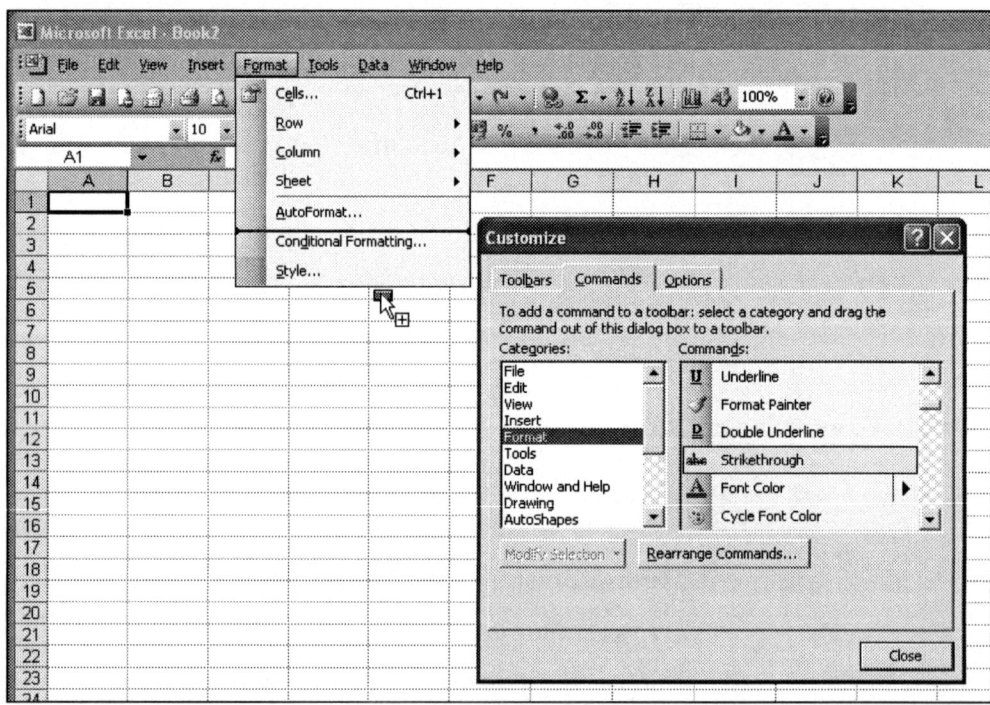

A black bar shows the new option's position on the menu; when this is correct, release the mouse button.

* Click **Close** to close the **Customize** dialog box.

Renaming a menu or an option

- Click the **Commands** tab in the **Customize** dialog box.

- In the application window, on the menu bar, click the name of the menu or option you wish to rename.

- Click the **Modify Selection** button on the **Customize** dialog box.

- In the text box next to the **Name** option, type the new name for the option or menu; type an **&** character in front of the letter that should appear underlined.

- Press the ⏎ key.

- Click **Close** to close the **Customize** dialog box.

Adding a new menu

- Click the **Commands** tab then choose **New Menu** in the **Categories** list.

- Drag the **New Menu** option from the **Commands** list onto the required position on the menu bar (in the application window).

- Use the **Modify Selection** button to give a new **Name** to the menu.

- Click the name of the new menu on the menu bar to open it, then add the options of your choice.

- When you have added all the options you require, click the **Close** button on the **Customize** dialog box.

5 ▪ Changing Excel's default settings

Changing the default font

- **Tools - Options**

- Click the **General** tab.

CONFIGURATION
Lesson 4.1: Toolbars/Default settings

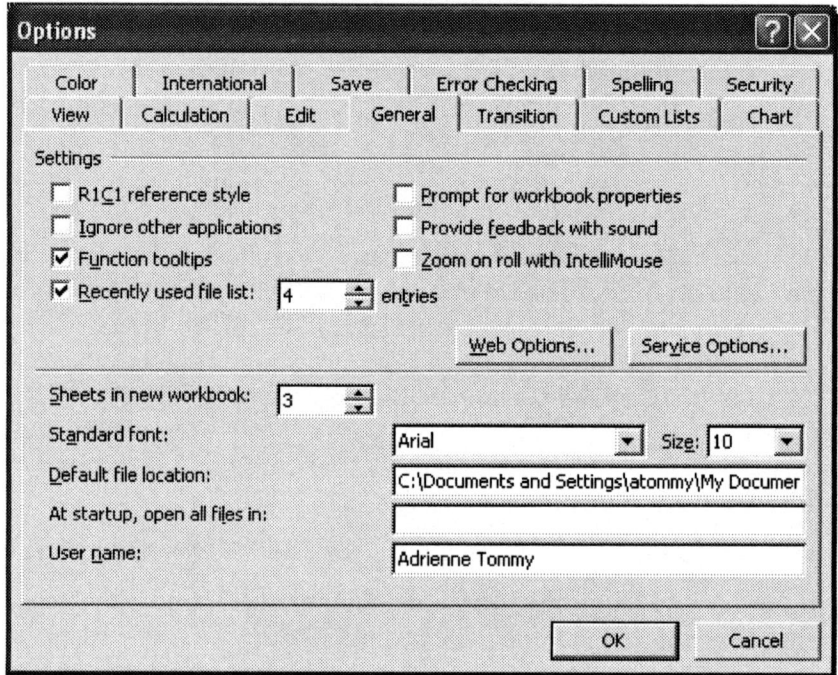

- To change the default font, open the **Standard font** drop-down list and choose another font.

- To change the default font size, open the **Size** list and choose the new size.

- Click **OK** to confirm.

The changes you make apply to new workbooks created the next time you restart Excel.

Changing the default number of sheets in a workbook

- **Tools - Options**

- Click the **General** tab.

- In the **Sheets in new workbook** box, enter a new value or click the increment buttons to choose how many worksheets are inserted by default in each new workbook.

▪ Click **OK** to confirm.

The new value applies immediately; any new workbooks you create will have the number of worksheets you specified.

Changing the default templates

When you start Excel, it creates a blank workbook using a template called

***Book.xlt**; this template is also used when you create a new file using the* ⬚ *tool button on the **Standard** toolbar.*

*Similarly, the **Insert - Sheet** command uses the **Sheet.xlt** template which defines the layout and potentially the contents of any new worksheets.*

It is possible to create your own customised Book.xlt and/or Sheet.xlt templates and/or change the folder in which Excel looks for them.

▪ To create your own standard workbook and/or worksheet template, create a template as you normally would, using **File - Save As** and choosing **Template** as the file type. Name your template **Book.xlt** or **Sheet.xlt** as is appropriate.

▪ If you want Excel to use your custom templates automatically each time it creates a new workbook or worksheet, save your templates in the startup template folder: depending on your system, this could be **C:\Program Files\Microsoft Office\Office11\XLStart** or **C:\Documents and Settings\user name\Application Data\Microsoft\Excel\XLStart**.

▪ If you want to save them in another folder, you need to define that folder as the new startup template folder: to do this, use **Tools - Options - General** tab. In the **At startup, open all files in** box, give the path to the alternative folder, then click **OK**.

▪ To restore the default settings for workbooks, delete your custom **Book.xlt** template.
To restore the default settings for worksheets, delete your custom **Sheet.xlt** template.

CONFIGURATION
Exercise 4.1: Toolbars/Default settings

Below, you can see **Practice Exercise 4.1**. This exercise is made up of 5 steps. If you do not know how to do one of the steps, go back to the title that corresponds to that particular lesson. When you have finished, you can check your work by reading the **Solution** that follows.

Steps in the exercise that are likely to be tested on the exam are preceded by this symbol: ▦. However, it is a good idea to complete all the steps in the exercise, to ensure that you have understood all the points discussed in the lesson.

☞ Practice Exercise 4.1

To work on practice exercise 4.1, open a new workbook.

1. Display the **Web** toolbar then hide it again.

▦ 2. Create a toolbar called **Formulas** and add these tool buttons to it:

▦ 3. On the **Formulas** toolbar, delete the [" "] tool button and move the [Σ ▾] tool button to the end of the toolbar (if you wish, delete the **Formulas** toolbar).

▦ 4. Create a menu called **Email** in the menu bar and in it, insert the command **Send for Review** which is in the **File** category. Next, delete the **Email** menu.

▤ 5. Modify Excel's default settings in the following ways:

- Change the default font to **Tahoma** in **12 point** size.

- Insert **4** worksheets in each new workbook.

If you wish, close and restart the Excel application and create a new workbook, entering any text you like in the first cell, to check the new settings.

Finish by restoring the default settings, namely Arial police , size 10, and 3 worksheets for each new workbook.

If you would like to practise these features more, on another document, you should work through Summary Exercise 4, on CONFIGURATION. You will find the summary exercises at the end of the book.

CONFIGURATION
Exercise 4.1: Toolbars/Default settings

It is often possible to perform a task in several different ways, but here, only the easiest solution is presented. You can go back to the corresponding lesson if you want to see other techniques you could use.

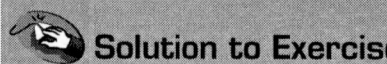 **Solution to Exercise 4.1**

1. To display the Web toolbar, use **View - Toolbars** or right-click one of the toolbars already on the screen, and choose the **Web** option.
   To hide the Web toolbar, use **View - Toolbars** or right-click one of the toolbars already on the screen, and click the **Web** option again to deactivate it.

2. To create the Formulas toolbar, use the **View - Toolbars - Customize** command and click the **Toolbars** tab.
   Click the **New** button, type **Formulas** in the **Toolbar name** box then click **OK**.
   To add the tool buttons to the Formulas toolbar, click the **Commands** tab on the **Customize** dialog box and click the **Insert** category.
   For each tool button to be added, select the tool in the **Commands** list and drag it onto the **Formulas** toolbar in the application window until you obtain the result below:

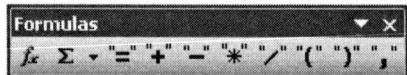

   Click the **Close** button on the **Customize** dialog box.

3. To delete the ![icon] tool button from the Formulas toolbar, start by displaying the **Formulas** toolbar on the screen if it is not already there.
   Use **View - Toolbars - Customize**.

   Drag the ![icon] tool button away from the **Formulas** toolbar.

   To move the ![icon] tool button to the end of the **Formulas** toolbar, drag the ![icon] tool button to the end of the **Formulas** toolbar. If you wish to delete the **Formulas** toolbar, go into the **Customize** dialog box (**Tools -**

Customize, Toolbars tab), select its name in the **Toolbars** list and click the **Delete** button. Confirm the deletion with **OK** and click **Close** on the **Customize** dialog box.

4. To create a menu called **Email** in the menu bar of a new workbook, first click the ☐ tool button to create a new workbook.

Use the **Tools - Customize** command and click the **New Menu** option in the **Categories** list.

Drag the **New Menu** option from the **Commands** box onto the menu bar in the application window; you can place it to the right of the **Help** menu.

Click the **Modify Selection** button in the **Customize** dialog box and in the list that opens, click the text box next to the **Name** option: in this text box, enter **Email** and confirm by pressing the ⏎ key.

Click the new **Email** menu to open it (for now it contains just a grey space).

Click **File** in the list of **Categories** in the **Customize** dialog box to see all the accompanying commands.

Click the **Send for Review** command to select it.

Drag the selected command onto the blank space in the **Email** menu.

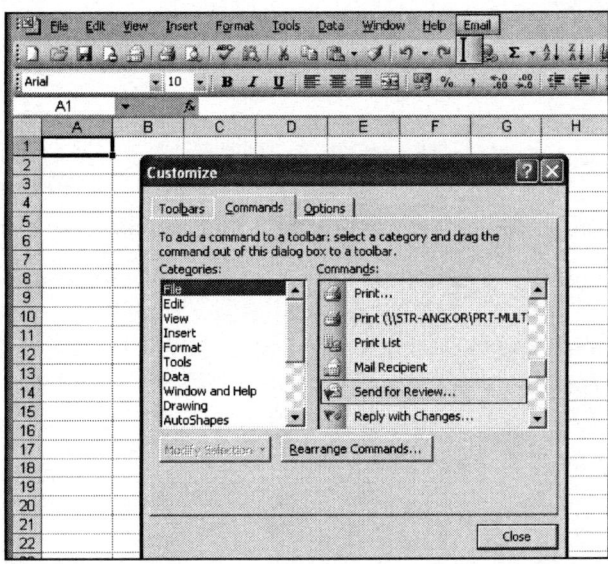

When you release the mouse button, you will see this result.

To delete the **Email** menu you have created, make sure the **Customize** dialog box is still open and drag the **Email** menu clear of the menu bar and any toolbars.

Click the **Close** button on the **Customize** dialog box.

5. To modify the default Excel font, use **Tools - Options - General** tab.

In the **Standard font** box, choose **Tahoma** from the drop-down list. In the **Size** list, choose **12**.

To modify the default number of worksheets in each new workbook, delete the contents of the **Sheets in new workbook** box and type **4** in the box. Click **OK** to confirm your changes and close the dialog box then click **OK** on the message that reminds you that you must restart Excel for your changes to the settings to take effect.

To check the new settings you have defined, close Excel with **File - Exit**, then re-open it using **start** on the Windows taskbar - **All Programs - Microsoft Office - Microsoft Office Excel 2003**. Excel automatically creates a new workbook: if you look at the bottom left corner, you should see 4 sheet tabs. Type a text of your choice into the first cell of the active worksheet: the text should appear in Tahoma font, size 12.

To restore the original settings, open the **Options** dialog box (**Tools - Options**), enter **3** in the **Sheets in new workbook** box, choose **Arial** in the **Standard font** list and then choose **10** in the **Size** list. Next, click **OK** on the **Options** dialog box and click **OK** on the message that reminds you that you must restart Excel for your changes to take effect. Finish by quitting Excel and re-opening it, as described earlier.

MACROS
Lesson 5.1: Macros

🖳 1 ▪ Recording a macro

- ▪ If necessary, open the workbook in which you wish to record the macro.
- ▪ **Tools - Macro - Record New Macro**
- ▪ Type the name of the macro in the **Macro name** box.

  Do not put any spaces in the name of a macro.

- ▪ Indicate, if necessary, the shortcut key that will run the macro.
- ▪ Indicate where the macro should be recorded: in **This Workbook** (if the workbook is open) or in a **New Workbook**. If the macro is to be available all the time, choose **Personal Macro Workbook**.

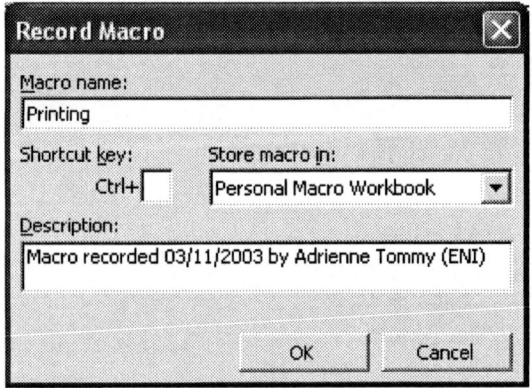

- ▪ If necessary, enter text in the **Description** box to change or add to the information about the macro.
- ▪ Click **OK**.

  The macro toolbar (with two tools) appears on the workspace and the word ***Recording*** *can be seen on the status bar.*

- ▪ Carry out all the actions you want to record in the macro.

■ Once all the actions have been completed, click the button on the macro toolbar (or use **Tools - Macro - Stop Recording**).

> *Macros recorded in this way are created in a file called Personal.xls, which is where personal macros are stored. This workbook is opened automatically with Excel (and then hidden), which means these macros are always available.*
>
> *Remember that you can check the level of security set for macros by using* ***Tools - Macro - Security****. The macro security features disable certain types of macro, depending on the level set.*

 ■ **Running a macro**

■ If the macro was recorded in a workbook other than Personal.xls, open the workbook.

■ Open the workbook in which you want to run the macro.

■ **Tools - Macro - Macros** or ⌨ Alt F8

■ Indicate where the macro you want to run is saved, using the **Macros in** list.

■ Double-click the macro you want to run from those in the list.

> *To delete a macro, use* ***Tools - Macro - Macros****, select the required macro in the list and click the* ***Delete*** *button.*

> *If the macro is in an open workbook or in Personal.xls, you can also use the shortcut key defined when the macro was recorded.*

▦3 ▪ Editing a macro

▪ If the macro is in Personal.xls, unhide this workbook using **Window - Unhide**, click **PERSONAL.xls** and click **OK**.

▪ **Tools - Macro - Macros** or Alt F8

▪ Select the macro in question then click **Edit**.

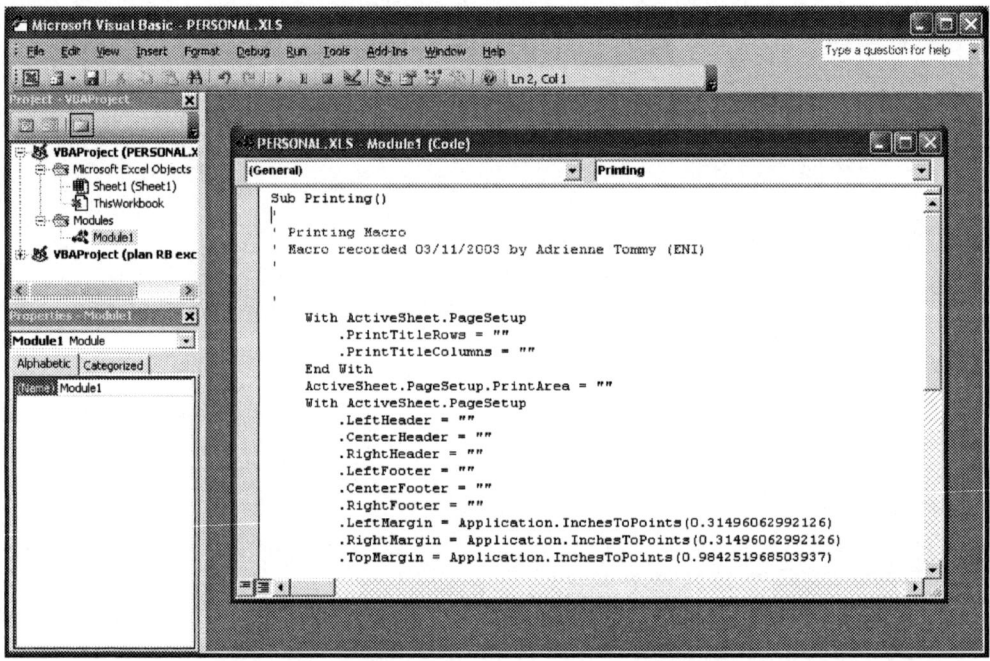

The contents of the macro appear in a Visual Basic window. This language lists the variables that have been recorded (here the print settings controlled by the Page Setup dialog box, such as the margins) and the values that have been set for each one.

- Without knowing the Visual Basic language, you can make simple changes, such as changing cell references, changing a number of copies, turning options on or off with a true/false value and so on. You could also copy and paste parts of the code to repeat actions on a different part of the sheet, editing the cell references accordingly.

- Click the tool button to save the changes.

- Close the Visual Basic window by clicking the button or with the **File - Close and Return to Microsoft Excel** command.

- If necessary, hide the **Personal.xls** workbook using **Window - Hide**.

MACROS
Exercise 5.1: Macros

Below, you can see **Practice Exercise 5.1**. This exercise is made up of 3 steps. If you do not know how to do one of the steps, go back to the title that corresponds to that particular lesson. When you have finished, you can check your work by reading the **Solution** that follows.

All the steps of this exercise are likely to be tested in the Microsoft Office Specialist exam.

☞ **Practice Exercise 5.1**

*To work on practice exercise 5.1, open the **5-1 Exams.xls** workbook in the **MOS Excel 2003 Expert** folder.*

1. Create a macro called **Printing** in this workbook. This macro will activate the **Landscape** page layout, reduce the scale to **95%** of normal size, centre the data **Horizontally** on the page and print two copies of the active sheets. This macro should be recorded in the **Personal Macro Workbook, Personal.xls** so that it can be used in any workbook.

2. Run the **Printing** macro in **5-1 HI-FI.xls** in the **MOS Excel 2003 Expert** folder.
   This macro was recorded in the **Personal.xls** workbook.

3. In the **Printing** macro, change the zoom to **100%**.
   This macro was recorded in the **Personal.xls** workbook.

If you would like to practise these features more, on another document, you should work through Summary Exercise 5, on MACROS. You will find the summary exercises at the end of the book.

It is often possible to perform a task in several different ways, but here, only the easiest solution is presented. You can go back to the corresponding lesson if you want to see other techniques you could use.

Solution to Exercise 5.1

 1. To create the **Printing** macro in the 5-1 Exams.xls workbook, use the **Tools - Macro - Record New Macro** command.

Type **Printing** in the **Macro name** box, select **Personal Macro Workbook** in the **Store macro in** list and click **OK**.

Use the **File - Page Setup** command and click the **Page** tab. Activate the **Landscape** option and type **95** in the **Adjust to** box in the **Scaling** frame.

Click the **Margins** tab, activate the **Horizontally** option in the **Center on page** frame then click **OK**.

Run the **File - Print** command, leave the **Active Sheet(s)** option active, enter **2** in the **Number of copies** box then click **OK**.

Click the ■ tool button on the macro toolbar.

 2. To run the Printing macro in 5-1 HI-FI.xls, open the **5-1 HI-FI.xls** in the **MOUS Excel 2002 Expert** folder if necessary, then use the **Tools - Macro - Macros** command.

In the **Macros in** list, make sure the **All Open Workbooks** option is selected, and double-click the **PERSONAL.XLS!Printing** macro

 3. To change the zoom to 100% in the Printing macro that is recorded in the personal macro workbook Personal.xls, use the **Window - Unhide** command, then click **OK**.

Use the **Tools - Macro - Macros** command, select the **Printing** macro and click **Edit**.

Press `Ctrl` `End` to see the bottom of the window, select **95** in the **.Zoom = 95** line and press `Del` then type **100**.

Click the tool button then use the **File - Close and Return to Microsoft Excel** command.

Finish by hiding **Personal.xls** with the **Window - Hide** command.

▌ SUMMARY EXERCISES

Summary Exercise 1   MANAGING DATA

Open the **Valley Fruits.xls** workbook in the **Summary** folder in the **MOS Excel 2003 Expert** folder.

In the **Customer list** worksheet, copy the table from the **Valley Customer base.xls** file that is stored in the **Summary** folder of the **MOS Excel 2003 Expert** folder (the first destination cell is cell A1). Create a link when you make the copy. Once you have copied the data, adjust the width of columns **A** to **G**.

Name the cell range **A1** to **G52 Customers**.

In cells **D5**, **D6** and **D7** of the **Invoice** worksheet, enter a formula that will automatically display the name, address and city that correspond to the code entered in cell **B10**; the data concerning the customers are in the **Customer list** worksheet.

Apply a comma format, with no decimal places, to cells **B9** to **F27** in the **Report** worksheet.

Use conditional formatting in cells **B27** to **E27** to show annual totals greater than or equal to 15000 in red.

Create an automatic outline of the table in the **Report** worksheet then use this outline to display only the results shown on the screen below:

FRUIT PRODUCTION (in kilos)				
	Apples	**Pears**	**Peaches**	**Nectarines**	**Total**
1st Quarter	4,495	5,015	3,685	985	14,180
2nd Quarter	5,125	6,320	3,940	595	15,980
1st Semester	9,620	11,335	7,625	1,580	30,160
July	1,300	1,800	1,000	860	4,960
August	1,490	1,820	1,100	1,600	6,010
September	1,500	1,830	1,000	2,200	6,530
3rd Quarter	4,290	5,450	3,100	4,660	17,500
4th Quarter	6,825	6,760	2,415	2,510	18,510
2nd Semester	11,115	12,210	5,515	7,170	36,010
ANNUAL TOTAL	20,735	23,545	13,140	8,750	66,170

The following changes need to made to the list in the **Customer list** worksheet, using the data form:

- Mrs CHEYNE is no longer a customer: delete her record.

Filter the data list in the **Customer list** worksheet to display only male customers from the **Three Rivers** and **Mapleton** districts.

Display all the records again then sort the list by district, then by city and finally by surname.

From the list in the **Customer list** worksheet, display different selections to obtain the result below:

List of women customers in Mapleton

Title	Surname	Address	City	Postcode
Mrs	FIELDING	60 The Crescent	Fern Grove	4120
Miss	CRAMMOND	45 Bethel Rise	Herston	4150
Miss	JONES	39 Blackfriar's Drive	Herston	4150
Mrs	PARK	55 Tulip Avenue	Herston	4150
Mrs	STOLL	34 Barns Road	New Grove	4121

List of women customers in Three Rivers plus all customers in Lake Greer

Title	Surname	Address	City	Postcode
Mr	BARTON	22 Harrison Avenue	Greerton	7520
Mrs	BIRKETT	64 Hamden Gardens	Greerton	7520
Mr	GREENE	2 Seaview	Greerton	7520
Mrs	HOLDERBY	45 Seaview	Greerton	7520
Miss	GREEN	45 West Road	Gunston	5230
Miss	MILLER	18 King's Road	Gunston	5230
Mrs	ANDERSON	17 Abbey Crescent	St Lucia	5235
Mrs	BROWN	14 King Street	St Lucia	5235
Miss	RAY	122 Cross Avenue	Trout Lake	5260
Miss	SUNDERLAND	80 Clement Grove	Trout Lake	5280

Finally, in the list in the **Customer list** worksheet, enter lines of statistics that will show the number of customers per district.

A solution is saved under the name **Solution 1.xls** in the **Summary** folder.

Open the **TEMPO & CO.xls** workbook that is in the **Summary** folder in the **MOS Excel 2003 Expert** folder.

Display the **Formula Auditing** toolbar, then use the auditing arrows to find the precedents of cell **L4** and the dependents of cell **F5** in the **Employee list** worksheet.

From the list in the **Employee list** worksheet, use pivot table tools to obtain the table below:

	A	B	C	D
1	SURNAME	(All)		
2				
3	Sum of GROSS☐TOTAL	NIGHT☐WORK		
4	JOB☐DESCRIPTION	N	Y	Grand Total
5	Accountant	7990		7990
6	Janitor		1140	1140
7	Mechanic		2340	2340
8	Office manager	1260		1260
9	Production manager	1450	4400	5850
10	Receptionist		1140	1140
11	Secretary	3605		3605
12	Supervisor	2665	4155	6820
13	Technician	3410	1240	4650
14	Typist	2330	1220	3550
15	Grand Total	22710	15635	38345
16				

This new pivot table should be inserted in a new sheet that should be called **Analysis** and should not be based on the existing pivot table in the **Pivot table** worksheet.

Change the pivot table so that the **Production manager** and **Supervisor** jobs are no longer shown, then apply AutoFormat **Table 10**.

In the **Pivot table** worksheet, change the pivot table by grouping the items in the **DATE OF ENTRY** field by year.

In a chart sheet that should be called **Chart Analysis**, create the pivot chart associated with the pivot table in the **Analysis** worksheet. Modify the chart type and show all the available job descriptions to obtain the pivot chart below:

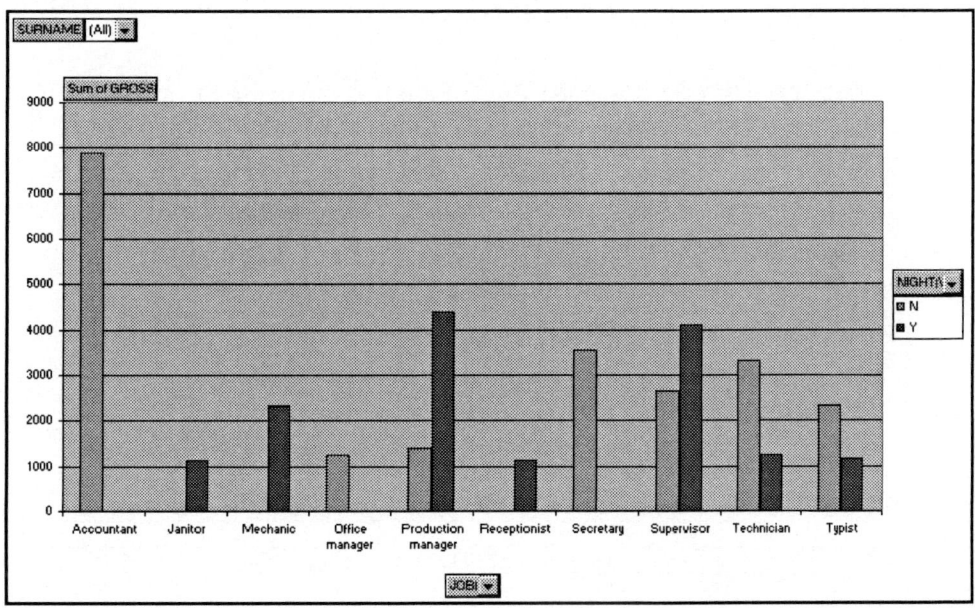

In the **Auditing** worksheet, there is an error in cell B24. Examine this error then correct it (it should refer to cell A21). Then create 2 scenarios in this worksheet, one to show the current situation and one called **Bonus increase** to reflect an increase in the night bonus, by changing cell **G24** to **70**. Run this scenario to see the changes then return to the original figures.

A solution is saved under the name **Solution 2.xls** in the **Summary** folder.

Summary Exercise 3 — TEMPLATES, WORKBOOKS AND WORKGROUPS

Change the **Sales by Semester.xlt** template (which is in your **Templates** folder) so that cells **B6** to **D6** and **A8** to **A15** have a **Gray - 25%** fill. Save and close the template.

Create a workbook based on the **Sales by Semester.xlt** template and complete it as shown below:

SALES ANALYSIS BY SEMESTER					
LIST OF SALES PEOPLE	JANUARY	FEBRUARY	MARCH	TOTAL	BONUS
PETER	45,689.00	39,580.00	45,785.00	131,054.00	1,965.81
CALLUM	25,870.00	32,500.00	23,560.00	81,930.00	
SUE	65,891.00	38,450.00	45,789.00	150,130.00	3,002.60
JOSH	63,450.00	78,900.00	78,451.00	220,801.00	6,624.03
ANNE	28,900.00	45,600.00	35,890.00	110,390.00	1,655.85
WENDY	45,789.00	71,250.00	45,600.00	162,639.00	3,252.78
BEN	38,750.00	45,000.00	52,300.00	136,050.00	2,040.75
PHILIP	45,800.00	58,450.00	23,560.00	127,810.00	1,917.15
TOTAL	360,139.00	409,730.00	350,935.00	1,120,804.00	20,458.97
AVERAGE	45,017.38	51,216.25	43,866.88	140,100.50	2,922.71
MINIMUM SALES	25,870.00	32,500.00	23,560.00	81,930.00	1,655.85
MAXIMUM SALES	65,891.00	78,900.00	78,451.00	220,801.00	6,624.03

Save the workbook as **Sales Semester1.xls** in the **Summary** folder of the **MOS Excel 2003 Expert** folder.

Change the properties of the workbook as shown below:

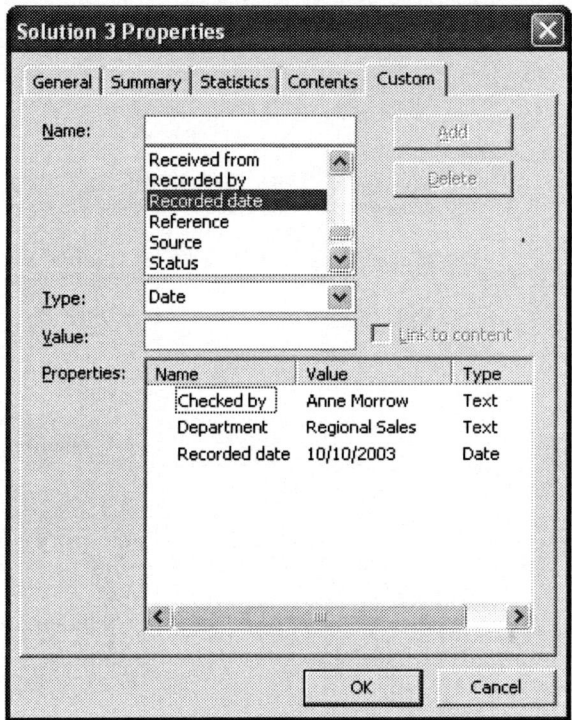

Protect all the cells in **Sheet1** except cells **A6** to **D15**, in which data can be entered. Add the password **sem1** (in lower case) to this protection.

A solution is saved under the name **Solution 3.xls** in the **Summary** folder.

Create a **Rows/columns/cells** toolbar and add the tools below:

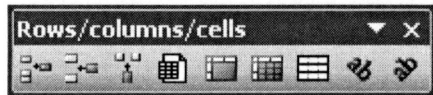

Create a menu called **Print** and insert the **Print Preview** and **Print** commands into it.

Unfortunately, no solution is available for this exercise, as this would add the toolbar and the menu to Excel before you undertake the exercise!

Summary Exercise 5   MACROS

Open the **Due Date.xls** workbook and create a macro called **Print_formulas**. This macro should be saved in this workbook and it should perform the following actions:

- display formulas instead of values in the worksheet, using the **Formulas** option in **Tools - Options - View** tab.

- apply a **Landscape** orientation to the worksheet.

- print gridlines and row and column headings.

- print the workbook name in the right of the header and the page number in the middle of the footer.

- print two copies of the selected worksheets. (when the message 'Microsoft Excel did not find anything to print' appears, click **OK**).

- Run the **Print_formulas** macro.

A solution is saved under the name **Solution 5.xls** in the **Summary** folder.

*As the solution contains a macro, you may need to change your macro security settings in order to check the results. Use **Tools - Macro - Security** and choose **Medium** level or below. Re-open **Solution 5** and if prompted, choose to **Enable Macros**. Don't forget to set the security level back to its original setting once you have finished (cf. Lesson 3.4 - Checking the macro security level).*

Microsoft Excel 2003 Expert Table of objectives ⊞				
Tasks	**Lessons**	**Pages**	**Exercises**	**Pages**
Organizing and Analyzing Data				
Use subtotals	Lesson 1.4 Title 4	88	Exercise 1.4 Point 4	91
Define and apply advanced filters	Lesson 1.5 Titles 3, 4, 5 and 6	102 to 105	Exercise 1.5 Points 3, 4, 5 and 6	111
Group and outline data	Lesson 1.4 Titles 1, 2 and 3	86 to 88	Exercise 1.4 Points 1, 2 and 3	91
Use data validation	Lesson 1.5 Title 7	106	Exercice 1.5 Point 7	112
	Lesson 2.1 Title 3	139	Exercice 2.1 Point 3	145
Create and modify list ranges	Lesson 1.5 Title 1	94	Exercise 1.5 Point 1	111
Add, show, close, edit, merge and summarize scenarios	Lesson 2.2 Titles 1 and 2	150 and 151	Exercise 2.2 Points 1 and 2	154
Perform data analysis using automated tools	Lesson 2.5 Titles 1, 2, 3 and 4	180 to 188	Exercise 2.5 Points 1, 2, 3 and 4	197 and 198
Create PivotTable and PivotChart reports	Lesson 2.3 Titles 1 and 2	158 and 160	Exercise 2.3 Points 1 and 2	164
	Lesson 2.4 Titles 1, 2 and 3	170 to 172	Exercise 2.4 Points 1, 2 and 3	174 and 175
Use Lookup and Reference functions	Lesson 1.1 Title 4	17	Exercise 1.1 Point 4	20
Use Database functions	Lesson 1.5 Title 8	109	Exercise 1.5 Point 8	112
Trace formula precedents, dependents and errors	Lesson 2.1 Titles 2 and 3	136 and 139	Exercise 2.1 Points 2 and 3	149
Locate invalid data and formulas	Lesson 2.1 Titles 3 and 4	139 and 142	Exercise 2.1 Points 3 and 4	145 and 146

Tasks	Lessons	Pages	Exercises	Pages
Watch and evaluate formulas	Lesson 2.1 Title 4	142	Exercise 2.1 Point 4	145 and 146
Define, modify and use named ranges	Lesson 1.1 Titles 1, 2 and 3	14 to 16	Exercise 1.1 Points 1, 2 and 3	20
Structure workbooks using XML	Lesson 1.6 Titles 1, 2, 3, 4 and 5	118 to 128	Exercise 1.6 Points 1, 2, 3, 4 and 5	131 and 132
Formatting Data and Content				
Create and modify custom data formats	Lesson 1.3 Title 2	60	Exercise 1.3 Point 2	79
Use conditional formatting	Lesson 1.3 Title 3	62	Exercise 1.3 Point 3	79
Format and resize graphics	Lesson 1.3 Title 4	63	Exercise 1.3 Point 4	79
Format charts and diagrams	Lesson 1.3 Titles 5 and 6	68	Exercise 1.3 Points 5 and 6	80
Collaborating				
Protect cells, worksheets, and workbooks	Lesson 3.4 Titles 1, 2 and 3	238 to 241	Exercise 3.4 Points 1, 2 and 3	257
Apply workbook security settings	Lesson 3.4 Titles 4, 5, 6, 7, 8 and 9	244 to 256	Exercise 3.4 Points 4, 5, 6, 7, 8 and 9	257 and 258
Share workbooks	Lesson 3.2 Title 2	217	Exercise 3.2 Point 2	225
Merge workbooks	Lesson 3.2 Title 3	220	Exercise 3.2 Point 3	226
Track, accept, and reject changes to workbooks	Lesson 3.3 Titles 1, 2 and 3	230 to 233	Exercise 3.3 Points 1, 2 and 3	234

TABLE OF OBJECTIVES

Tasks	Lessons	Pages	Exercises	Pages
Managing Data and Workbooks				
Import data to Excel	Lesson 1.2 Titles 1, 2 and 3	24 to 31	Exercise 1.2 Points 1, 2 and 3	51
Export data from Excel	Lesson 1.2 Title 4	38	Exercise 1.2 Point 4	51
Publish and edit Web worksheets and workbooks	Lesson 1.2 Title 5	41	Exercise 1.2 Point 5	52
Create and edit templates	Lesson 3.1 Titles 1, 2 and 3	204 to 207	Exercise 3.1 Points 1, 2 and 3	209 and 210
Consolidate data	Lesson 3.2 Title 4	222	Exercise 3.1 Point 4	226
Define and modify workbook properties	Lesson 3.2 Title 1	214	Exercise 3.2 Point 1	225
Customizing Excel				
Customize toolbars and menus	Lesson 4.1 Titles 2, 3 and 4	264 to 267	Exercise 4.1 Points 2, 3 and 4	272
Create, edit and run macros	Lesson 5.1 Titles 1, 2 and 3	278 to 280	Exercise 5.1 Points 1, 2 and 3	282
Modify Excel default settings	Lesson 4.1 Title 5	269	Exercise 4.1 Point 5	273

A

ADD-IN

ANALYSIS

APPLICATION

AUDITING

C

CALCULATION

CATEGORY

CELL

CHANGES

CHART

COLOUR

CONSOLIDATION

INDEX

INDEX

N

NAME

O

OBJECT

OPENING

OUTLINE

P

PASSWORD

PICTURE

PIVOT CHART

PIVOT TABLE

PROPERTIES

PROTECTION

..

INDEX

List of available titles in
the Microsoft Office User Specialist collection

Visit our Internet site for the list of the latest titles published.
http://www.eni-publishing.com

ACCESS 2002
ACCESS 2000
EXCEL 2000 CORE
EXCEL 2000 EXPERT
EXCEL 2002 CORE
EXCEL 2002 EXPERT
EXCEL 2003 CORE
EXCEL 2003 EXPERT
OUTLOOK 2000
OUTLOOK 2002
POWERPOINT 2000
POWERPOINT 2002
WORD 2000 CORE
WORD 2000 EXPERT
WORD 2002 CORE
WORD 2002 EXPERT
WORD 2003 CORE
WORD 2003 EXPERT